The Cinematic Influence

The Cinematic Influence

Interaction and Exchange Between the Cinemas of France and Japan

Peter C. Pugsley and
Ben McCann

BLOOMSBURY ACADEMIC
NEW YORK • LONDON • OXFORD • NEW DELHI • SYDNEY

BLOOMSBURY ACADEMIC
Bloomsbury Publishing Inc
1385 Broadway, New York, NY 10018, USA
50 Bedford Square, London, WC1B 3DP, UK
29 Earlsfort Terrace, Dublin 2, Ireland

BLOOMSBURY, BLOOMSBURY ACADEMIC and the Diana logo are trademarks of Bloomsbury Publishing Plc

First published in the United States of America 2023
Paperback edition published 2024

Copyright © Peter C. Pugsley and Ben McCann, 2023, 2024

For legal purposes the Acknowledgements on p. x constitute an extension of this copyright page.

Cover design: Eleanor Rose

Cover images: The Tokyo Tower, Tokyo, 29 May 2020. © Charly Triballeau / AFP / Getty Images; The Eiffel Tower, Paris © Alexander Spatari / Getty Images

All rights reserved. No part of this publication may be reproduced or transmitted in any form or by any means, electronic or mechanical, including photocopying, recording, or any information storage or retrieval system, without prior permission in writing from the publishers.

Bloomsbury Publishing Inc does not have any control over, or responsibility for, any third-party websites referred to or in this book. All internet addresses given in this book were correct at the time of going to press. The author and publisher regret any inconvenience caused if addresses have changed or sites have ceased to exist, but can accept no responsibility for any such changes.

Library of Congress Cataloging-in-Publication Data
Names: Pugsley, Peter, author. | McCann, Ben, author.
Title: The cinematic influence: interaction and exchange between the cinemas of France and Japan / Peter C. Pugsley and Ben McCann.
Description: 1st. | New York: Bloomsbury Academic, 2023. | Includes bibliographical references and index. | Summary: "Using extensive examples of films and filmmakers from French and Japanese cinemas, this book tracks the longstanding and multiple cultural, aesthetic and stylistic links that are found in films from the two countries" – Provided by publisher.
Identifiers: LCCN 2022023511 (print) | LCCN 2022023512 (ebook) | ISBN 9781501382949 (hardback) | ISBN 9781501382932 (paperback) | ISBN 9781501382956 (epub) | ISBN 9781501382963 (pdf) | ISBN 9781501382925
Subjects: LCSH: Motion pictures, Japanese–French–Influence. | Motion pictures, French–Japanese–Influence. | Japan–Civilization–French influences. | France–Civilization–Japanese influences.
Classification: LCC PN1993.5.J3 P84 2023 (print) | LCC PN1993.5.J3 (ebook) | DDC 791.450952/eng/20220914–dcundefined
LC record available at https://lccn.loc.gov/2022023511
LC ebook record available at https://lccn.loc.gov/2022023512

ISBN: HB: 978-1-5013-8294-9
PB: 978-1-5013-8293-2
ePDF: 978-1-5013-8296-3
eBook: 978-1-5013-8295-6

Typeset by Deanta Global Publishing Services, Chennai, India

To find out more about our authors and books visit www.bloomsbury.com and sign up for our newsletters.

Contents

List of illustrations	vii
Preface	ix
Acknowledgements	x
Introduction	1
Two cinematic ecosystems: France and Japan	6
History	8
Reception	11
Chapter structure	14

Part One History and Style

1	Historicizing French and Japanese cinemas	19
	Before the *nouvelle vague* . . . and after	20
	The impact of Japan's *Nūberu bāgu*	23
	The rise of the female auteur: Naomi Kawase and Claire Denis	24
	Conclusion	31
2	Cinematic engagement between France and Japan	33
	Kurosawa connections	36
	Formalizing co-productions	38
	Conclusion	45
3	Directorial styles, influence and exchange	47
	Styles and technologies	59
	Theatrical antecedents	61
	Monochrome	63
	Conclusion	74
4	Tora-san and the Monsieur Hulot influence	75
	Tati: choreographing meaning through movement	77
	Icons from another era	78
	Ambivalence to modernity (and love)	82
	Conclusion	88

Part Two Themes, Ideas and Approaches

5 Unemployment and the isolating self ... 93
   The personal toll of unemployment ... 93
   Unemployment in France ... 98
   Isolation ... 105
   Conclusion ... 113

6 Location and the sense of place ... 115
   Imagining the nation through rural–urban divides ... 122
   Country living in French cinema ... 130
   French colonialism ... 135
   Reflections of Japan as colonizer ... 139
   Absences ... 141
   Conclusion ... 143

7 Confrontational cinema ... 145
   Eroticism and sexploitation ... 146
   Violence ... 151
   Conclusion ... 162

8 Life, death and states of being ... 164
   Hirokazu Kore-eda: Contemplations on life ... 174
   The connectivity and disconnectivity of family in French cinema ... 181
   Conclusion ... 188

9 Adapting literary and visual texts ... 189
   Adaptations ... 189
   Fantasy ... 195
   Drama ... 198
   Conclusion ... 208

Conclusion: Where to next for the cinematic influence? ... 210
   Audience and reception ... 213

Films cited ... 217
Bibliography ... 231
Index ... 239

Illustrations

Figures

0.1	France meets Japan; Deneuve meets Kore-eda in *The Truth* (2019)	2
1.1	Finding solace in the final shot of *Let the Sunshine In* (2017)	28
1.2	Masaya struggles to focus in *Radiance* (2017)	30
2.1	Frenchness elided in *The Fifth Element* (1997)	36
2.2	Lou de Laâge and Isabelle Huppert in *Pure as Snow* (2019)	42
3.1	Minimal movement in *Postcard* (2011)	50
3.2	Visual exuberance in *Mood Indigo* (2013)	54
3.3	Frame within a frame in *Stray Dog* (1949)	58
3.4	Centralizing performance in *2 Autumns, 3 Winters* (2013)	61
3.5	Devastation in *The Whispering Star* (2015)	70
4.1	Tora-san in his hat and *haramaki* in the *Tora-san* series	76
4.2	Monsieur Hulot in his hat and trench coat in *Playtime* (1967)	76
4.3	Hulot as passive, curious observer in *Monsieur Hulot's Holiday* (1953)	80
4.4	Tora-san oblivious to the chaos in *Tora-san: Our Lovable Tramp* (1969)	81
5.1	Ryûhei by the riverbank in *Tokyo Sonata* (2008)	95
5.2	A developing rift in *All Is Forgiven* (2007)	100
5.3	Precarity and uncertainty in *Rust and Bone* (2012)	102
5.4	Mika and Daigo kneeling in *Departures* (2008)	108
6.1	Establishing a sense of place and mood in *The 400 Blows* (1959)	116
6.2	Tightly framed views of Tokyo in *Tokyo Story* (1953)	118
6.3	Confusion and displacement in *Tokyo Fiancée* (2014)	125
6.4	Isolated motel in *Black Snow* (1965)	128
7.1	The calm before the storm in *Enter the Void* (2009)	150
7.2	Schoolgirl carnage in *Tag* (2015)	152
7.3	Angry Ishihara in *Outrage Beyond* (2012)	157
7.4	Three bodies in *Titane* (2021)	163
8.1	Jean-Louis Trintignant watches and listens in *Amour* (2012)	167

8.2	Static shot as Eiko emerges in *Tony Takitani* (2004)	171
8.3	Framing the grandfather in *Still Walking* (2008)	178
8.4	A father and son divided in *You Will Be My Son* (2011)	187
9.1	Comic-book aesthetic in *Valerian & the City of a Thousand Planets* (2017)	190
9.2	Al and Ed in *Fullmetal Alchemist* (2017)	198
9.3	Eroticized close-up in *The Cherry Orchard* (1990)	200
9.4	Albert Dupontel as a stuntman in *In Harmony* (2015)	208

Table

2.1	UNIJAPAN Creative Contribution Points	43

Preface

The Cinematic Influence: Interaction and Exchange Between the Cinemas of France and Japan draws on films that are generally accessible in subtitled format for foreign audiences through the use of DVDs and streaming services, including (in Australia) Netflix and Stan, and the public broadcasting service, SBS On Demand. The accessibility of films was a key issue for us – while obscure experimental films may tell us much about a particular film culture, we feel that it is more effective if we discuss films that you, the reader, will be able to locate without too much difficulty. Our selection of films favours live-action dramas, comedies and occasional musicals, with some reference to anime; however, given the enormity of the anime market, we have generally avoided close readings of animated works.

Films have been listed by their title in English followed by their original French or Japanese title, except in those instances where the film was released internationally with its original title. In the later pages of the book, we have provided an extensive list of the films cited, along with details of the production company(ies) and place of origin. Japanese names have been listed in the Japanese order of surname first unless the artist uses the Westernized form in regular use. Quotations used throughout are from the subtitles provided with the film, to ensure consistency, and rather than having us attempt to muddy the waters with our own translations.

We approach these films and their cultures as outsiders, but with some understanding of the target cultures through our prior teaching and research experiences. We take full responsibility for any misreadings of texts, whether through simple misunderstandings or through ignorance (!). Our aim is to provide information on the selected films and their links to their respective cultures in the hope of furthering knowledge of the connections that exist between these two exciting film industries.

Acknowledgements

We wish to acknowledge the assistance of the Faculty of Arts and the School of Humanities at the University of Adelaide. The provision of Special Studies Leave through the Faculty of Arts in 2018 allowed Peter the ability to conduct preliminary research in France and build on his familiarity with Japanese cinema. Peter acknowledges the love and support of Mandy, Charlie and Louisa while he toiled away in the loft before and during various homebound Covid-19 lockdowns. He wishes to thank Jan and Chris for their assistance in navigating (both geographically and linguistically) film museums and archives in France. And thanks must go to Professor Aki Nakamura in Kyoto for his wonderful insights into Japanese cinema. As always, Peter is thankful to those students in *Asian Film Studies* and *Japanese Media Cultures* that alert him to films that may have sat beyond his radar but ultimately helped to inform the writing of this book.

Ben wishes to thank his family – as always – who have provided much-needed support and respite over the last two years, and who were introduced to a new selection of French films. Thanks are also due to Raphaëlle Delaunay, *directrice* of the Alliance Française in Adelaide, and Karine Mauris, Cultural Attachée to the French Embassy in Australia, for their support of the project, their invitation to present portions of the book at a conference and their willingness to provide screeners of French films. He also wishes to thank his students in *Screening the World: Global Film Aesthetics* and *Introduction to French Cinema*: many of their sophisticated and elegant observations about French cinema and its place in the world have made their way into the book.

Introduction

A woman walks her dog along an autumnal Parisian boulevard. Resplendent in a leopard-print coat, she strolls out of the distance and slowly towards the camera in one long, unbroken take. It is a beguiling moment, not least because the sequence is an extended outtake that plays out over the film's end credits. Equally captivating is the fact that the woman is Catherine Deneuve, that icon of French post-war cinema and a key figure in the glamorous exportability of French national cinema, and that the director is Hirokazu Kore-eda, who, for his first non-Japanese film, *The Truth* (2019), chose to set his elegant family drama in France. It is a fascinating contact point between stardom and auteurism, the frivolous and the downbeat, the elegant and the bathetic, and between France and Japan. Here, in a brief instance, do the cinemas of France and Japan harmonize (Figure 0.1).

This book explores the long-standing cinematic connections between two major regional, cultural and linguistic players: France (in Europe) and Japan (in East Asia). Taken separately, the history of the cinema in France and Japan is well known and has been written about from countless perspectives. But the converging and intersecting of the two industries – what we call the transformative 'cinematic influence' of France on Japan and Japan on France – has rarely been explored. This, therefore, is not another book 'about' French and Japanese cinema. It is not our intention to revisit old theoretical debates, cast fresh light on classic films or critique previous discussions of esteemed directors. Instead, our aim is to put under an analytical lens the relationship that exists between two geographically and culturally distant countries – France and Japan – and expose how these two different cinemas have cross-fertilized in interesting and dynamic ways over more than a century. Our central focus is how this cinematic meshing has taken a number of transnational forms; through, for instance, financial and co-production arrangements, the role of film criticism and film festivals, and the ways in which French and Japanese filmmakers approach particular social problems.

Figure 0.1 France meets Japan; Deneuve meets Kore-eda in *The Truth* (2019).

The influential French film journal *Cahiers du cinéma* (established in 1951) is an important contributor to this meshing. Each year, *Cahiers* critics would list their annual 'Top Ten' best films. In the years 1959 and 1960, widely regarded as a period in which enduring masterpieces of the cinema were released, it was not Alfred Hitchcock's *Vertigo* (1959) or François Truffaut's *Les 400 coups/The Four Hundred Blows* (1959) that topped the list. Rather, it was Kenji Mizoguchi's *Tales of Ugetsu/Ugetsu Monogatari* (released in Japan in 1953 but not in France until six years later). The following year, Mizoguchi's *Sansho the Bailiff/Sanshô Dayû* (1954 in Japan) did the same again, pushing out Hitchcock's *Psycho*, Michelangelo Antonioni's *L'avventura* and *Cahiers* favourite Jean-Luc Godard's *Breathless/À bout de souffle*. If, as Isadora Kriegel-Nicholas notes (2016: 1), such polling suggests an over-privileging of Japanese film by the journal at this time, it nonetheless reveals the importance of the 'newness' of Japanese cinema to French critics and audiences during the period when auteur theory was gathering influence.

We are also particularly interested in professional trajectories, such as the careers of Kiyoshi Kurosawa and other Japanese filmmakers and actors who have been recognized for their work in France, like Takeshi 'Beat' Kitano (who was awarded France's prestigious *Ordre national de la Légion d'Honneur* [Legion of Honour] in 2016). *The Truth* was Kore-eda's follow-up to *Shoplifters/Manbiki Kazoku* (2018), which, in a fine example of the ongoing intertwining of French and Japanese cinema, was the Palme d'Or winner at Cannes. Japan had not won the Palme d'Or since Shōhei Imamura shared the prize (with Abbas Kiarostami's

Taste of Cherry) for *The Eel/Unagi* in 1997. This was Imamura's second Palme win, following his bleakly dramatic *The Ballad of Narayama/Narayama Bushikô* in 1983. Ryusuke Hamaguchi and Takamasa Oe won the Best Screenplay at Cannes for *Drive My Car* (2021), and, as we write this Introduction, the film has just won the Best International Feature Film award at the 2022 Oscars. Clearly, this ongoing fascination with and high regard towards Japanese film culture by French cultural organizations like Cannes and *Cahiers du cinéma* is indicative of a sensitivity towards and appreciation of the films themselves: their stories, their visual textures and their ways of seeing the world.

In a reciprocal gesture, we also look at the ways that Japanese film has influenced French filmmakers such as Luc Besson, through the appropriation of visual techniques such as framing and long-takes, the use of particular performance styles, narratives and structures, and the choice of Japan as a setting or location for a film. Conversely, Japanese filmmakers from Akira Kurosawa through to Seijun Suzuki and Naomi Kawase have expressed their appreciation of French film as playing a formative role in their personal development as directors. Our approach is therefore wide-ranging: the close textual analysis of French and Japanese film aesthetics, themes and narratives; the reception of French and Japanese films based on their exposure at film festivals, the critical response and box-office figures; modes of exchange in French and Japanese cinema through their cultural crossover and co-production practices; film adaptations from other media; and the history of the cinematic relationship between France and Japan.

This book draws on our prior experiences in dealing with close textual studies of cinema as a form of cultural communication. As the editors of *Cahiers du cinéma* wrote back in 1969 the critical function of film and its analysis demands no less than 'a necessary stage of going back to the material elements of a film, its signifying structures, its formal organization' (Comolli and Narboni 1971: 34–5). As teachers of and writers about Japanese and French cinema, we attempt the same, drawing parallels where possible, but fully aware that there are limits to analysis. Our focus is on those links that can be determined whether through aesthetic styles shared by the films under analysis, or by concrete, material links that can be supported by empirical approaches. The connections we seek to uncover tell us much about the relations between Japan and France, and show that filmmaking does not occur in isolation, nor does it rely on one culture alone.

To achieve this, we shall explore the ways that filmmakers utilize cinematic techniques to create an aesthetic that either reflects a specific cultural view or carries a more universal tone. We investigate the ways that, for instance, the iconic films of Seijun Suzuki in the mid-1960s draw upon Jean-Luc Godard's fast and loose editing styles from the late 1950s, and how the incorporation of jazz-style, often atonal, musical scores that work both with and against Suzuki's films, create a sense of urgency and unease for the audience. In our exploration of the acknowledgement of Japan's contribution to the French appreciation of cinema, we explore the films of Kitano, Besson and others to track their reception through the availability of their films (when and where were they shown), and the ways in which their films were received by audiences and critics. The role of film festivals as 'distribution circuits' (Carroll Harris 2017: 46) is important in this regard, not least because many of the films mentioned in this book first gained attention by appearing in competitions such as the *Festival de Cannes*, the *Tōkyō Kokusai Eigasai* (Tokyo International Film Festival) or smaller competitions such as the *Festival des 3 Continents* and the Deauville Asian Film Festival. Such festivals are part of the extensive networks at play that facilitate the dissemination and mutual appreciation of French and Japanese cinema and are increasingly intertwined with broader funding opportunities for filmmakers.

In covering two specific national cinemas in this book, we are wary of what Pierre Bourdieu once cautioned against; namely, an approach based on 'casual inspection' undertaken by 'someone with a taste for the exotic, that is for *picturesque differences*' (1991: 628). Bourdieu gives the example of what has been said and written, in the case of Japan, about the 'culture of pleasure' (628), the orientalizing of the East where all texts are seen through an exotic, and at times erotic lens. Instead, following Bourdieu, our task is to seek out the 'particularities of different *collective histories*' (629) between France and Japan. Similarly, we are aware that just as French films are not representative of European cinema, Japanese films are not representative of Asian cinema. The concepts of 'Asian', 'European' or even 'East Asian' cinemas are, of course, reductive and serve best only as geopolitical references. The disparity of cultures, languages and traditions across either of these regions makes our insistence on looking at cinemas as a national project (itself a high-risk venture) a matter of convenience, to then be broken down into temporal or even personal/personnel analysis of films and film styles. Takeshi 'Beat' Kitano, for instance, addresses such problematic delineations when he says, 'I feel like when anyone calls me an "Asian director" it's loaded with preconceptions' (in Davis 2001: 55). Kitano warns of the dangers of creating a 'blatantly stereotypical Asian look' (Davis 2001: 55), something that we are keen to avoid in our choice of films for analysis in this book. In comparing and contrasting films from Japan (not 'Asian films') with films from France, we are keen to investigate the ways that the essence, the language, of a film can be both culturally determined and universal, and how it can speak to audiences both within or without its own cultural, national or linguistic group.

In this age of co-productions and the global accessibility of films, exploring the connections between different national cinemas allows a stronger understanding of the cinematic process, and the extent to which cultural differences impact the final aesthetic of a film. Cinema plays a large role in the identity of any nation, and certainly in France and Japan where the film is often seen as part of national conversations around the sense of self-identity and national identity. The role of filmmakers and critics is seen as an essential component in representations of each nation's land and cityscapes, and the cultures that they inhabit. In this book, we direct our focus to feature films, mostly live-action fictional works, not because 'factual' films, animations or documentaries are not important, but because the cinematic world is one of fantasy that is based on elements and aesthetic approaches that are recognizable to us, the audience. We come to understand the significance of actions, colours, narrative structures, personalities and a range of other variables through culture and traditions that provide meaning and comfort to us. The meanings created are, of course, different once we move beyond our own, known, culture, and here this book unpacks the reasons why film as a form of cultural exchange is so important.

The understanding (or misunderstanding) of culture that may be found in the cinema audience's reaction to a film can add to its appreciation of an aesthetic style. Standish, for instance, notes how the Japanese concept of *mono no aware* (the pathos of things) is often seen as deeply rooted in tradition reaching back to the ninth century, yet she argues that it actually 'represents a modern reflexive reappropriation of a traditional aesthetic as a response to the changing nature of man's relationship to time, space and knowledge in the late nineteenth and early twentieth centuries' (2012: 6). This reappropriation could be viewed as an essential component of Japanese cinema from the 1950s and onwards that helped it to create such an impact in international film markets and festivals.

It is worth pointing out that, during that halcyon period of the late 1950s during which the films of Kurosawa, Ozu and Mizoguchi were first exhibited in France, box-office success did not follow. *Ugetsu Monogatari*, for example (released as *Les Contes de la lune vague après la pluie* in France in March 1959) may have topped *Cahiers*' 'Best Film' poll that year but sold only 283,000 tickets across France (for a film to be considered a commercial success in France, 1 million entries remains a long-standing industry benchmark). *Sanshô dayû* (*L'Intendant Sansho*) did not even figure in France's National Centre for Cinema and the Moving Image box-office figures for the following year. Nevertheless, by following the release of films over concurrent or overlapping periods, trends and patterns in the use of particular filmmaking behaviours and images across French and Japanese cinema can be tracked. The use of specific cinematic techniques, narrative structures and the creation of cinematic auteur and star fandoms can also be traced – for instance, as stars move from film to film, genre to genre, year to year, we explore how their performance styles reflect temporal understandings of national cultures.

This book will also explore the proliferation of film adaptations of existing texts, whether from literary novels, comics (*manga*) or animation (*anime*). We will examine how these adaptations feature in both French and Japanese cinemas as a legitimate form of source text. The importance of these films is, as Robert Stam notes, heightened because '[e]ach medium has its own specificity deriving from its respective materials of expression' (2000: 59). In other words, the cinematic form of visual and audio representation can develop or exploit the individual traits of its medium that may not be reproducible in the medium of the source text; for instance, the addition of a musical score to set a particular mood. As we shall see, the presence of an existing, popular text does not necessarily guarantee box-office success, and we discuss various examples of adaptations that may or may not have benefitted from the move to a cinematic format.

Two cinematic ecosystems: France and Japan

The French and Japanese film industries are prolific in these two nations where cinema is held in high regard as an art form: France produces around 250 feature films per year; in Japan that number increases to around 600 per year (UNESCO), with a record 698 releases in 2019 (EIREN 2021). The last few years have seen global disruptions and shutdowns that affected production, distribution and screenings due to the Covid-19 pandemic. In 2017, for instance, Japan saw 175 million cinema admissions (Schilling 2018), from a population of 125 million, roughly equivalent to each person seeing 1.4 films per year (compared to the United States where the figure is around 0.3). This had grown to 194.9 million in 2019 (EIREN 2021), before dropping to 106 million in 2020 and then climbing to 114 million in 2021, still affected by cinema closures and restrictions on movement. While the overall box office in 2017 was down on the previous year (bolstered by the US$235 million draw of the romantic anime, *Kimi no Na wa/ Your Name* (dir. Makoto Shinkai), it nevertheless reached US$2.1 billion, and saw the release of 594 locally made films against 593 foreign films. By 2019, box-office revenue had reached US$2.29 billion, but the impact of the pandemic in 2021 saw revenue down to US$1.42 billion, with just 490 locally made films released (Schilling 2022). In France, the admissions per capita ratio is even stronger, with each person seeing around 3.12 films per year, or 209 million admissions from a population of 66 million (Keslassy 2018). Box-office grosses for France in 2017 reached US$1.64 billion, with three domestic films, *Raid: Special Unit/Raid Dingue* (2016, dir. Dany Boon), *Valerian and the City of a Thousand Planets/Valérian et la Cité des mille planètes* (2017, dir. Luc Besson), and *Alibi.com* (2017, dir. Philippe Lacheau), reaching the top ten (Keslassy 2018). Awareness of French culture can be seen in Japanese films such as *Shimotsuma Monogatari* (aka *Kamikaze Girls*, 2004, dir. Nakashima Tetsuya), a film heavy on riot-grrrl attitudes illustrated via an aesthetic derived from the French Rococo (Late Baroque) subculture, most visibly recreated in the 'millennial street fashion of gothic Lolitas' (McKnight 2010: 118–19). *Shimotsuma Monogatari* and the manga series that inspired it, *Berusaiyu no bara/Rose of Versailles*, 1972–3), both draw on (French) historicist narratives that show how '[t]he court, with its hermetic world of artifice and ritual, offers tropes for examining how a feminine subject becomes self-sufficient and free' (McKnight 2010: 122). Therefore, across the decades between the introduction of the manga to the release of the film, Japanese audiences have been able to reflect on their own culture through a romanticized, dislocating lens of French Renaissance society.

There is also one other, perhaps more tangible connection that can be made when looking at the cinematic links between France and Japan, and that is the movement of people through migration. Sylvie Blum-Reid (2003: 4) picks up on this when she notes that 'a sizable segment of France's population consists of people of Asian origins and their children, whether they be first-, second- or third-generation'. Although her focus is centered around the Southeast Asia of the former Indochina region, particularly the cinematic history of Vietnam, Blum-Reid points to the temporal shifts (namely post–Second World War decolonization and Cold War-era communist insurgencies from 1965–75), that resulted in massive evacuations and humanitarian shifts from the region. The constant movement of peoples across the globe is hardly a new phenomenon, but for well over a century film has played a role in how people communicate because '[i]t is in cinema's nature to cross-cultural borders within and between nations, to circulate across heterogeneous linguistic and social formations' (O'Regan 2004: 262).

History

The extensive links between French and Japanese cinema owe a lot to a chance meeting between a young Japanese entrepreneur studying in France at a college attended by one of the Lumière brothers. Extensive historical accounts of the arrival of the moving picture in Japan have been written, detailing the earlier arrival of Eastman's Kinetoscope in 1896, but trumped just a year later by the Lumière Cinématographe (Anderson and Richie 1982: 21–2). The opening of Japan to foreign influences following the Meiji Restoration saw an influx of goods and, of particular concern for this study, the screening of images from the *cinématographe* Lumière in Kyoto in February 1897 following a recent trip to France by businessman Katsutaro Inabata. In his younger years, Inabata had studied weaving and dyeing techniques at La Martinière in Lyon, where he first met Auguste Lumière. On his return to France in 1896 he was reacquainted with Lumière (and his brother, Louis) and learned of the new *cinématographe*. The keen businessman saw the potential in the new technology as a form of commodifiable entertainment. Inabata returned to Japan with filmmaking equipment from the Gaumont company, an experienced technician, and the rights to project the more than fifty films he had purchased from the Lumière brothers. Thus, the introduction of film to Japan had an element of serendipity. As the ability to capture paying audiences gained momentum, studios were quickly set up to capture the new medium, with Nikkatsu Studios (then Japan Motion Pictures Limited Company), constructing a glass-roofed studio in 1913 to take advantage of natural light when filming (Sato 2008: 7).

Technologically, Japan had a precursor to the Lumière brothers' invention early in the nineteenth century with a simple projection method known as the *utsushi-e* (Komatsu 1996: 431), but its static nature failed to attract the kind of audiences that the Lumière's moving pictures would. Japan's economic drive at the dawn of the new century (of which cinema played a role) was a site where 'ideas of Japanese tradition were being produced for both foreign and domestic consumption' (Bordwell 1995: 14). This was not a wholesale export venture, however, and Bordwell argues that Japan was in fact working to 'redefine its own culture over and against the Europe and America it was coming to know' (1995: 14). The importance of cinema was to become paramount by the mid-1930s, as Japan became even more deeply embedded in regional conflicts, and its film industry 'was second only to Hollywood as a mass-production, vertically-integrated studio system' (Bordwell 1995: 15). As Japan's involvement in military conflicts deepened, its film industry became devoted to serving the nation through the creation of propaganda films for the government.

Japan's rebuilding after its surrender to the United States and Allied forces, saw filmmakers quick to return to their craft, and by the late 1940s had begun to capture international attention. It was then that the relationship with French cinema began to take a more reciprocal tone. In a recent (unpublished) thesis, Isadora Kriegel-Nicholas investigates the privileging of Japanese cinema in the newly arrived journals *Cahiers du cinéma* (from 1951) and *Positif* (from 1952) citing 'the entwining of their two trajectories' (2016: 1). The importance of film to national debates was later outlined by *Cahiers* in an editorial in 1969 where it set out to define not just its own Marxist-based approach to film, but to the idea of film as both a national product, and as part of an increasingly global system of image exchange. Film, for the *Cahiers* editors, was a manufactured product, and 'as a result of being a material product of the system, it is also an ideological product of the system, which in France means capitalism' (Comolli and Narboni 1971: 29). For *Cahiers*, cinema was defined as 'one of the languages through which the world communicates itself to itself' (30), in other words, its role moved way beyond national borders, driven not only by ideologies but also the global flows of capitalism found in production, distribution and even in the technology, such as the supply and exchange of film stock.

The international profile and influence of French cinema are well established, especially in the West. Less obvious are its influences in non-Western environments. China's cinematic connections to France, for instance, are less obvious than those between France and Japan. The effect of a tumultuous twentieth century in which China found itself marshalling energies to deal with civil disturbances, Japanese aggression, concessions to foreign powers (including France), revolutions and an eventual, guarded, opening to the outside world saw its film industry lacking the continual threads of development that other national cinemas, such as the United States (Hollywood), France and even India, could nurture. Through its colonial links to Britain (and to a lesser degree to Europe and nations such as France), Hong Kong was able to continue developing its film industry, even providing a home for filmmakers who had fled their mainland homes and the studios of Shanghai to work in exile, eventually leading to Hong Kong creating its own brand of action cinema. More recently China has entered the co-production arena. *Yǒngshì zhī mén/ Warrior's Gate* (aka *Enter the Warrior's Gate*) (Hoene 2016) is a Chinese–French co-production, an English-language, action fantasy co-written by Luc Besson and created through Besson's EuropaCorp in partnership with Shanghai's Fundamental Films. Besson was also a co-writer, and his production company was behind 2015's *The Transporter Refueled/Le Transporteur: Héritage*, the fourth instalment of the *Transporter* action series that were all co-produced and co-written by Besson. For this instalment, directed by Camille Delamarre, Besson had also teamed up with Fundamental Films and Belga Film Funds to create a French–Chinese–Belgian production. Luc Besson's *Lucy* (2014) was shot in Taipei, Paris and New York, and starred, among others, Korean actor Choi Min-sik, best known for his intense lead role as Oh Dae-su in Park Chan-wook's *Oldeuboi/Old Boy (2003)*. Besson also established a clear connection with Japan when he used Tokyo as a setting for his 2001 action film *Wasabi* and had chosen Japanese yakuza as the 'bad guys' in the Paris-based sequel *Taxi 2* (2000, dir. Gérard Krawczyk), following the success of *Taxi*, the 1998 blockbuster action film he had written and produced, and continued until *Taxi 5* in 2018.

One particular area where this book seeks to expand on ideas of exchange, interaction and overlap is through a close analysis of the French and Japanese 'New Waves', which emerged in the 1950s and early 1960s. As David Desser (1988) reminds us:

> [s]uperficial comparisons between the Japanese New Wave cinema and the French New Wave, typically to imply greater integrity to the latter, have served the cultural cliché that the Japanese are merely great imitators, that they do nothing original . . . To see the Japanese New Wave as an imitation of the French New Wave (an impossibility since they arose simultaneously) fails to see the Japanese context out of which the movement arose (4)

In other words, we need to look closer at how the Japanese New Wave emerged, to a degree, in tandem with the more prestigious French *nouvelle vague*, and explore how the broad range of technical, thematic, artistic, historical, cultural and industrial frameworks in both countries enabled two distinctive national cinemas to emerge.

Reception

One of the key means of keeping the Franco–Japanese cinematic connection alive is the support of international Film Festivals. Japan's presence at the Cannes film festival has been notable since the early 1950s, and the announcement of director Naomi Kawase (who has had six films presented at the festival) as presiding over the 2016 *Cinéfondation* and Short Film Jury, indicates the level of mutual respect for Japanese cinema (Keslassy 2016). *Cinéfondation* founder, Gilles Jacob, praised Kawase's contributions to cinema, stating that she has 'helped generate a cinematic intelligence and a subtle art full of poetic mystery and graceful simplicity' (Keslassy 2016). Japan's cinematic reputation does not seem to have suffered in terms of its profile at Cannes, despite what Czach sees as a 'radical departure from the first generation of French cinephiles, who adored and venerated American cinema as one of genres, directors, and actors as opposed to stars' (2010: 141). Czach sees a threat to the credentials of the film festival arising from an atmosphere where: 'parties, scenes and events overpower the status of film as an art form [so that] the cineaste, as exemplary of the cinephiliac disposition, appears as an endangered species' (2010: 142). Yet both French and Japanese cinemas remain much less star-driven than Hollywood and other national cinemas such as India and, increasingly, China. Czach refers to 'the perceived threat of stars' (2010: 142), that looked to overshadow festivals such as Sundance, where specific attempts were made to restore 'film's status as the principal object of desire' (2010: 143). Responding to Susan Sontag's treatise on 'The Decay of Cinema', Czach sees the rise of the multi-screen megaplex as symptomatic of a turn from the big-screen experience so that 'it is no surprise that film festivals emerge as one of the last refuges for the cinephile' (2010: 140). Czach notes that:

> Film festivals occupy a liminal space between the older forms of first-generation, pretelevisual cinephilia, where the only access to films was in movie theaters, and contemporary forms of cinephilia, in which DVD collecting and digital downloads bypass the moviegoing experience altogether. (2010: 140)

Borrowing from Mark Peranson, Abé Mark Nornes (2014) notes the distinction between 'audience festivals' and 'business festivals', although in terms of branding, these two types often converge under the one masthead. Czach maintains that the 'explosion of the international film festival network suggests that cinephilia is far from dead' (2010: 140), and that festivals offer 'a seductive return to classical cinephilia' (141) despite the concern that they are being prostituted in the name of the 'consumption of stars and celebrity culture' (141). Czach notes that even in the 1950s there were concerns that stars were being promoted as more significant than their films, conceding that the 'extra-cinematic or paracinematic events at film festivals are key to their success' (2010: 144–5). In other words, the economic survival of a festival hangs largely on the success and exposure of each year's festival. Not only do the films have to make an impact by drawing favourable reviews, but the festival's visibility must be maintained by capitalizing on the bankability of the personal appearance of stars. As Czach reasons, a 'film festival without stars and parties would be as impoverished as one without cinephiles' (2010: 145).

The role of France was paramount in establishing the importance of film festivals, and as Evans notes, 'there seems to have been a tacit acceptance on the whole that Cannes essentially established the mould of the contemporary film festival and has attracted the principal focus accordingly' (2007: 23). Evans investigates whether the privileging of Cannes comes at the expense of other festivals that may provide a more representative view of the European festival experience. The influence of the International Federation of Film Producers Associations (FIAPF) creates a hierarchical structure of festivals that receive assistance from the European Coordination of Film Festivals (ECFF) such as the Berlin festival that demonstrate 'an element of national specificity rather than difference from the more internationally oriented Cannes' (Evans 2007: 24). For Japanese filmmakers, the approval of European festivals assists in wider recognition of their art and helps to address the 'multiple factors involved in restricting and regulating the circulation of Japanese films and texts, from the limits of language and representation to cultural imperialism, racism and gender discrimination' (Nygren 2007: ix). In a 1998 interview, Jun Ichikawa lamented that even though he had won Best Director at Montreal for *Tôkyô Yakyoku/ Tokyo Lullaby*, he felt that 'I would still feel better if I could win something at Cannes, Venice or Berlin' (Schilling 1999: 103). Jun is open about his need for recognition and box-office success, claiming that 'My films aren't exactly big hits in Japan [laughs], so it would be nice if foreign audiences liked them . . . I'd like to make a film that was a hit abroad' (Schilling 1999: 103).

This desire for recognition on the international stage is not unusual for Japanese filmmakers, with Kore-eda once remarking that 'we have to try harder if we want our films to reach average filmgoers' (Schilling 1999: 117). The difficulties seem to lay deeper than just gaining popular support, with one scholar suggesting that '[t]the dilemma of Asian film cultures – desiring recognition from the European other and being greeted by indifference – is an old and enduring dynamic that goes back to the silent era' (Nornes 2014: 247). The problem, as Kore-eda sees it, is that 'when it comes to moving beyond film festivals to general release, there is still a long way to go', adding that '[i]n Europe for example, there are still barriers to a wider release' (Schilling 1999: 117). It remains to be seen whether the international success of South Korean cinema, led mostly by *Parasite*'s Academy Awards success in 2020, opens the barriers for more Asian films to receive mainstream recognition.

Kitano's success at Cannes and other festivals with *Hana-Bi/Fireworks* could be seen as a response to his reinterpretations of Japanese cinema. The violence of Akira Kurosawa and the samurai codes were mixed with an urban sensibility, clearly inspired by Martin Scorsese's New York in *Taxi Driver* (1976), or John Woo's Hong Kong in *Ying hung boon sik/A Better Tomorrow* (1986). The craggy, stony-faced visage of Kitano (the actor) not only drew on these cinematic icons but also, according to Davis (2001: 72) the traditional, fixed masks of *Noh* theatre. Like fellow actor/director Hitoshi Matsumoto (*Dai Nipponjin/Big Man Japan*, 2007), Kitano started out as one half of a comedy duo, essentially the dimwit (*boke*) in the duo 'Two Beats' (hence the 'Beat' nickname), but his constant TV and film appearances in everything from comedic to dramatic roles, meant that he became 'everything to everybody' in Japan (Jacobs 2008: 95). Kitano's agility saw him recognized, according to Aaron Gerow, as a 'super auteur' that 'could not be captured by auteurist criticism, undermining each iteration of the Kitanoesque by doing the opposite in his next film' (2016: 345), an evasiveness that continues to this day.

The beginnings of Japanese success in European film festivals is said to have started when a programmer at the Venice International Film Festival in 1950 saw Kurosawa's *Rashomon*, and was so impressed that he 'selected it against the wishes of studio head Nagata Masaichi, and screened it unbeknownst to the director: the film won the Golden Lion, and suddenly every festival desired a Japanese film in its lineup' (Nornes 2014: 245). So, while European festivals have proven beneficial (at times) to Japan's filmmakers, the success of local or regional film festivals has proven more challenging. Nornes writes of the early iterations of the 'cringe-worthy' Tokyo International Film Festival, that was 'never taken seriously', despite its ambitions to be a worthy part of the circuit that includes festivals and industry meets in nearby Busan and Hong Kong (2014: 247). For Nornes, this leads to a situation where '[m]ore fascinating are the subtle inflections of Europe's dominance – and by extension indifference – on the ground' (2014: 247).

At various points throughout this book we return to the important role played by film festivals in legitimizing the 'worth' of individual films, and in maintaining connections between the cinemas of France and Japan.

Chapter structure

The structure of this book is designed to firstly guide the reader through a brief, and selective, history of film in each of the selected nations, France and Japan. Secondly, through comparative studies in successive chapters, we explore thematic elements found or reproduced in films from the two countries. In each chapter, we investigate the reception of the 'other' cinema and its filmmakers in terms of accolades and film festival appearances, and, where possible, highlight connections of a more formal, industrial nature such as co-productions and talent exchanges.

To undertake a study such as this, we begin with an awareness of the vast array of cinematic materials before us. Even as we write, new films are being released at a constant rate, totalling around a thousand per year in France and Japan alone! To guide our way through, we look at a selection of films across several decades that illustrate the key themes and ideas that we wish to explore when we consider connections and synergies between the two nation's cinemas. We call upon the vocabulary of film studies, perhaps best summed up in this (extended) extract from Tom O'Regan:

> We speak of film, filmmakers, and audiences alike indigenizing, adapting, appropriating, poaching, resisting, co-opting, and remaking films, filmmaking styles, practices, and technologies drawn from other filmmaking traditions – national and otherwise. We speak of filmmakers entering into a dialogue with the dominant international cinema and other cinema traditions. We speak of the cross-cultural reception of film and television. We speak of too little and too much cultural exchange, of unequal and reciprocal exchanges. (O'Regan 2004: 263)

To put it another way, there is much to be said. Even with the focus of our attention on the cinematic outputs from just France and Japan, the list of considerations is immense. In order to work through the wealth of connections between the two cinemas, we commence our study with Part One – History and Style – in which we offer an alternative historical overview of some of the exchanges and interactions that have taken place between France and Japan. We then explore the 'hardware' – the commercial, technical and industrial elements that have driven the two cinemas over more than one hundred years. In Chapter 1, we explore the idea of cinema and how France has played an instrumental role in not just the technicalities of film, but in the creation of narratives, styles and techniques that would go on to have a significant impact on the history of cinema, and to what extent the emergence of the Japanese *Nūberu bāgu* (a simple phonetic transliteration of *nouvelle vague*) was in part contingent on its French counterpart. We also look at how gender impacts the opportunities and potential for success for the female auteur in both nations. In Chapter 2, we turn our attention to the formal and informal connections that have grown between French and Japanese cinemas, and how these links are recognized beyond the borders of their respective countries. We examine, therefore, the crucial role of institutional support through public and private organizations, and demonstrate how important film festivals are in promoting film as a prestigious, exportable national project. In Chapter 3 we begin to more closely analyse how particular French and Japanese filmmakers establish their own styles and techniques, and how they may 'trade' these through influencing or being influenced by other directors. We look in particular at the deployment of monochromatic imagery as a visual distinction in a range of films that reflect a formalist approach to cinema production.

In Chapter 4 we focus on two iconic film 'series' based around lone comedic protagonists – Jacques Tati's Monsieur Hulot and Yoji Yamada's Tora-san – to illustrate the ways that specific cultural and historical traits can work equally well alongside universal cinematic styles in film.

In Part Two – Themes, Ideas and Approaches – we turn our focus onto the films themselves: the narratives, the social environments, the locations and the emotions that they create. What we are particularly interested in is how French and Japanese cinema engage with the real world to express universal truths about the human condition in ways that pivot between the comedic, the traumatic, the political and the emotional.

Chapter 5 explores the social impact of unemployment and how the filmmakers of France and Japan persistently turn to this theme as a way of showing the breakdown of the social contract. In turn, this breakdown can lead to isolation from the family and the community, often with harmful repercussions.

Chapter 6 is concerned with the geographical setting of films and the specific use of locations to connect with audiences and to provide a shorthand, visual use of iconography to situate characters and plots. This chapter also highlights how institutional incentives are often provided to filmmakers in France and Japan to encourage them to shoot films in selected locations. In Chapter 7, we explore the idea of confrontational cinema, films that sit in the margins of mainstream release, yet tell a story every bit as important as big-budget films. The focus of Chapter 8 is on the ways that cinema allows us to consider the major issues of life and death, and the struggles that may take place in between. Chapter 9 explores the many adaptations, translations and reworkings that provide filmmakers from Japan and France with visual inspiration and literary context for their works, often across national cultures. Our concluding chapter outlines possible areas for further research and looks ahead to suggest how the richness and diversity of the cinematic influence between France and Japan continue to develop alongside each other in parallel.

Part One

History and Style

1

Historicizing French and Japanese cinemas

The renowned French film theorist and critic André Bazin once famously posed the (rhetorical) question 'What is Cinema?'. To a degree, he already had an answer at the ready, arguing that a 'complete harmony of image and sound' (1967: 29) had been achieved in films such as John Ford's *Stagecoach* or Marcel Carné's *Daybreak/Le Jour se lève*, both released in 1939. Bazin sees in such films 'the ripeness of a classical art', where he defines them as a site where 'art has found its perfect balance, its ideal form of expression, and reciprocally one admires them for dramatic and moral themes to which the cinema, which may not have created them, has given a grandeur, and artistic effectiveness, that they would not otherwise have had' (Bazin 1967: 29). Although Bazin is here referring primarily to the concept of cinematic form and pre–Second World War cinema, he also captures the intimacy of content, as without content no meaning could be created from the 'dramatic and moral themes'. Indeed, influences from Japan could be seen in the mirroring of styles earlier in French cinema, such as 'when Mizoguchi's technique of the "one scene-one shot" became popular in the West around the 1950s and was highly acclaimed in France' (Sato 2008: 97). But it was not just France heaping acclaim on the cinema of Japan. In Italy, Elio Ruffo (1955: 270) was to write that *Ugetsu Monogatari* was a worthy winner of the Venice Silver Lion (1953) because of 'its truly superlative rendering of manners and environment', and scenes that are 'the product of a refinement of taste, of a culture, and therefore of a civilisation which are quite unmistakable' (270). Ruffo's obvious deification of Japanese cinema is even found in his hopes that 'this year the Italian cinema has given us a film which may be linked up with the trend of the Japanese films', and what he sees as 'the rejuvenated cinema art of Japan' (1955: 273).

Before the *nouvelle vague* . . . and after

In March 1960, Godard's and Truffaut's debut features – *Breathless/A Bout de souffle* (1960) and *The 400 Blows/Les 400 Coups* (1959) – were both released in Japan. Yet the beginnings of the French New Wave (the *nouvelle vague*) had an earlier explicit link to Japan with the 1959 Alain Resnais film, *Hiroshima, My Love/Hiroshima, Mon Amour*. Set mostly in Hiroshima as it reconstructs after the 1945 bombing, Emmanuelle Riva plays a French actress (Elle) starring in an anti-war film. Elle has a brief affair with Lui (Eiji Okada), a local architect (Nochimson 2010: 59). Resnais uses the couple's affair to explore not just universal themes of human attraction and fidelity (both Elle and Lui are already married) but also the complexities in trying to understand the politico-cultural differences between two nations and their ability to communicate. The film creates a space where 'thoughts like memories and the terrors of trauma are fragmentary, incomplete, lingering and subjective' (Standish 2011: 148), especially so for Lui, who has lived through the bombing and desecration of his homeland and has given in to the temptation of a foreign muse.

While the *nouvelle vague* shook up French filmmaking, its impact created a series of films (and film styles) that served to complement traditional French cinema rather than destroy them. The concept of the *nouvelle vague*, and later, Japan's *New Wave* is both helpful and limiting in dealing with cinema at the national level. It can also run counter to *auteur* theory, which seemed to push for cinema to be treated with the 'high seriousness of hushed museums and other temples of art' (Tweedie 2013: 71).

Limiting the parameters of French cinema to select filmmakers through auteur theory is contestable though, 'because of its inability to fully explain the production of a distinct body of films by a diverse group of individuals within an historic moment' (Standish 2011: 148). By the 1980s there was a return to nostalgic 'heritage' films that '[a]dapted old, reassuring stories taken from French literary classics and produced them as lush, color, star-filled spectacles that rivalled those of Hollywood' (Nochimson 2010: 63). As if to compensate for the move towards safer, populist or mainstream cinema, new directors such as Luc Besson and Jean-Jacques Beineix burst on to the scene with their heavy, formalist accent on visual style, surreal cinematography and a highly kinetic use of montage. These films, which accentuated form over function, were newly coined as *cinéma du look* and instigated a key aesthetic mode in 1980s France. Directors took their cues from the glossiness of the new MTV era, and Besson's

Subway (1985) in particular became the standard-bearer of the so-called *cinéma du look*. Will Higbee sees films of this kind as possessing:

> a spectacular visual style which manifests itself through a highly stylised mise en scène (elaborate framing, a preoccupation with decor and colour), a cinéphile tendency to reference or recycle from other films, and a focus on youthful protagonists who are often marginal or romantic figures. (Higbee 2006: 154)

Such characteristics inflected – and continue to inflect – Besson's work. *The Big Blue/Le Grand Bleu* (1988) was a critical, if not commercial, success, acclaimed for its breathtaking underwater cinematography framed by long takes and extended, dialogue-free scenes. He achieved greater international commercial success with his English-language, science fiction and made-for-Hollywood *The Fifth Element* (1997), but later films such as his 2004 produced and co-written, parkour-based *District 13/Banlieue 13* (directed by Pierre Morel) failed to attract the same attention at the box office.

The idea that French cinema sits beyond Hollywood is complicated by the relationship between the two, where 'desire and repulsion for the same cinematic phenomena are to be found among the same people' (O'Regan 2004: 276). So, while French filmmakers and critics may be critical of the Hollywood hegemony, they may also be drawn to its new techniques, its star actors or its latest auteur. Take Besson's later career: *Lucy* (2014), his science-fiction-inflected thriller, starred Scarlett Johansson as an unsuspecting drug mule who gains psychokinetic abilities after she is surgically implanted with a powerful chemical substance. *Valerian and the City of a Thousand Planets* (2017), an adaptation of a series of French science-fiction comics, marked a return to form for Besson, a director who has frequently, and unashamedly, imitated Hollywood in both visual and industrial terms. As David Pettersen acutely notes, Besson's cultural strategy over the last decade 'is not a negation of French culture but rather a creative adaptation of Frenchness to the constraints of global, transnational film markets' (2014: 27). Such unashamed mirroring of Hollywood is far from new, though. Éric Rohmer, for example, openly cited his adoration of the work of Alfred Hitchcock and Howard Hawks, 'praising long takes and static camerawork that did not interfere with the presentation of events' (Neupert 2007: 249). In his filmmaking, Rohmer was not afraid to draw on such techniques as can be observed in scenes in his later films such as the iconic observational-style footage of Pauline's (Amanda Langlet) languid walk along the beach in the aptly titled *Pauline at the Beach/Pauline à la plage* (1983), or the hilltop scenes above

Annecy between Jerome (Jean-Claude Brialy) and the much younger Laura (Béatrice Romand) in *Claire's Knee/Le genou de Claire* (1970). During the peak of the *nouvelle vague* though, despite Rohmer's commitment to cinema, his time at *Cahiers du cinéma* was curtailed by those wanting a 'more modernist slant' to the journal (Neupert 2007: 258).

Besson's appeal, both in France and abroad, has always been popular, not critical, and his career is a useful test case for the viability of a Hollywood-style reliance on genre, star and 'the cinema of attraction' in a domestic film culture traditionally skewed towards the intimate and the personal. Perhaps Besson's most notable achievement has been the establishment of Paris's vast Cité du Cinéma studio complex, and EuropaCorp, one of the biggest film companies in Europe. Besson's interest in and engagement with Asian cinema has primarily stemmed from his perspective as a producer; the aforementioned *Banlieue 13* exemplifies a 'global' action cinema that reaches back to Hong Kong and Japanese genre cinema, while *Wasabi* (2001, directed by Gérard Krawczyk) is an action-comedy set in Japan. Here, Besson acts as a 'gatekeeper' figure (Hunt 2008), 'Asianising' European action cinema by displaying a connoisseurship of Asian cinema, casting Asian actors and being attuned to the demographics and crossover cults of the target audience.

Since the late 1990s, French cinema's international visibility has grown considerably, mainly due to its push to make crowd-pleasing forms of cinema. Action buddy films like the *Taxi* series (1998–2018) or slasher horrors such as *Them/Ils* (2006), *Inside/A l'intérieur* (2007) and *Frontiers/Frontière(s)* (2007) 'imitate Hollywood production models through the deployment of star actors and hyper-real mise en scène but also through their progressive erasure or elision of specific linguistic and cultural markers' (McCann 2008: 236). French horror films in particular were successful both within the Hexagon and on the international cult circuit because for a brief moment they offered a third-way alternative to American and Asian horror tropes. This complicated play of imitation and reworking of conventional genre codes functions as part of a broader debate in France on the emergence of new forms of popular cinema and the wisdom of competing with Hollywood. Comedy, too, is the most dominant genre in French cinema, in terms of films made and tickets sold (Moine 2014; Harrod and Powrie 2018). The phenomenal success of *Welcome to the Sticks/Bienvenue chez les Ch'tis* (2008) and *Intouchables* (2011) discredited the myth that French comedy does not travel – the former grossed nearly US$200 million in France and over US$50 million in international markets; the latter grossed over US$160 million in France with a further US$250 million worldwide. As Charlie Michael concludes, 'while some onlookers view successful French films as healthy symptoms of an industry pursuing a combination of survival strategies, others see them as harbingers of destruction, wherein an infatuation with corporate success could eventually destroy the distinctive qualities of a culture and its cinema from the inside' (2019: 20).

The impact of Japan's *Nūberu bāgu*

Japan's twentieth century saw complex societal and economic changes, leading Nygren to posit that it is 'a tutelary site for understanding the processes of inversion, displacement, and appropriation that mark the end of Western imaginary universalism and the opening of a postcolonial possibility' (2007: 118). In other words, Japan's resistance to the West was entwined with its embrace: to move forward required advancements beyond the shackles of 'colonialism' (in this case, the occupation of Japan), while maintaining its own identity through tradition. Filmmaking was no different. Despite initial resistance by some filmmakers to the *nūberu bāgu* tag (Nygren 2007: 164), the essence of its renegade nature was linked closely with the more adventurous young filmmakers emerging from production houses and studios such as the Art Theatre Guild (ATG), Nikkatsu, Shochiku, Toho and Daei, and consolidated the political and artistic links to the highly respected cinema of France.

Nygren suggests that Kurosawa's *Ikiru/To Live* (1952) could be seen as 'a prototype for the nouvelle vague', perhaps because it 'defies the humanist ideology of authenticity and transparency by narrativizing the difficulty and obscurity of becoming a humanist individual' (2007: 118). But it was not until later in the decade, spilling over into the 1960s, that the more excessive features of Japanese filmmaking began to mirror what was happening in French cinema. New films began to challenge what, to some, was seen as 'Japan's complicity with Western Orientalism' that resulted in 'self-Orientalising representations' (Tezuka 2020: 541) through films that were beginning to gain international attention. Unlike in France though, it was within the confines of Japan's studio system that these new filmmakers were able to produce, and fund, their 'B' films that were to push the limits of filmmaking. The emergence of Shōhei Imamura at Nikkatsu (after learning the trade at Shōchiku) saw the creation of films that were increasingly dark in their satirical tone, from *Pigs and Battleships/Buta to gunkan* (1961) to his notorious *The Pornographers/"Erogotoshitachi" yori jinruigaku nyūmon* [lit. "Pornographers": An anthropological introduction] in 1966. Meanwhile, at Shōchiku, Masahiro Shinoda emerged with the yakuza-themed *Pale Flower/Kawaita hana* (1964), a film influenced by Charles Baudelaire's 1857 collection of morally introspective and controversially erotic poems, *Les Fleurs du mal*. Shinoda's film plays down the eroticism of Baudelaire's work, focusing on the protagonists' moral and ethical dilemmas. It bursts onto the screen (in black and white), with busy scenes of a crowded Tokyo train station and snippets of industrial Japan intercut with bleak images of suburban life. A voiceover narrated by Muraki (Ryō Ikebe), a man returning to the city after some years away (later revealed to have been in jail), sets a nihilistic tone:

> **Muraki**: People. Such strange animals. What are they living for? Their faces are lifeless, dead. They're desperately pretending to be alive.

Then, after a pause, he gives a preview into the sort of man he might be:

> **Muraki**: Why make such a big deal about slaughtering one of these dumb beasts?

Shinoda's sleazy world of yakuza, gamblers and general ne'er-do-wells is presented through the use of sharp cuts, canted angles and montages of the type found in Godard's *Breathless*, and in the numerous films of his increasingly feted contemporary, Seijun Suzuki.

While there were degrees of mutual admiration for each other's film industries, there were anomalies, such as Ōshima Nagata's oft-cited dichotomous stance where although 'Europe was a pompous gatekeeper for the international film market; he strategically sought European awards for his films while simultaneously reviling the European perspective' (Tezuka 2020: 553). Of course, neither the *nouvelle vague* nor the *nūberu bāgu* were defined by any singular genre or style, or even strictly, a particular chronological period, but they both help to indicate that a shift was occurring, from the old guard to the new.

The rise of the female auteur: Naomi Kawase and Claire Denis

One area where French cinema surpasses Japan is in its recognition and support of female filmmakers, although this did not occur during the early days of the *nouvelle vague*, as Tweedie notes (2013: 48):

The absence of a single first-time female director between 1958 and 1962, the key years when the new wave developed into a cultural force, suggests that there was nothing genuinely innovative about the representation of gender in the films ... and even less in the sexual politics of an ostensibly transformed industry.

From the 1960s onward, though, luminaries such as Agnès Varda (*Cleo from 5 to 7/Cléo de 5 à 7*, 1962) have been joined by Claire Denis (*Chocolat*, 1988; *White Material*, 2009), Catherine Breillat (*Romance*, 1999), Coline Serreau (*Three Men and a Cradle/Trois Hommes et un Couffin*, 1985) and Céline Sciamma (*Tomboy*, 2011 and *Portrait of a Lady on Fire/Portrait de la jeune fille en feu*, 2019). Former child actor (and former wife of Besson) Maïwenn Besco (mostly known simply as Maïwenn) was nominated for the Palme d'Or in 2015 for her fourth feature (and fourth as writer/director), *My King/Mon Roi*. In a number of ways *Mon Roi* points to a difference between the *mono no aware* (pathos of things) so prevalent in Japanese films, and the metaphysical search for meaning that permeates many French films. There is no acceptance of the self in *Mon Roi*; as Tony (played by actor, director and recipient of the esteemed *Ordre national de la Légion d'honneur* for her services to the film industry, Emmanuelle Bercot) recovers from a skiing accident, she becomes self-absorbed, partly prompted by a psychologist who suggests that the accident did not just 'happen' but that events must have led to Tony's skis crossing and her subsequent fall, stating that 'we're looking ahead, never behind'. Tony tries to piece together the emotional journey that preceded the accident, told through a series of flashbacks. Maïwenn's focus on a female protagonist, Tony (a shortening of 'Marie-Antoinette'), nearing middle age and divorced, is said to be based on her own life. Tony finds a new love – successful restaurateur Georgio (Vincent Cassel) – becomes a mother, and seems to find some contentment before suffering an injury requiring an extensive period of rehabilitation. *Mon Roi* navigates the fragile nature of a woman filled with uncertainties and hesitations; as Maïwenn refuses to settle for a sense of *mono no aware*, her narrative becomes driven by the search for happiness.

More broadly, the recent proliferation of young girl/female coming-of-age dramas in European cinema, and in particular the French format of the genre developed by female directors like Diane Kurys and Catherine Breillat back in the 1970s, has evoked child and youth narratives to revisit colonial history, interrogate national myths and expose current political and religious turmoil. More recent French films have offered cutting-edge depictions of female subjectivity and have explored the multiple effects that social conventions might have on the formation of female identities. As Judith Franco notes: '[a]dolescent girlhood is primarily associated with loss, frustration, and self-estrangement . . . that show young women confronted with predatory male sexuality and limited options in their quest to develop a sense of self' (2017: 2). Franco's list of French films that are directed by women and offer a child-centred narrative perspective include *Water Lilies/Naissance des pieuvres* (Céline Sciamma 2007), as well as *Stella* (Sylvie Verheyde 2008), *No and Me/No et moi* (Zabou Breitman 2010), *Love Like Poison/Un poison violent* (Katell Quillévéré 2010), *17 Girls/17 filles* (Muriel and Delphine Coulin 2011) and *Tomboy* (Céline Sciamma 2011). These works, and many others, are frequently 'anchored in self-inscription and marked by a strong focus on the role of lived/embodied experience in girls' identity formation' (Franco: 2). *Bandes de filles/Girlhood*, Sciamma's 2014 coming-of-age film, recounts how 16-year-old Marieme (Karidja Touré) must navigate the unsettling transition into adulthood while at the same time struggle against the institutional inequities and disadvantages of being black and living in the underprivileged *banlieues* of outer Paris. This focus on identity construction and self-actualization is a common motif in contemporary French films about young people.

Claire Denis burst onto the international cinema arena with the release of *Chocolat* in 1988. A drama set in colonial Cameroon, *Chocolat* proved to be a festival favourite. It offers a detailed character study of a young woman, Aimeé Dalens (Giulia Boschi), who has accompanied her husband Marc (François Cluzet) and their young daughter with the nationalist-inspired name of France (Cécile Ducasse) to a desolate outpost. Denis captures the harsh physical environment and the ongoing racial and class tensions that underpin the colonial experience, a common theme in many of her films. The sexual tension of the hot, languid environment is heightened when Aimeé's husband is away for days at a time, leaving Aimeé in close contact with their servant, the muscular, soft-spoken Proteé (Isaach de Bankolé).

Later work by Denis has looked closer to home and the hedonistic desires of particular characters. Denis's *Let the Sunshine In/Un beau soleil intérieur* (2017), for instance, focuses firmly on the romantic and sexual relationships of Isabella (Juliette Binoche), divorced and in her middle age, seeking male companionship, but strictly on her own terms. *Let the Sunshine In* is close, almost claustrophobic in its presentation of Isabella, an artist, as she moves around Paris trying to create some kind of structure in her personal and professional life. In this dialogue-heavy film, Denis captures Isabella's frustrations and somewhat impetuous nature that creates constant conflict with her various lovers (and ex-husband). Seemingly economically independent through the success of her artworks and exhibitions, Isabella's self-centred behaviours create tensions that remain mostly unresolved throughout the film, and lead to awkward conversations as she tries to measure the level of commitment she wants from her lovers. When one of these men, the unnamed 'actor' (played by Nicolas Duvauchelle), a younger, married man, drops her home after a dinner, they sit for a moment as the engine idles.

> **Actor**: So . . .

Isabella does not react, and stares ahead, out the window.

> **Actor** (*cont.*): So.

Isabella takes off her seatbelt, and still staring ahead responds:

> **Isabella**: I feel like we said nothing. We got nowhere. (*pause*). I'm just tired.

She glances across at him, as he remains silent, bemused.

> **Isabella**: We said things . . . then we said the opposite.
> **Actor** (*sighs*): I'm off tomorrow. We can go see a movie.

Isabella reaches for the car door handle to let herself out, but instead pauses and refrains from opening it.

> **Actor** (*cont.*): I'll call you. So. See you tomorrow. (*Pause.*) I'll call you when I wake up.

While this appears to be a mostly banal conversation, the tension builds throughout. It is noticeable that the actor is not asking Isabella but stringing together a series of statements, as if there is no discussion to be had.

> **Isabella**: I don't know.
> **Actor** (*frustration building*): So I'll call you and we'll see.
> **Isabella**: I don't know if you should bother calling.

Denis again shows Isabella's hand clutching the door handle, her grip tightening. They barely glance at each other.

> **Isabella**: Park! So we can talk about it for a minute. No use beating around the bush for hours.

Reluctantly, he turns the engine off.

> **Actor**: Whatever you say.

They sit silently for a moment, both staring ahead. Finally, Isabella blurts out:

> **Isabella**: Let's not meet again. It's going nowhere.

He sighs again.

> **Isabella** (*cont.*): What is that face?
> **Actor**: I feel like a spurned lover, that's why. And you don't get it.
> **Isabella** (*laughs*): I don't understand how you can feel like a spurned lover. I don't get it.
> **Actor**: You said 'no use meeting again, it's going nowhere'!
> **Isabella**: Yes, I said that. And you don't see why?
> **Actor**: No.
> **Isabella**: I said it, but don't listen to everything I say.

The argument continues for some while before the actor acquiesces and joins Isabella upstairs. The constant interplay between Isabella and all the other characters is a feature of the dialogue that threads through the entire film. Denis leads the viewer on a journey that looks to have no suitable conclusion for Isabella. The final fourteen minutes of the film (including as the final credits roll) consists of a slightly odd postscript where Isabella consults a psychic, named Denis (Gérard Depardieu), who dispenses his sage advice, culminating in the suggestion that Isabella remains 'open' to any love offered to her. The final shot is of Isabella nodding and smiling, suggesting that at last she has found some kind of solace (Figure 1.1).

Naomi Kawase's continued success and recognition at Cannes since 1997 (just four years after her first short films were released) indicate the esteem with which she is held in the global film community. She released the Japanese/

Figure 1.1 Finding solace in the final shot of *Let the Sunshine In* (2017).

French co-production, *Radiance/Hikari* (2017) in the year following her appointment as jury president for both the short films section and the student film awards, La *Cinéfondation* at Cannes. *Radiance* saw her nominated for the *Palme d'Or*, and it won the *Prix du Jury Œcuménique*. Kawase's emotionally enduring style is on full display in *Radiance* when audio describer Misako (Ayame Misaki) is shown trialling the scripted descriptions she will record for films for those who are sight-impaired. A process done in conjunction with a select number of those who will eventually make up her potential audience, the young Misako is taken aback when one of the test audience members, a middle-aged man, Masaya Nakamori (Masatoshi Nagase), critiques her work in a way that seems to breach the unofficial codes of politeness that operate in Japanese society. A stern-faced Masaya prompts one of the other members (played by J-pop icon, Saori Koide):

> **Masaya**: Don't you think it was intrusive?

Kawase's camera cuts to Misako's slightly shocked face.

> **Other member**: I wouldn't say 'intrusive'. Having all those descriptions is undeniably very helpful, but if all the gaps are filled with words, it can be a bit too much.
> **Masaya** (*in close-up*): For example. [he repeats in a slightly mocking, higher-pitched voice] 'As if he can see the absent Tokie . . . ' Or: 'Overflowing with the hope of life.' Maybe? Aren't those subjective feelings?

The shots cut between extreme close-ups of Masaya and his target.

> **Misako** (*barely audible*): No.
> **Masaya**: Frankly, (*pause*) like that, it just gets in the way.
> **Misako** (*shaking*): There's no need to be so blunt. I wrote it that way . . . for all of you.
> **Masaya**: That's why it's intrusive.

Misako's elder co-worker Tomoko (Misuzu Kanno) draws back a long breath, shifting in her seat at the tension that has suddenly intercepted the discussion. Misako's co-worker interjects to try to diffuse the moment:

> **Co-worker**: Mr Nakamori is a bit different from the rest of you. He does have partial sight, so . . .

Cutting back to Masaya's stern face filling the screen, Misako can be heard in acknowledgement.

Misako: I understand. [the camera cuts back to her staring wide-eyed at Masaya] Before the next session . . . I'll try to put it right. [pause] I'll try to put right all the intrusive elements. [pause] I'll do my best not to upset you Mr Nakamori.

In this short sequence, Kawase sets up the initial dynamic between Misako and Masaya and captures the essence of contemporary Japanese culture and its attitudes towards politeness and gender (with ultimate deference to Masaya's needs).

Radiance continues Kawase's fascination with nature and the often documentary style of her earlier films such as *Suzaku* (see Chapter 3), with the use of frequent close follow-shots (especially of Masaya as he navigates his way through hallways and downstairs, as if to amplify the sensory loss that he must combat in order to get from one place to another). The use of amplified sounds of nature with rustling leaves and windblown grasses is a common trope in film (frequently used in Zhang Yimou's films) that also evokes the aural tone in the animated Studio Ghibli films, where the soundscape is often as important as the visual imagery. Masaya's vision loss is itself a commentary on nature and his frustration at no longer being able to experience it. As he desperately aims his camera towards what he perceives as light, and the hope of picking out the details of a subject, he experiences a type of trauma and his camera is basically rendered impotent because he can no longer control the images (Figure 1.2).

Kawase's use of the widescreen anamorphic lens (with cinematography by Arata Dodo, who worked again on Kawase's next film) fills the screen almost in mockery of Masaya's increasingly diminishing sight. The wide vistas, lavish sunsets and open skies are intercut with extreme close-ups of Misako and

Figure 1.2 Masaya struggles to focus in *Radiance* (2017).

Masaya: one who has the gift of sight, and the other so cruelly denied. Kawase also drops between showing us what the characters see (or don't see) and the 'film-within-a-film' that Misako is audio describing, which itself has widescreen shots of lakes and beaches.

While *Radiance* continues Kawase's theme of emotionally charged, melancholy films, the sense of loss portrayed through Masaya's vision impairment is paralleled by Misako's mother, Yasuko (Kazuko Shirakawa), and her swift decline into dementia. But while Masaya is intently aware of his loss, Yasuko is thankfully unaware and wanders away from her home. When Misako finds her mother, standing at the edge of the forest in a favourite place she used to visit to watch the sunset when Misako was young, and her husband (Misako's father) was alive, weeping, Misako confronts her:

> **Misako**: Mum!
> **Yasuko**: Ah, Misako. You've come home. It's starting to get cold.
> **Misako**: Mum. But what are you doing?
> **Yasuko**: What am I doing? I'm waiting for your father to come home. (*Turning away from her daughter*) Once the sun goes down behind that mountain, your father will be home.

They stand in silence, watching the sun disappear, and Misako suddenly recalls standing there, in her father's arms, sharing the same event. Again, Kawase uses the natural environment as a site for emotional human interaction.

Conclusion

What we have shown in this initial excavation of the state of French and Japanese cinema since the 1950s is the central role France has played in developing the technical possibilities of film, as well as the laying down of templates in terms of image, storytelling and techniques that continue to resonate across the intersecting and overlapping ecosystems of global cinema. The French *nouvelle vague* undoubtedly inspired the emergence of Japan's *nūberu bāgu*, even if this movement, unlike its European counterpart, emerged from within the studio system as a conscious attempt to counter the growing popularity of television. A further connection between the two nations lies in the way both French and Japanese 'new waves' were contingent on the emergence of film criticism and a new way of thinking about film theory and praxis. We are by now familiar with the story of *Cahiers du cinéma* and the seismic role the journal played in European film circles in cementing the idea of the auteur. In Japan, too, the emergence of sophisticated film criticism went hand-in-hand with the emergence of a new cinema style. Eizo Yamagiwa founded the film journal *Eiga Hihyo* (*Film Criticism*) and made films at Taiho studios, while Toshio Matsumoto and Shinkichi Noda edited and wrote for *Kiroku Eiga* (*Documentary Film*). This fusion of theory and practice would have important industrial implications for the post-war Japanese film industry.

2

Cinematic engagement between France and Japan

As we have already discussed, the Inabata-Lumière connection began the cinematic connection between France and Japan as early as 1897. From that point on, a series of important criss-crossing 'moments' reveal the strong links between the two nations. William Gardner (2004) rightly focuses on the increased exposure of European modernist art, avant-garde culture and critical writing in Japanese circles throughout the 1920s that had a direct influence on emerging Japanese modernist sensibilities. Films such as *The Cabinet of Dr. Caligari/Das Kabinett des Dr. Caligari* (1919) and Abel Gance's *The Wheel/La Roue* (1923) were screened in Japan in 1925 and their visual extravagance would be clearly visible in the work of Teinosuke Kinugasa, whose *Crossroads* (1928), a *jidaigeki* (period action film), blends German expressionist and French impressionist visual styles. *Crossroads* was one of several important Japanese films that screened in the West (after touring Paris, Berlin and London, it continued its run in New York). In 1931, *Under the Roofs of Paris/Sous les toits de Paris* made the opposite journey: the first French talking picture to be exhibited in Japan. The increasing rapid transmission of European cinema to Japan, coupled with an enthusiastic domestic audience, meant that French films found a receptive audience. Film journals like *Kinema Junpō* would compile yearly top ten lists: from 1931 to 1939, French films routinely placed first or second. Director Heinosuke Gosho regarded Julien Duvivier's *Le Paquebot Tenacity* (released in 1934, topping the *Kinema Junpō* list in 1935) as one of cinema's purest examples of romanticism, and praised the French director for creating 'a lyrical poem' (Anderson and Richie 1956: 80–1). This elegance and craftsmanship identified in Duvivier's work were qualities admired by many Japanese writers and directors of the time, who also held up the work of René Clair and Marcel Carné as exemplars of French cinema's formal and pictorial beauty.

Subsequent events were to see parallels between the two nations, not the least the experimental 'new waves' that refigured approaches to cinema in each country and influenced filmmakers around the globe. Political events were also to play a role, with opposition to the Vietnam War a common platform, but local issues sparking the student protests, strikes and revolutionary air of France in May 1968 that were echoed in similar protests in Japan later that same year, and into 1969. In both instances, these were youth-led insurgencies aimed at disturbing the status quo in a push for generational change. It was perhaps only natural that this provided a fertile ground for avant-garde cinema.

As France struggled with its own conceptions of identity in the 1960s, its intellectuals began to look further afield in a precursor to the debates on post-colonialism that would follow in subsequent decades. Roland Barthes, for instance, penned *L'Empire des signes* in 1970, where he 'speaks of an East/West encounter, under the mode of resistance, producing an unrestrained passion for everything Japanese' (Blum-Reid 2003: 6). While directors such as Jun Ichikawa show their reverence for earlier local filmmakers, such as Ozu, they also draw from other fields, with Ichikawa stating that:

> [o]n the whole, I think I like European films the best, especially those by British or French directors. My favourite, though, is probably Truffaut's *Les Quatre Cents Coups* (*The Four Hundred Blows*). It's an old film, but no matter how many times I see it, I never get tired of it. (Schilling 1999: 104)

By the mid-1980s, both the French and Japanese industries began to recognize the need to raise the international profile of their films in order to offer stronger competition from Hollywood blockbusters. The projects that followed (in France, films like *Valmont* [1989], *The Lover/L'Amant* [1992], and *1492: Conquest of Paradise* [1992]; in Japan, *Nausicaä of the Valley of the Wind* [1984]; Kurosawa's *Ran* [1985]; and *Akira* [1988]) were both financially ambitious – in essence, mimicking Hollywood's modes of production – and strategically released and promoted so as to attract a wider global market. Martine Danan calls such policies 'postnational', or 'depthless commodified images detached from the complexity of history and from concrete, situated life' (2000: 356). Though Danan is referring here to a French industrial strategy, her comments can be usefully applied to the Japanese context as well. While these films may look and feel 'French' or 'Japanese' on a surface level, their marks of 'Frenchness' and 'Japaneseness' are elided, obscured or even jettisoned. Instead, there is an emphasis on action, the deployment of international actors, and a glossy mise-en-scene.

By the 1990s, ties between French and Japanese cinemas became even more closely associated with continued attempts towards global box-office success, with intended blockbusters exemplified by the likes of Hayao Miyazaki's *Porco Rosso* (1992) and *Princess Mononoke* (1997) – both huge financial and critical successes at home and abroad – or Luc Besson's similarly lucrative *Léon* (1994) and *The Fifth Element/Le Cinquième Élément* (1997). The steady decline of Japan's studio system (from the 1960s onward) resulted in filmmakers now finding themselves part of an industry where, as Wada-Marciano (2012: 15) points out, 'new production modes and thematic focuses ... distinguish[ed] their films from previous ones – in particular, the assimilation of digital media and the representation of the transnational', in order to survive. It was the same in France – successive waves of filmmakers and policymakers since the mid-1980s have formulated canny strategies to counter the hegemonic reach of a globalized Hollywood. One of the most remarkable trends in recent film history has been the sustained emergence and success of the 'French blockbuster' – whether comedy (*Intouchables* [2011]), genre film (*Lucy* [2014]) or prestigious award winner (*The Artist* [2011]). For Charlie Michael (2019: 20), this eclectic range of work exemplifies a 'collective aesthetic outcome of a vigorous and ongoing campaign to foster a more competitive, commercialised Gallic production sphere'. In other words, playing (and in some cases, beating) Hollywood at its own game (Figure 2.1).

At the 2010 Tokyo International Film Festival, Jason Gray, *Screen International*'s Japan correspondent, gloomily noted in a presentation to delegates the steady decline over the previous decade in the number of European films screened in Japan (from ninety-two released in the Japanese market in 2004 to eighty-four in 2010, with only seventy-two in 2008). Gray also outlined the number of European films to have screened at the prestigious Berlin, Cannes and Venice film festivals and then to have subsequently had a release in Japan; once again, the numbers were dispiriting: fourteen in 2004 down to five films in 2009. Yet there was a glimmer of hope: Gray also listed the number of films Japan had acquired for local distribution from the European Union: by far the most popular market was France: thirty-one deals in 2004 and 2006, and a consistent mid-20s range for the rest of the time (Foreman 2010). French cinema's continuing appeal to Japanese audiences remains strong.

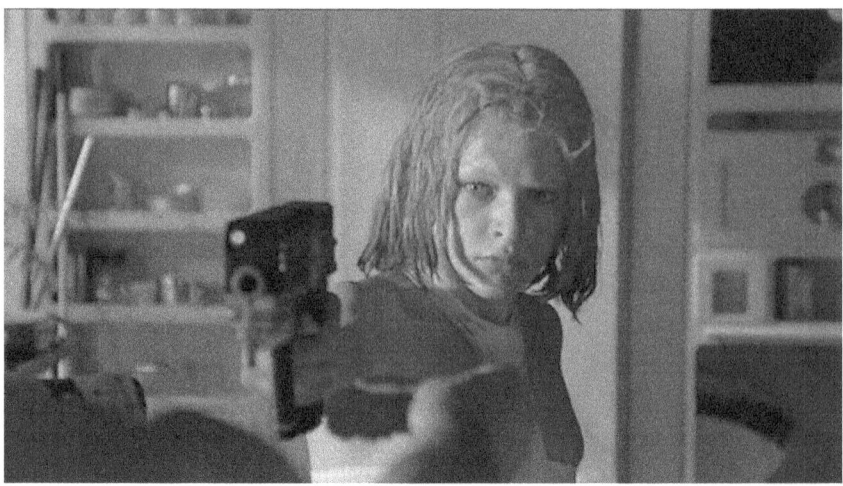

Figure 2.1 Frenchness elided in *The Fifth Element* (1997).

Kurosawa connections

The ability to grow each national cinema during the late twentieth century seemed to depend on formal and informal cultural exchange. Tezuka (2012: 3), for instance, notes that through successive generations, Japan's filmmakers' 'subjectivity has been shaped by their transnational experiences'. The key factors that initiated change in Japanese films, according to Tezuka, were Japan's introduction to the international cinema market in the 1950s, and the moves within the global industrial complex of film finance, including Sony's bold takeover of Columbia Pictures, in the 1990s (2012: 3).

Japan's links to the West, and particularly the United States, in the post-war period saw a complex relationship that appeared to be developed along paternal lines, with the United States as the economic, military and cultural hegemony. For the non-West, and Japan specifically, Tezuka maintains that 'it [Japan] seeks recognition from the West of the particularity of its culture as an exceptional case' (2012: 41). Thus, recognition of Japanese films at major festivals such as Venice and Cannes helped to delineate the 'exotic' Japan not only from the West but also from the rest of Asia. Renowned scholar and critic André Bazin was to write of the 'exemplary merits of Japanese film', further waxing that:

> There are undoubtedly no other productions in the world that give us the feeling of being more perfectly homogenous with the artistic spirit of a civilization. I've

already seen some twenty or twenty-five Japanese films, diverse in genre and quite unequal in result. (Bazin 1982: 188)

Bazin continues to list several films that he regards as highlights of Japanese cinema, before concluding, 'what I have not seen, even when the performance was boring, naive, or, in my Western eyes, worthless, is a Japanese film that is vulgar or just in bad taste' (188).

Tezuka (2012: 42) notes that in the year before *Rashomon* became feted in the West, 'the Motion Picture Association of Japan had considered sending *Mata au hi made* (*Until We Meet Again*, Tadashi Imai, 1950 [aka *Till We Meet Again*]), a love story set in modern times, to the Cannes Film Festival but decided against it when . . . , it was pointed out that the story of the film resembled perhaps too closely that of a certain Romain Rolland novel'. In fact, the film was said to be a direct adaptation of Rolland's 1920 First World War–based romance, *Pierre et Luce*, simply reset in Second World War Japan. Ultimately, Rashomon was sent to the 1951 Venice Film Festival, resulting in Japan's first major international cinema success. Japan's reputation in the West was still recovering during this period, and in Japan itself, the nation struggled in its reflections about what it meant to be Japanese, so a film like *Until We Meet Again*, which reminded audiences of the immediate war, was deemed too controversial. The types of film that Japan sent out had to be carefully selected, and representative of a nation where its society 'relied on a sense of discipline originating within and imposed throughout the collective consciousness to maintain social order' (Wren 2016: 234).

Nygren contends that any attempted historicization of *Rashomon* means it can be considered 'a hinge text, between two epistemes or cultural configurations, that constitutes the possibility of a recognizable national cinema in a world context' (2007: 108). Indeed, in the aftermath of the Second World War, the trauma felt across Europe echoed that of Japan, and Kurosawa was able to capture the subsequent despondency in *Rashomon*. Its specific references to Japan's history are seen by Nygren as a 'refolding of time', where the opening scenes of the ruined gate 'marks the decline and disintegration of the Heian period [794–1185, when the film is set], as well as the devastation of the bombing at the end of the Pacific War (2007: 111). The argument can be expanded to include the fall of Japan's other great eras, the Meiji, the Taisho and the early Showa (Nygren 2007: 111).

To focus on Kurosawa alone is quite obviously a reductive approach to thinking about Japanese cinema and its impact beyond the nation itself. As

Phillips and Stringer note, 'the brand name of the *auteur* continues to provide the terms of reference through which cultural institutions both inside and outside Japan present and promote Japanese cinema' (2007: 15). But these 'terms of reference' can increasingly be challenged by the significant industry links that see the global flow of capital across studios, film funding bodies and state apparatus.

Formalizing co-productions

By the mid-1950s, co-productions with the West had begun to emerge in Japan, mostly with the United States, but also with France when Yves Ciampi (who later married Japanese actress Keiko Kishi, best known for Ozu's 1956 *Early Spring*) teamed up with Shōchiku and several other Japanese companies to direct *Typhoon Over Nagasaki/Typhon sur Nagasaki/Wasureenu Bojo* (Tezuka 2012: 46). The idea of the co-production, though, may create concerns around the meaning of cinema as a national product, after all, the 'integrity and autonomy of a culture and an identity formed in auto-identificatory fashion (constructing an identity in relation to itself rather than in relation to another) seem compromised by processes which . . . must question, even corrode, the bounded, coherent, and placed character of a cultural formation' (O'Regan 2004: 280). In other words, while the sense of *Nihonjinron* (Japaneseness) may seem to play a pivotal role in defining what it is to be Japanese, of equal importance may be what one measures one's Japaneseness *against* (i.e. French or Spanish or American or Australian).

Akira Kurosawa's grand epic, *Ran* (1985), based on Shakespeare's 'King Lear', was an early French–Japanese co-production, with the link apparent from the opening credits where the text mostly consists of French, Japanese and Romanized Japanese ('English'), with minor actors' names only presented in the latter two forms. As Wada-Marciano notes, 'Kurosawa's reiteration of grand themes from Western literary humanism also secured Japan's place within the cosmopolitan community' (2012: 22). This was further exemplified by the inclusion of Polish-born, French film producer Serge Silberman, who saw opportunities to extend the impact of Kurosawa's work with *Ran*. With a solid body of productions and co-productions (mostly with Spain) behind him, including a close association with Luis Buñuel on *That Obscure Object of Desire/Cet Obscur Objet du Désir* (1977), *The Discreet Charm of the Bourgeoisie/Le Charme Discret de la Bourgeoisie*

(1972) and even the notorious, highly sexualized sci-fi horror film *The Diabolical Dr. Z/Miss Muerte* (1966, dir. J. Franco), Silberman threw his support behind Kurosawa's ambitious project. Silberman's enthusiasm to work with Kurosawa seemed to echo Bazin's fascination with Japan and its cinema, where the esteemed critic exclaimed that '[i]t is a fortunate country where the most controversial films still appear in our eyes as miracles of balance and perfection' (1982: 186).

Further links can be found in French filmmaker Chris Marker's 1985 behind-the-scenes documentary *AK* where he follows Akira Kurosawa as he directs the epic *Ran*. Or in the French/Japanese co-production helmed by Iranian filmmaker Abbas Kiarostami, *Like Someone in Love/Raiku Samuwan in Rabu* (2012), filmed entirely in Japan, which followed Kiarostami's first film shot outside Iran, the mostly French-funded *Certified Copy/Copie conforme* (2010). Utilizing the streets of Tokyo as a backdrop, *Like Someone in Love* is a measured, intimate drama that features an all-Japanese cast and seems to have few overt links to either France or Iran in its narrative or visual styles.

At the 2005 Cannes Film Festival, UniJapan, the Japanese entertainment industry umbrella organization, signed an agreement with CNC to enable a greater number of films to be seen in each other's countries and to build grounds for future Japan–France co-productions. CNC's financial and technical assistance has continued to benefit Japan's filmmakers, with Kiyoshi Kurosawa's *Daguerreotype/Le Secret de la chambre noire* (2016) a recipient of support. Utilizing a strong cast of recognizable French actors, including Constance Rousseau, Mathieu Amalric, Olivier Gourmet and Tahar Rahim, the broody, slow-burning *Daguerreotype*, about a photographer obsessed with old-style photographic techniques, was critically hailed a 'cinematic ghost tale par excellence' (Christley 2018), yet failed to have quite the international box-office impact that was expected. This brings into question the 'value' of a co-production where economically the arrangement has not necessarily been successful, but as a cultural exchange and the development of a text that can be shared, its impact can be seen as immeasurable.

Institutional encouragement

The use of a particular setting or location may not always be at the whim of the filmmaker but closely dependent on the economic gains that can be accrued through financial incentives offered by state and tourism institutions. In attracting foreign filmmakers to France, for instance, a number of institutions work together to promote the nation as a favourable shooting location, claiming that:

> France enjoys a breathtaking range of locations, from mountains to surf spots, from deserted landscapes to idyllic coastal locations. You will also find the greatest number of historical monuments in the world, enough to satisfy the needs of any period film or heroic fantasy piece. Scroll on Film France qualified set database and view up to 17,000 locations. (CNC 2015: 12)

The use of France as a cinematic location is given institutional state support through the *Centre National du Cinéma et de l'image animée* (CNC) and its various funding schemes, especially for co-productions through tax rebates and programmes (CNC 2015: 4), such as the *Aide aux cinémas du monde* – co-managed with the *Institut Français*. This programme supports up to fifty projects per year, with its remit to 'allow and encourage international co-productions and the creation of works that help promote cultural diversity' through either 'a "pre-filming" subsidy of up to €250,000, awarded to the French production company to cover production and post-production costs', or an 'after-production subsidy' up to €50,000 (CNC 2015: 6). Of note is that the programme is designed, and funding allocated, on the somewhat subjective criteria of 'artistic quality and the ability to present different views and new ways of looking at things' (CNC 2015: 6), rather than the more objective reasoning (found in many other national funding schemes, including Japan as outlined shortly) of potential economic return.

The CNC offers structured agreements for international 'Bilateral Co-productions' and regional 'European Co-productions' that require a minimum of three signatory countries (CNC 2015: 5). Funding can also be contingent on such factors as being 'mainly filmed in French', or adaptations of literary works by European authors (CNC 2015: 5), with levels of funding contingent upon the film having been 'granted production approval by the President of the CNC' (CNC 2015: 5). There is also a TRIP (Tax Rebate for International Productions) scheme for projects 'wholly or partly made in France and initiated by a non-French company' (CNC 2015: 11). There have been few Japanese beneficiaries of this model to date. The first of these was a retroactive payment in 2009 for *Nodame Cantabile: The Final Score – Movie I*/*Nodame Kantâbire: Saishu-gakushou – Zenpen* (2009, dir. Hideki Takeuchi), based on the highly successful Nodame Cantabile manga and anime series that features young classical musicians seeking fame and glory in their musicianship. The film was produced through co-production with

Japan's Cine Bazar, Fuji TV, Kodansha and Toho companies, and through production services provided by France's Commes des Cinémas. Other successful ventures include two films funded in 2014: *Foujita* (2015, dir. Kōhei Oguri, an Academy Award nominee for his 1981 *Muddy River/Doro no Kawa*), a biographical drama about Japanese artist Tsuguharu Foujita who lived periodically in Paris, and *Chateau de la Reine/Ohi no Yakata* (2014, dir. Hajime Hashimoto), a flamboyant comedy, based on a novel, set in Paris where a Japanese travel agency lures tourists to stay at an historic chateau. More recently, support was provided for a new animated TV series of *Little Astroboy* (2019, dir. Virgile Trouillot).

CNC's economic support for international filmmaking also includes attractive rebates of 30 per cent allowable on salaries, transportation and catering, expenditures on technical goods and services, or as depreciation, with the central pre-condition that the film includes 'elements related to the French or European culture, heritage, and territory' as determined by the CNC's 'cultural test' (CNC 2015: 11).

Support for the use of new technologies is also available through the CNC's 'New Technologies in Production' scheme, with the provision for twenty-three feature films in 2014, of an average of €185,000 for 3D films and €137,000 for non-3D films (CNC 2015: 7). In a global context, this helps to keep French film competitive in a market swamped by Hollywood special-effects, franchise films through this 'selective fund to help mitigate risk-taking on the part of producers of movie or TV projects who work in 3D, or who use innovative digital technologies (digital visual effects, synthetic imaging, development of specific processes)' (CNC 2015: 7). At the institutional level, France is well equipped to manage international productions, with forty local film commissions across the nation that provide 'free assistance with contacting appropriate agencies regarding immigration/work permits and filming permits, as well as information regarding labour rates, studio facilities, post-production facilities and suppliers' (CNC 2015: 12). The Commission du Film Rhône-Alpes, for instance, offers assistance with location shooting around the historic city of Lyon, the Rhone and Loire rivers, and the glaciers of Mont-Blanc. While not an international production, a recent example is the Commission's assistance with filming for the 2019 Snow White-based comedy, *Pure as Snow/Blanche Neige* (dir. Anne Fontaine), starring Isabelle Huppert, that recently began in the region, a co-production between Mandarin Cinéma and Cine @ (Figure 2.2).

Figure 2.2 Lou de Laâge and Isabelle Huppert in *Pure as Snow* (2019).

The previous examples indicate that France has several strong funding incentives in place to encourage co-productions and international location shooting on French soil. On the other hand, Japan has a less visible approach to dealing with or encouraging international filmmakers to its shores. Regular requirements such as visas and shooting permits need to be obtained, but to apply for a Co-production Subsidy (known as the *Bunka-cho* Subsidy) through the Agency for Cultural Affairs, Japanese filmmakers or producers must apply for a UNIJAPAN Certificate. Created under the national government in 1957, UNIJAPAN (Japan Association for International Promotion of the Moving Image) is a non-profit organization established to promote Japanese cinema abroad, and since 2005, has been the responsible organization for the Tokyo International Film Festival (TIFF) (UNIJAPAN 2017a). In listing its main activities and goals, UNIJAPAN states:

> The Association holds an international film festival, supports the discovery and nurture of future talent, and assists in the preservation of cultural assets. In addition, the Association promotes Japanese moving images overseas to develop the Japanese moving image culture, and promotes the export of Japanese moving images, in line with its goals of contributing to furthering of international friendship and cultural exchange. (UNIJAPAN 2017b)

While this sounds encouraging, the relationship between UNIJAPAN and the state agency is perhaps not as close as one might expect, with the UNIJAPAN website 'Partnering with Japan' offering a frank assessment of the level of support available to foreign filmmakers:

In terms of financial support Japan is not the most coproduction friendly country.
- There is NO system of production tax incentive programs.
- There is NO co-production treaty except for a document signed with Canada.

Films are financed as businesses, and overseas producers seeking to coproduce with Japan must first and foremost convince the Japanese counterpart of the project's commercial feasibility in Japan (UNIJAPAN 2017b).

Unlike France, then, support for international filmmaking in Japan has a much clearer economic focus. The *Bunka-cho* Subsidy has strict requirements, including the completion of the film within the applicable financial year, with payment only after completion of the film and its screening 'to *Bunka-cho* [the funding committee] as proof of completion before the end of the fiscal year' in which the project was funded. As most people involved in the film process would recognize, given the myriad difficulties and delays that arise while locking in funding arrangements, attempting to write, produce, shoot and finalize post-production to a schedule that fits neatly within a fiscal year means that these requirements could be difficult to fulfil.

In terms of film production (including content and crew), based on a points system, the film must feature a 'creative contribution' of at least three points (out of fifteen, for a live-action feature) by a Japanese national or permanent resident, with points allocated as per Table 2.1.

Further to the Creative Contribution points system, the UNIJAPAN Certificate will only be awarded if the (Japanese) producers can show that a minimum of 20 per cent of production funding is from Japan and a minimum 5 per cent (which must total over JPY10 million) from overseas. The producers

Table 2.1 UNIJAPAN Creative Contribution Points. (UNIJAPAN 2017a)

	[Live action]	
(a)	Director	Two points
(b)	Screenwriter	Two points
(c)	Director of photography	One point
(d)	Composer	One point
(e)	Production designer	One point
(f)	Main cast (up to four)	One point each
(g)	Original author	Two points
(h)	Shooting in Japan	One point
(i)	Post Production in Japan	One point
	Total Points Available	Fifteen points

must also show evidence that a distribution plan is in place for the film's Japanese and international distribution.

In working towards its goals (stated earlier), UNIJAPAN (2017c) is responsible for the following operations:

1. The holding of [an] International Film Festival, symposiums and research meetings regarding moving images.
2. The holding of [an] International Contents Trade Fair.
3. The creation, display and distribution of material and literature deemed necessary for the widespread [sic] of Japanese moving image overseas.
4. Conducting studies on the situations and circumstances pertaining to the moving image in foreign countries.
5. Performing services related to the display or participation at international moving image events, including international film festivals and international film competitions.
6. Performing services pertaining to the holding of touring previews of Japanese moving image[s] in foreign countries.
7. The overseas dispatch of those connected to moving images or invitation of foreign persons related to moving images, and any services pertaining thereof.
8. Providing facilities to any foreign persons involved in research related to Japanese moving image.
9. Assist international co-production of the moving image.
10. Pursuing of international contact and communication with personnel connected to the moving image.
11. The submission of proposals, opinions and findings to relevant organizations.
12. Focusing on artistic and outstanding moving images to assist and focus on young talent.
13. To research, investigate and help preservation of the moving image culture and technology.
14. To edit and publicize journals and other publications of printed matters related to international moving image information.
15. Any other operation not listed above but deemed necessary to achieve the goals of the Association.

Other support is available for fledgling Japanese filmmakers through competitive awards such as the transnational United States/Japan US$10,000

Sundance Institute/NHK Award, 'created to contribute to the world's visual culture and to promote cultural exchanges through finding and supporting emerging filmmakers' (NHK 2018). While NHK (*Nippon Hoso Kyokai*, or Japan Broadcasting Corporation) is most widely known as Japan's public television and radio broadcaster, it has a long association with films, especially in the documentary genre. The creation of this award, however, is not limited to a documentary but is open to any full-length feature film, short or other media such as television drama, music video or advertisement.

The Japan Film Commission (JFC, formerly the Japan Film Commission Promotion Council, or JFCPC) is another assisting body that can work with local film commissions to coordinate support for filmmakers, for example, finding volunteer film 'extras' for location or studio shoots, and for waiving or offsetting costs for location scouting, police or parking permits, or fee exemptions for public spaces (JFCPC 2009). Unlike other national film bodies (such as the British Film Institute, or Screen Australia), this is not a direct funding body. The practical nature of its activities initially saw the JFCPC set up within the Ministry of Land, Infrastructure and Transport, due to its function to promote tourism in Japan. In recognition of the cultural and historical importance of film, the JFCPC offices were moved out of the ministry in 2001 to relocate to the National Film Centre in Tokyo. The JFC's links to private production houses and organizations also assist in encouraging location shooting in Japan, where firms such as the recent merger of advertising companies Dentsu Creative X and Pict have become SAS (Sky, Air and Sea), under the banner of 'Shoot in Japan', offering experienced crew, equipment, location services and studios, and post-production facilities (SAS 2018). But location shooting is not always easy to arrange in a considerably bureaucratized Japan, with both Akira Kurosawa and Takeshi Kitano declaring that they had often experienced difficulties in obtaining permission to shoot (Schilling 1999: 95).

Conclusion

As we show in later chapters, cinematic interactions between France and Japan are not wholly reliant on formal economic exchanges. These links may be more individualized through personal connections and the desire of particular filmmakers or actors who wish to work in an industry beyond the 'safety' of their own cultural or linguistic home. The role of institutional support through public and private organizations and festivals that promote film as a national and international project remain important markers of the contemporary French and Japanese industries. From the national to the transnational, from the state-funded and controlled to the independent and the grassroots, the flexible approach to economic exchange in France and Japan is revealing. While co-productions between the two nations remain the most noticeable industrial bridging point, the festival circuit remains, in the eyes of the audience at least, the clearest indication of engagement and recognition. The year-round festival circuit facilitates global flows of films across the world and allows for cultural exchange, the communal experience of film screenings – and the inevitable critical and theoretical discourse that swirls around them – and the construction of national identities. The festival circuit is therefore something akin to 'soft power': a form of cultural diplomacy that leverages a nation's cultural aspirations. But, more directly, they allow filmmakers to share stories and audiences to observe new styles in global cinema. Given the vagaries of exhibition and distribution practices, and the frequent difficulty in getting hold of films, festivals provide opportunities for films to be shown, directors and writers to emerge, and new formal practices to be disseminated.

3

Directorial styles, influence and exchange

Historical links between the states, industries and individuals in both France and Japan, as we have shown, have been instrumental in the development of the two national cinemas. Equally important, though, are the stylistic influences and exchanges that have informed filmmaking across physical and temporal divides. In 1995, David Bordwell wrote of the importance of visual style in Japanese films, focusing on the cinema of the 1925–45 period, but drawing conclusions that inform later periods. His examination of Japanese national cinema is framed in terms of how Japanese film might differ from Western film and to what degree any differences are informed by traditional culture, and to what degree social conditions, especially Japan's role in regional and global wars, may have influenced film style (1995: 5). Bordwell proposes that a number of 'major stylistic trends' are visible in Japanese film by arguing that these occur 'through the mediation of international filmmaking norms and contemporary popular culture' (1995: 5). Following this line of thought, the uniqueness of early Japanese cinema arose from 'extensions and transformations of norms governing Western filmmaking' (1995: 28). In fact, Japan had begun to toy with realism and even what was later to be known as method acting, when director Suzuki Kansaku ordered a film-set extra to not eat in preparation for a short role as a starving man in *Man's Pain* [*Ningen Ku*] (1923) (Sato 2008: 8). In other words, this cinema and its approaches were not entirely 'new', but a recasting of the 'cinematic style current in both West and East' where Japanese traditions began to be 'largely absorbed through second-degree conceptions of "Japaneseness"' (1995: 29).

Bordwell writes that 'French chase films and serials were the predominant influence' around 1910, and that the arrival of the Nikkatsu company and US film influences 'marked the beginning of awareness of international stylistic developments – chiefly, the proto-continuity style bred in North America and Western Europe' (1995: 6). The close affiliation of Japanese cinema with theatre, and the *benshi* style (where a narrator would sit at the front or side of the stage and narrate the events, live, as they unfolded on screen), nevertheless singled out Japanese cinema from its foreign counterparts. Visually, though, Japanese films reflected 'virtually every device of Western editing technique[s]', albeit with slightly 'longer takes' (Bordwell 1995: 6). But there is more to cinema than this, and as Standish points out, culture plays an important role where, 'in the western view, man impacts upon his environment, and narrative and "continuity editing", within the "classic" Hollywood mode, subordinate space to action with action being the measure of time' (2012: 11).

Bordwell goes to some lengths to delineate Japanese films from Western films, mindful of becoming too prescriptive, explaining that '[a] group style includes not only a repertoire of recurrent devices but also functional principles and a range of choices operating at distinct levels of composition' (1995: 7). In other words, there is scope for Japanese cinema to rely heavily on Western cinematic and narrative techniques, while still forging a unique approach to the aesthetics of cinematic imagery. For Bordwell, Japan's directors 'embraced classical *découpage* as a system', while challenging elements such as the expected modes of continuity editing (1995: 8). In our reading, Bordwell's use of *découpage* is here used to refer to the director's final say in the post-production editing (vision, sound and dialogue) for the continuity of a film.

The importance of a visual aesthetic in Japanese cinema emerged through a number of different techniques, including the long takes and distant framings of 1930s films, that, Bordwell maintains, serve to underscore each 'individual shot as a rich visual design, summoning light, texture, and geometric shape to create stable, graceful compositions' (1995: 22). These compositions are, as Kuhn proposes, part of the way that cinema is able to 'evoke the experiences that are fundamental to some of the processes through which we become human beings' (2005: 414). It is important to explore how these processes might be culturally determined in Japanese cinema, rather than universally realized. One example can be found in Tomiyasu Ikeda's 1930 film, *The Twenty-Six Japanese Martyrs/ Les Vingt-Six Martyrs Japonais*, one of several to experiment with tight framing in action sequences, in this case with swordsmen that 'plunge' in and out of shot. Importantly, from a global cinema point of view, the film was released with a French title due to being written and financed 'by Belgians, presumably to proselytize for Christianity' (Bordwell 1995: n. 33, 30).

The concept of style is, of course, highly subjective, as is the concept of national cinema. Debates such as the one on slow cinema (mostly attributed to Jonathan Romney and spurred on by Nick James) are often tagged to national cinemas, with, for instance, Grady Hendrix in 2014 suggesting that 'slow movies are Japanese cinema's middle name' (2014: 1). Using the term CCC (contemplative contemporary cinema), Hendrix refers to the 'slow, fast, end' tempo known as *jo-ha-kyu* in traditional Japanese music and theatre to explain the pacing of Japanese film. But slowness in cinema is a charge equally levelled at French cinema, and at what broadly sit under the umbrella term of art cinema in which '[d]istinctive uses of style and idiosyncratic narrational stances in turn become associated with individual directors, around which the marketing of art films centre' (Smith 2000: 18). Claims against Mizoguchi's style, for instance, centre on the ways that his 'one scene-one shot technique, and the extreme long shot have acted as a conservative and reactionary influence on the progress of cinematic language because they come out of a theatrical and not a cinematic style' (Sato 2008: 99). This is, of course, a highly reductive argument that ignores the ability for cinematic realism, a neutering of a film's teleological ability to relate a story in a way that directly reflects the passing of time.

As noted, existing literature often provides detailed analysis of individual directors or national cinemas, such as Bordwell's work on Ozu, or Sato's on Mizoguchi, each with a strong emphasis on cinematic style. This provides a strong foundation for the search for differences and similarities between the two national cinemas. Others have written direct comparisons of films, such as Lehman and Luhr's (2018) examination of narrative structure in Hollywood's *Jurassic Park* (Spielberg 1993) and *Rashomon* (Kurosawa 1950), despite the obvious differences in content, special effects and date of production. Darrell William Davis's analysis of Takeshi Kitano's internationally acclaimed *Hana-Bi* [*Fireworks*] (1997) notes how iconic Japanese images (such as Mt. Fuji and cherry blossoms) 'not only are metonymic, standing in for Japanese tradition in much the way palm trees or the Hollywood sign represent Los Angeles, but are also strongly coded as timeless, sacred and feminine' (2001: 71–2).

Early Japanese cinema borrowed heavily from *kabuki* theatre and its exaggerated performance and musical styles. These styles were relatively popular, but the theatre itself was undergoing changes in the early 1900s, with a move towards realism in the *shinpa* (new) style that rejected the highbrow nature of *kabuki* (Sato 2008: 20). Instead, *shinpa* films 'were influenced by Western romantic melodrama' (Sato 2008: 20) that helped them reach a wider, more receptive audience. The *shinpa* style helped to shape the successful career of Kenji Mizoguchi, 'a pioneer in bringing modern realism into Japanese film' (Sato 2008: 22).

The markings of tradition meant that Japanese realism of the 1930s and 1940s was portrayed very differently from Western realism. The use of space and time (slow cinema?) was exploited by Mizoguchi, and later by others such as Ozu, Akira Kurosawa and Kaneto Shindo (up to and including his final film, *Postcard/ Ichimai no Hagaki* 2011), where the long, static shot would be broken only by an actor 'sitting, standing or reclining' creating for the audience 'a powerful means of expressing how the psychological barrier between two people is slowly broken down' (Sato 2008: 22) (Figure 3.1).

The role of film as a metaphor for larger social or political issues was apparent in many Japanese films, even, or especially, in the period post–Second World War where film moved from a relatively straightforward device for unambiguous propaganda to texts that delved deeper into the psyche of the audience. For instance, the tripartite story structure of Kurosawa's *Rashomon* 'had already identified a crisis of 'truth' by exposing the unreliability of memory as a testament to past events' (Standish 2011: 147). Japan's filmmakers were faced with the challenge of creating unique, new stories in a climate where '[a]ny attempt to address difference becomes an affront to the homogeneity of the nation-state and its self-legitimising meta-narratives' (Wren 206: 233).

The role of cinema as a reflection of contemporary society was especially apparent in Japan from the 1960s as filmmakers from the major studios made

Figure 3.1 Minimal movement in *Postcard* (2011).

use of their licence to create low- and lower-budget films. Seijun Suzuki was one such director who rose to fame in the 1960s when he 'used parody and visual artifice to satirize the established conventions of the action thriller' (Jacobs 2008: 289). One of Suzuki's later films, *A Tale of Sorrow and Sadness/Hishū monogatari* 1977 reflected his move from *pinku* films, through *yakuza-eiga* (gangster films), to combine a sport that was immensely popular at the time, golf. *A Tale of Sorrow and Sadness* featured a young female model, Reiko (Yuko Shiraki) being trained and promoted as the next big sensation on the financially lucrative Japanese golf circuit. The premise of an attractive young golfer allowed nudity to feature as a relatively seamless part of the narrative, with Suzuki again employing screenwriter (and another *pinku* director) Atsushi Yamatoya, who had penned 1967's *Branded to Kill/Koroshi no rakuin*, to create this 'tale' of greed, corruption and *yakuza*. As Reiko's fame and earning capacity grows, the stakes get higher for promoters and gamblers, and it is not long until deals sour and pistols are drawn. Bourdieu picks up on the 'practice' of golf in Japan (perhaps unintentionally elevating its status – one does not refer to the 'practice' of football or boxing) as being 'nominally identical' (1991: 631) to golf in France but warns of the danger of 'unduly identifying structurally different properties' (631). While Bourdieu's arguments are based in support of his own theories on class structure and capital, the golf example is useful. Golf is often seen as an elitist Western sport, refined and well-mannered (fitting nicely with stereotypical views of Japanese society), yet Suzuki's film undermines this by first glamourizing (and sexualizing) the sport, then dragging it through the mire of sleaze and corruption.

The recognition of directorial style is, in the auteurist reading of filmmaking, that which marks the work of an individual artist. Writing of Naomi Kawase's individual approach to direction, Jacobs remarks that 'Kawase's hyperrealist style has at times derived from chance events: for instance, the cleansing rain that falls during the festival in *Shara*' (2008: 105). Produced in 2003, Kawase's third feature, *Shara/Sharasôju*, continued her observational, documentary-style approach, based around the disappearance of a young boy, an event that immediately opens the film. Rather than milk the theme for its drama or shock value with rapid jump-cuts and frenetic searches, '[t]he aesthetics of the opening scenes lack the menace we associate with the disappearance of a child; the soft light, slowed-down shots, beautiful trees, neat houses, all are the antithesis of the action that occurs' (Taylor-Jones 2013: 168). The use of a focused, restrained directorial style reflects Kawase's understanding of cinema, where her links to French cinema run deeper than just her success at Cannes, where she was the youngest director to ever win the Camera d'or in 1997 with the gentle family drama, *Suzaku/Moe no Suzaku*. Kate Taylor-Jones draws links between the ways Kawase and Truffaut both see film as focusing in on personal stories, governed by notions of temporality and the audio-visual capture of something now that will be realized afterwards (2013: 154–5). As her first full-length feature, *Suzaku* opened up opportunities for Kawase, and by 2000 her funding for *Firefly/Hotaru* had extended to include French production house Les Films de L'Observatoire, suggesting that the style of her films had struck a chord with those involved in filmmaking in France.

Jeunet's *Amélie* enjoyed international success, including in Japan, where it had over 40,000 viewers within three weeks of opening and some 550,000 viewers before being released beyond the major cities (Vanderschelden 2007: 86). Its impact at home in France was credited to its 'commitment to spectacular aesthetics . . . as a reaction against the gritty realism of French cinema in the 1990s, and the critics' stigmatisation of beautiful images as suspect' (71). Jeunet's success for what was 'planned as a modest, personal film, designed to make people feel happy, but unlikely to become a box office hit' (2007: 1) was in no small part due to its 'distinctive mise-en-scene strategies' (72) that seemed to borrow from another popular and influential European film, Tom Tykwer's *Run Lola Run* (1998). Vanderschelden (2007: 72) concludes that *Amélie* was successful because it

> rejects the superiority of classic art over popular culture. It brings together all sorts and origins (posters, videos, newsreels, adverts and paintings), which are appropriated to be consumed again, initially by the characters and, by extension, the viewers.

In other words, Jeunet's bricolage approach was an invitation for the audience to join the on-screen adventure, using a style that was inclusive, intimate and nostalgic – even for audiences with no direct experience of Paris, as shown by the film's success in territories such as Japan.

Burch notes that '[a]ny Japanese film set in a traditional interior offers Mondrian-like patterns, many large or small sections of which may at any time slide back to reveal a new, *framed* element: a person, a fragment of a garden, a painted *fusuma* [sliding panel], etc.' (1979: 199). Such scenes are perhaps obvious in Ozu's films, but in more recent films such as Shindo's *Postcard*, Fukada's *Hospitalité*, Masayuki Suo's musical comedy, *Lady Maiko/Maiko wa Redi* (2014) and even Sion's *Why Don't You Play in Hell?*, all feature extensive use of this diegetic framing. For Shindo, who had been an assistant to Mizoguchi in his early years, his work appeared to shift from 1950s realism to a more aestheticized approach in his later films. The result, according to a somewhat harsh appraisal from Alexander Jacobs (2008: 277), was that Shindo 'never truly evolved a coherent visual style, or a way of commenting on the world through images'.

Seijun Suzuki's directorial style continued to surprise right up until his last films, with the 2005 musical comedy *Princess Raccoon/Operetta: Tanuki Goten*, starring Chinese superstar Zhang Ziyi, 'an inventive but inane postmodern musical, which retold a traditional legend on stylized sets . . . like many of Suzuki's films, it was more interesting to look at than to think about' (Jacobs 2008: 290). Referring back to his lack of box-office success or studio support in the 1960s, Suzuki related to (the much younger) Tom Mes in an interview for Midnight Eye that 'either my films were too early or your generation came too late' (Mes 2001).

Michel Gondry's *Mood Indigo/L'écume des Jours* (2013), like Suzuki's films, also emphasizes the visual, in the style of *Amelie* and also reflective of Wes Anderson with a distinctive, vibrant colour palette and a postmodern mise-en-scene that includes 1950s kitsch, bizarre inventions made of existing technologies (a gramophone coffee grinder, a piano that makes cocktails – a 'pianocktail'), stop-motion imagery and rapid montage sequences. The film begins with a pool of brightly dressed typists each writing a line of a story about someone named Colin, before sliding their typewriter across to the next typist to continue the story. Gondry's international credentials as a filmmaker were cemented with the US-produced *Eternal Sunshine of the Spotless Mind* (2004) that took over US$70 million at the box office (Figure 3.2).

The jazzy film score in *Mood Indigo* also brings to mind *Amélie*, but also Suzuki's *Branded to Kill*, and reinforces Gondry's expertise as a music video maker for artists as diverse as the Rolling Stones, Björk, the White Stripes and Kanye West. Gondry frames characters through all manner of windows, openings and obstructions, an almost overwhelming collection of images, sounds and obscure sequences of dialogue. The eccentric, and seemingly independently wealthy, Colin (Romain Duris) falls in love with Chloe (Audrey Tautou), but far from a simple romance, Gondry appears to be channelling the Theatre of the Absurd as the film's narrative structure skips from episode to episode in what at first appear to be puzzling ways. Colin's personal manservant/butler/chef, Nicolas (Omar Sy), serves up incredible meals, often with living or moving objects, at an astonishing rate.

Figure 3.2 Visual exuberance in *Mood Indigo* (2013).

Although *Mood Indigo* is set in Paris and draws from iconic landmarks such as Notre Dame and Les Halles, things are not quite right. The currency used is the 'doublezoon', and transport is via a range of odd cars and suspended or floating vehicles. Colin's best friend and confidante, Chick (Gad Elmaleh), is obsessed with a celebrity philosopher, with the Spooneristic name of Jean-Sol Partre, Gondry's parodic dig at academia. Partre arrives at a speaking engagement in a huge smoker's pipe that swings out over his audience of screaming fans, and spouts the line, 'The athletic exocytosis I reproduce is more repressed and declericalises . . .', and the cult-like crowd goes wild with appreciation. A TV crew covering the event are told, 'Don't try to follow [understand], we can play it back later', as Partre cryptically (nonsensically) continues, ' . . . it has a shelf life through which the excerpt pre-estimates destiny . . .'. The absurdity continues, Chick discovers that Partre is writing a twenty-volume 'Encyclopedia of Nausea' and, when Chloe is struck down by a mysterious illness, Colin is sent to an old-style apothecary where Chloe's medicine is prepared through a bizarre series of plastic tubes that run through a taxidermied rabbit (that soon explodes).

While *Mood Indigo* is filled with oddities, Gondry in many ways is sticking to the traditional three-act narrative of equilibrium (Colin is lonely, then he meets Chloe, they fall in love and they are married), disequilibrium (Chloe becomes ill and Colin faces economic hardship in looking after them; tragedy strikes) and a return to equilibrium (Colin is alone). The narrative path is also indicated by Colin's vibrant penthouse apartment (with an interior that resembles a train carriage) that begins the film as brightly lit, and sparklingly clean, but starts to gather more and more cobwebs, and deteriorates rapidly into a dark cavernous space of matted webs, as Chloe becomes more ill. Nicolas begins to age rapidly and only manages to serve up spartan dishes. Chloe undergoes a surgery to remove a large flower that has been growing in her lung, but it seems to be to no avail. The film itself begins to take on a washed-out look, then sepia and then recedes into monochrome, as the possibility of tragedy looms. Colin takes on a job working for 'the administration', where he travels the city administering bad news a day before it happens, knocking on the door of an old woman, for instance, to tell her that tomorrow she will fall and break her hip, so she needs to ensure there will be someone to call the ambulance for her. His next errand is to his own house, where he realizes that Chloe will die.

Mood Indigo tests the boundaries of cinema, in effect reflecting Vsevolod Meyerhold's concept of 'theatricality' (*teatral'nost*) in relation to performance, which was later adapted by Sergei Eisenstein for his analysis of cinema (Arsenjuk 2018: 67). Meyerhold was perhaps the first to map the 'experiences of *commedia dell'arte* and the grotesque' onto theatrical performance (pre-dating Bakhtin). Meyerhold established his reading of 'theatricality' as one which 'unlike the illusionism of bourgeois "naturalism", makes visible and, by bringing them to the surface, displaces its own conventional limits, without at the same time leading us out of theater altogether' (Arsenjuk 2018: 67). In *Mood Indigo*, Gondry uses CGI and more prosaic visual effects to 'displace the conventional limits' of the medium, and to challenge the audience's reading of what is happening on screen. At the same time, of course, he ensures that the audience is aware of the 'theatricality' taking place before them – the surrealist images, manipulated colour palette and hyper-dramatic performances of his actors all combine to suggest a fantastical, but ultimately believable, diegetic framework for the film's narrative to play out.

It is worth briefly mentioning here a final intersection between French and Japanese cinematic styles: animation. French cinema has always been attentive to issues of animation. The International Animation Film Festival at Annecy entered its sixtieth year in 2020. The Paris premiere of Emile Cohl's 1908 *Fantasmagorie* is generally regarded as the first wholly animated cartoon, while the arrival of Polish émigré animator Ladislas Starewitch to France in 1920 is heralded as a key moment in the development magical realism animation narratives. Other key French animated films include *The Savage Planet/La Planète Sauvage* (René Laloux 1973); *The King and the Mockingbird/Le Roi et l'oiseau* (1980), the result of a long collaboration between influential animator

Paul Grimault and screenwriter and poet Jacques Prévert; *The Adventures of Tintin/Les Aventures de Tintin* (1990), an animated television series based on the famous Belgian detective; and *Kirikou and the Sorceress/Kirikou et la sorcière* (Michel Ocelot 1998) – notable for its soundtrack by Senegalese musician Youssou N'Dour. Whereas the large American animation studios were notable for their factory-assembly modes of productivity, recurring narrative templates and big promotional and post-production budgets, French animation practice has traditionally relied upon a small-scale artisanal approach and then hoped to be noticed at specialized conferences and festivals.

Interstella 5555: The 5tory of the 5ecret 5tar 5ystem (2003) marked the collaboration between French electronic duo Daft Punk and veteran Japanese manga artist Leiji Matsumoto. Combining arresting visuals with the music from Daft Punk's second album '*Discovery*' to create what reviewers routinely labelled 'a manga musical', *Interstella* is Japanese in its conception and delivery (Daft Punk took their idea to the prestigious Tokyo-based Toei studio; the visual style is reminiscent of classic 1980s anime series 'Battle of the Planets' and 'Ulysses 31'), but heavily inflected with 'French-ness' via its propulsive soundtrack. Like *Belleville Rendez-vous/Les Triplettes de Belleville*, another nostalgic animation released in France a year earlier that had enjoyed extended international coverage and kickstarted a new-found interest in French animation, *Interstella*'s slight plot, exuberant visual style and nostalgic intertwining of classic visual grammar suggested a potentially exciting direction for international animation.

Much has been written on the directorial stylings of Akira Kurosawa, particularly in relation to his martial arts epics. Even in his films set in the contemporary period, though, Kurosawa's style was apparent. He was also well aware of the drawing power of the cinematic star, and in Toshirô Mifune found a bankable proposition, exemplifying the idea that the 'economic importance of stars is of aesthetic consequence in such things as the centring of spectacle on the presentation of the star, and the construction of narrative's which display the star's image' (Dyer 1998: 12). Mifune was reasonably good (but not too-good) looking, which meant he could play a variety of roles without having to succumb to demands to only play romantic roles. He was also tallish (by Japanese standards in the 1950s), which Kurosawa used to effect when he wanted, but also not so gangly that he would appear ill-suited to the stealthy, crouching samurai roles, such as his leading roles in *Yojimbo/Yōjinbō* (1961) (the film most widely known for Sergio Leone's 1964 remake as *A Fistful of Dollars//Per un Pugno di Dollari*) and *Sanjuro/Tsubaki Sanjūrō* (1962).

Kurosawa's talent for sensing what the audience wanted could be seen in films such as *Stray Dog/Nora Inu* (1949) for instance, when junior homicide Detective Murakami (Toshirô Mifune) sets off on a lead to track down the woman who may have pickpocketed his gun during a bus ride on a sweltering day. Kurosawa's gritty, street-level film may have preempted the approaches taken by the burgeoning filmmakers over in France, who were 'forced to make films out of raw materials usually considered the opposite of cinema, the real world rather than the artifice of the soundstage' (Tweedie 2013: 54).

In *Stray Dog*, a simple narrative is honed down to a psychological journey into the mind of the detective. Mifune's highly anxious, sweating, Murakami brings to mind the later (1957) essay by Roland Barthes, 'Les Romains au cinéma', where he undertakes a semiotic deconstruction of the 1953 film *Julius Caesar* (dir. Joseph L. Mankiewicz). For Barthes, the sweat of the characters in *Julius Caesar* 'is an attribute with a purpose', that it is an outwardly visible sign of the internal torment borne by a character (1972: 27). The sequence of these scenes moves from the filing room where Murakami recognizes the woman from a file photograph. Kurosawa uses a wipe cut (a series of these is used later in quick succession when he chases after the woman) to move from the filing room to a transitory shot lasting just four seconds where the camera is inside a boat or a barge, looking forward through an opening that centrally frames Detective Murakami and the accompanying, more experienced, Detective Ichikawa (Reikichi Kawamura). To their immediate right, but in the distance, the boat's captain and first mate, and standing motionless inside the doorway in the foreground shadows, a young boy on one side, his mother and grandmother on the other, suggesting a family-run vessel, but also a portrait painting of many dimensions. The complexity of this shot conveys almost too much information to absorb in the short amount of time it is on screen. Kurosawa's ability to use the 'natural' borders of the scene to create a frame (the doorway) within a frame (the limits of the film itself on the screen) focuses attention on the central figure, or protagonist, but also feeds a wealth of establishing information to the audience (Figure 3.3).

This scene then cross-fades to another shot of equal length of the detectives arriving at a traditional-style wooden building, an old bar or perhaps even a brothel, but then immediately cross-fades to a profile shot of Murakami sitting inside (again the camera faces outward), framed first by a see-through screen, and then around this the doorway leading outside, the effect is to momentarily give the illusion that it is the same shot as when they were on the boat. The scene again contains a wealth of detail and depth, lasting twice as long as the previous

Figure 3.3 Frame within a frame in *Stray Dog* (1949).

shots as Murakami, alone, looks around the room, an unfamiliar space, while beyond him, outside young children can be seen running around in play. This then cuts immediately to a view from outside looking in at Murakami through the fringed doorway. Murakami fans himself in the heat before the fringing is pushed away and Ichikawa enters, his back to the camera. Ichikawa bends and places a tray holding a teapot and cups on the raised tatami floor, then steps up and turns to sit cross-legged to the side of Murakami but facing the audience in theatrical style blocking. He drinks tea, then pulls newspapers from his jacket and they begin their conversation, for forty seconds this part of the scene is filmed through the filter of the fringed screening that moves in the breeze. Finally, the shot switches to a closer, unfiltered shot as they read their newspapers. In less than two minutes, Kurosawa has conveyed a wealth of information, Murakami's sweat as it 'reveals a degraded spectacle' (Barthes 1972: 28), namely Murakami's anticipation that he will lose his job because his gun is missing, and the manner in which everyday life continues amidst and beyond the dramas of individuals (the children playing, the family on the boat).

Kurosawa is therefore adept at toying with the audience, veering from straightforward imagery to complex and unafraid to offer a proverbial 'red herring' that may have little to do with the narrative itself. The title scene of *Stray Dog* features a close-up of a panting dog, its teeth bared, but not necessarily in anger, but nevertheless somewhat frightening. As Hutchinson argues, this title scene is one where Kurosawa presents 'visual images, at first presumed to have some meaning in relation to the diegetic space, [but] reveal themselves as either arbitrary or suspect, throwing into doubt the omniscience of the narrator' (2006: 185, n. 9). Thus, the film is not about a dog at all, but serves as an allegorical reading, firstly of Murakami's wandering nature as he staggers from misadventure to misadventure, and then at around fifty minutes into the film when the wizened, superior, Detective Sato (Takashi Shimura) tries to impart his knowledge to a Murakami obsessed with finding the motives for criminal behaviour. Murakami learns that his stolen gun was hired out to another criminal, but that it wasn't used for a crime (a murder) until a day later. Sato is bemused at Murakami's neurotic approach to the case:

> **Sato**: Feeling sorry for the criminal too?
> **Murakami**: No, but he didn't rob the night he hired the gun. That means he hired it but didn't want to use it. He came to return it, but . . .
> **Sato**: (*interrupting*) Forget it. It's more important to stop the next murder. He stole 40,000. Easy come, easy go. And when it's gone, he'll strike again. Once doesn't make a habit, but twice . . . (*Pause.*) A stray dog becomes a mad dog, right?

Even at this relatively early point in Kurosawa's career, it was obvious that he was well schooled in the international realm of cinema and its techniques. He was, as Wren notes in relation to the corpus of Kurosawa's films, able to privilege 'symbolic representation, inviting a wider examination of some of the less savoury recesses of modern culture and unleashing a barrage of subliminal social and political commentary' (2016: 231). *Stray Dog* draws heavily from the *film noir* of Hollywood and Europe, although this was not a named genre at the time, there was only 'a cycle of films with enough similarities to strike critics, first in France in 1955, as a kind of genre, movement or mode' (Desser 2016: 113). The use of seemingly fresh narratives reflects the complexities arising in his films and 'the intertwined nature . . . based on so many different kinds of source texts, coupled with the self-reflexive consciousness of film as discursive act, gets beyond simple categorisations of "Japanese" or "Western" works, "original" and "adaptation", the "universal" and the "local"' (Hutchinson 2006: 183).

Styles and technologies

The use of stop-motion animation, CGI and other visual 'tricks' in films like *Mood Indigo* are hardly new. Early cinema, for instance, quickly latched onto the concepts of montage and continuity editing. Concerns that the use of manipulative techniques drew film from its representative, realist task were raised by critics such as Bazin, but these were countered by not only other critics but also by filmmakers themselves. As O'Brien states in relation (more broadly) to images of nature in cinema:

> Yes, the language surrounding digital capabilities emphasises manipulation and stimulation, and cinema can perhaps no longer lay claim to a particularly non-anthropocentric vision, at least not on the grounds for which it did throughout many decades. . . . But it would be a mistake to dwell too long on certain ontological properties, however fundamental they have been for many theorists, and lose sight of all those other qualities and techniques at cinema's disposal – such as movement in time, sound/image combinations and flexibility of scale. As it turned away from photo-based indexicality, the medium by no means became less able to register and imagine environmental details and experiences. (O'Brien 2018: 17)

The natural environment as presented in films by Kurosawa (in *Rashomon*'s black and white, or *Ran*'s colour), or more recent filmmakers such as Kawase, Shindo, Kore-eda or Ichikawa could be seen as drawing on all the medium has to offer, the clarity of digital reproduction, the use of widescreen formatting technologies, all allow for nature to be writ large upon the screen.

In searching for purity in cinema, in an ideal absolute 'realism', the pedantic cinephile might be better served to note that 'worrying over the relative artificiality of a film's constitutive technology is invariably a fruitless and short-sighted task' (O'Brien 2018: 18). While such fans or critics will gladly accept manipulated imagery under particular genre guidelines (e.g. science fiction), expecting only unadulterated images in 'serious' films shows an ignorance towards the fact that all film is mediated and therefore 'manipulated'; by the lens, the filmstock (or digital capture method), by its very projection (again through a type of lens and/or screen).

In the French comedy, *2 Autumns, 3 Winters/2 Automnes, 3 Hivers* (2013), director Sébastien Betbeder uses a masked format (1:33 aspect ratio) that serves to centralize the characters. This accentuates the performances because the characters often break the fourth wall to directly address the audience, whether mid-sentence within a scene, or in more formal interview styles against a staged background, the mid or close shot of the character frames them in an intimate, personal way (Figure 3.4).

Many Japanese films, manga and anime also utilize the fourth wall style. In the frenetic, video-game-influenced film, *We Are Little Zombies*/[lit.]

Figure 3.4 Centralizing performance in *2 Autumns, 3 Winters* (2013).

Watashitachi wa Ritoru Zonbī (2019, dir. Makoto Nagahisa), the young cast of orphaned children who form a rock band, often narrate their tragic story by staring back down the camera and delivering their lines in a deadpan manner. The style is used for comic effect in a number of high school-based Japanese films such as *Heroine Disqualified/Hiroin Shikkaka* [aka No Longer Heroine] (2015, dir. Hanabusa Tsutomu), *You, I Love/Ui Rabu* (aka *We Love*, 2018, dir. Yūichi Satō) and *My Brother Loves Me Too Much/Ani ni Ai Saresugite Komattemasu* (2017, dir. Hayato Kawai), but in *Little Zombies*, the tone is much more 'gothic' in style.

Theatrical antecedents

Influences from the theatre abound in cinema, most notably tracking back as far as the proscenium-based sets used by Georges Méliès in his 1902 *A Trip to the Moon/Le voyage dans la lune*, that make a clear link between stage arts and the cinema. In his 1986 film *Mélo* [lit. an abbreviation of *mélodrame/* melodrama], Alain Resnais adapted a Henri Bernstein play from 1929 for a cinematic release. While having all of the technologies of the cinema at his disposal, Resnais chose to keep *Mélo* (his eleventh feature film) restricted to a minimum of set changes, keeping the focus on the narrative and actions of its cast, still set in the 1920s. Resnais divides the film's three acts by showing a (painted) red curtain with gold brocade trimming at the bottom. In the opening transition from the curtains, Renais dissolves in through the curtains, opening onto the courtyard of the Belcroix couple, Pierre (Pierre Arditi) and Romaine (Sabine Azéma, who married Resnais over a decade after this film was made) who are hosting a visit from their friend Marcel (André Dussollier). As the titles have established, this is their home in the suburbs of Paris, and aside from their maid, the three inhabit that space for the first thirty minutes of the film as the charming Marcel regales them with stories about his musical career and thwarted attempts at love. The conversational style (albeit melodramatic as the title suggests), establishes the stage-like dynamic of the production. Romaine flirts with Marcel, first (while Pierre is momentarily absent) setting up a date with Marcel the next day to play music together, and then when Pierre returns, saying she will not be available to visit Marcel due to a conflicting appointment. The scene ends when Marcel has left and Pierre and Romaine enter the house firmly closing the door behind them, essentially leaving us, the audience, outside. When it dissolves into the next shot, it is in Marcel's apartment, with Romaine seated at the piano, confirmation of Romaine's interest in Marcel and a portent of her infidelity towards her husband.

The opaque windows in Marcel's luxurious Art Deco apartment establish a stage-like atmosphere, especially when the erratic Romaine (darting about the space, threatening to leave, then staying) comments on the apartment. She pulls her hat on, then reaches for her coat:

Romaine: This is a pretty place. These big windows, the view.

She steps towards the windows, pulling on her coat.

Marcel (*shrugs*): Yes, the view.

Romaine stands close to the window, her coat only slung across one shoulder. Marcel ambles across to her side, unsure of whether she is merely playing with him, or serious about a relationship. She delivers a series of lines, her face towards the windows as if gazing out upon something interesting (despite the windows obviously being nothing more than set dressing). Finally, she turns towards Marcel and again makes a pretence of leaving, only to soon discard her hat and coat again before Marcel romantically serenades her with his violin. In all, as with a theatrical production the film only has minimal (around ten) scene changes or set locations (four of which take place in Marcel's apartment).

Monochrome

The use of colour was firmly established in Hollywood cinema by the late 1950s, with forays into black and white purely a practice of the avant-garde filmmaker on the periphery of mainstream (and mostly) commercial success. France and Japan were exceptions to this notion that a film had to be in colour, and that realism demanded the full technicolour experience. The decision to return to, or stay with, monochrome was very much at the director's discretion, and one need look no further than Akira Kurosawa's films through the 1950s, and Godard's *Breathless* to see that a cinematic acclaim and reasonable box office were achievable. Godard, especially, was able to create films in which 'the hermeneutics of noir and its suspense structure becomes subject to digressions, some simply more lengthy suspensions than one would find in film noir, but others that are nearly extra-diegetic' (Turim 2016: 73).

A path can be traced into the 1960s and Seijun Suzuki's choice of a mix of vibrant, surreal colour and earthy black and white for *Tokyo Drifter* in 1966, with its 'cartoon-like imagery and deliberately exaggerated acting' (Jacobs 2008: 289), before returning to the simplicity of black and white for *Branded to Kill* in 1967. While Suzuki was comfortable with shooting in this style, he had planned for *Branded to Kill* to be shot in colour, but the studio had the final say, with Suzuki relenting at a time when Nikkatsu was 'split between colour and black and white' in the late 1950s–1960s (Desser 2016: 114–16). In 1969, Yoshishige Yoshida released *Eros + Massacre*, a twin-narrative film set partly around 1923 and partly in the present-day 1960s, yet maintaining the monochrome look throughout, even though it was not produced by the New Wave's most ardent supporters, the Art Theatre Guild (ATG).

Eros + Massacre opens with a highly stylized image of a young woman, dressed in contemporary black clothing of a see-through blouse and trousers, sitting in a chair against a grimy black background. She is facing a spotlight, as if being interrogated, and a woman's voice begins by telling us about the young woman. The narrator's voice begins asking questions, but the young woman remains silent as successive off-centre shots move in closer on the young woman, increasing the reflected brightness from her face. The narrator/interrogator becomes angry, her voice rising in frustration as she asks each new question. The film suddenly cuts to the stark white foyer and information desk of an airport, flooding the screen with whiteness. We are introduced to another young woman, dressed fashionably in a beret-style cap and trench coat. Yoshida continues the film in this alternating style of light and dark, cutting back to the young woman in the black room, and countering this with scenes such as one where a low shot of water spouting from a fountain is against a grey-white sky, filling the screen as a young woman crosses from right to left behind the fountain, obscured for much of the shot. This then cuts to a split-screen, the 'new' woman on the left of the screen against a white background, in front of a microphone, asking questions. To the right is the original young woman, in darkness, the only light reflecting off her hands shielding her face. Eventually she drops her hands and begins answering questions. Yoshida then jumps to a close-up, with a blazing white background, as the young woman with her face framed by her dark hair, points an accusing finger straight towards the camera (which is presumably aimed at the interrogator, but has the unsettling effect of being directed at us, the audience), and states, 'it's you!'. A fade to white then reveals explanatory title cards, and the opening credits, already four minutes into the film.

Yoshida's use of monochromatic imagery also favours his use of precise, linear shots, especially in interior scenes. Tables, doorways, and shelves provide surfaces either to track along or to interrupt the otherwise clean lines of a shot of white walls and gently blowing curtains (white, of course). His attention to detail in partly obscured shots and mise-en-scene of angular window frames and ducted air vents, all geometrically neat, reflect techniques not only established by Ozu and Kurosawa, with their focus on the ordered angularity of tatami-mat houses with their timber-linings and paper walls but also the *nouvelle vague* and its emphasis on form over content. Yoshida, however, tends towards the use of a static camera where often it is the actors that provide the movement, again mirroring Ozu's trademark style. Kurosawa tended towards a more visually dynamic aesthetic as in Rashomon, as Pettey notes (2016: 106), where he features 'expressive lighting, plays of shadows, and multiple oblique angles . . . to convey the narrative's multiple perspectives and interpretations'.

The early 1900s setting of *Eros + Massacre* does not appear until seventeen minutes into the film. It follows philosophical anarchist Ōsugi Sakae, a womanizing idealist, who is supported by his wife, a journalist. In these scenes, Yoshida floods the screen with light, often over-exposed through windows, silhouetting characters, suggestive of a time where control of light was almost beyond the control of filmmakers. The final scenes of the film shift the narrative realism of the film to a more surreal footing where the character Noe (the incestuous sister/lover) from the 1920s (and, it is established, has died in the Kanto earthquake of 1923) is interviewed by Eiko in 1969.

Kōhei Oguri's debut film, *Muddy River/Doro no Kowa* (1981) also drew on black-and-white imagery to capture Japan in the post-war period, in a simple tale of two young boys whose friendship develops along the banks of an Osaka river. The boys' families struggle to make a living, through a small restaurant and through prostitution, a stark reminder of the hardships faced by many Japanese as they struggled to rebuild their lives. The lack of colour in Oguri's film harks back to the days of Ozu. The form was also used in *Bullet Ballet*, a highly stylized 1998 revenge film by action director Shin'ya Tsukamoto (1989's surrealist *Tetsuo, the Iron Man*, also in black and white, and 1995's *Tokyo Fist*), but here the monochromatic look provides a gritty base for the plot to unfold as Goda (played by Tsukamoto) descends into a mental and physical breakdown following the death of his girlfriend. Violence quickly escalates from fist fights to the expected gunplay (as suggested by the film's title), and the mood shifts from empathy to astonishment. Taking cues from the be-bop stylings of Seijun Suzuki, and earlier, from Godard, *Bullet Ballet* also draws from the character intensity of Scorsese's *Taxi Driver*, and the stark use of greyed-out, muscular flesh that Scorsese used to great effect in his 1980 *Raging Bull*.

The surrealist *Labyrinth of Dreams/Yume no Ginga* (1997) is a mystery film directed and co-written by Gakuryû Ishii (aka Sogo Ishii) that tends towards experimental, a combination of Bunuel and David Lynch (especially the starkness of 1977's *Eraserhead* and the intercut shots of nature that frequent *Blue Velvet* from 1986). The relatively simple tale of a young woman, Tomiko (Rena Komine), who takes on a job as a bus conductor to a driver, Niitaka (Tadanobu Asano), whose previous conductors, all young, attractive women, have all been killed. Complications arise as Tomiko falls in love with Niitaka despite suspicions that he is a murderer. Throughout the film, the use of black and white, often (deliberately) poorly lit shots, jump-cuts and varying motions provide unnerving visions of dream or hallucination sequences that both help and hinder the forward movement of the narrative.

Director Ishii's fascination with black and white continued several years later with the fifty-four-minute *Electric Dragon 80.000 V/Erekuto Rikku Doragon 80000V* in 2001, written and directed by Ishii. Unlike *Labyrinth* though, *Electric Dragon* is a fast-paced rock and roll-fuelled cyberpunk fantasy, featuring Dragon-eye Morrison (*Labyrinth*'s Tadanobu Asano) as a self-electrocuting, hyped up and violent rocker. Coming across at times as an extended high-energy music video, *Electric Dragon* uses its lack of colour to achieve a grittier effect, sweat reflecting off Dragon-eye's torso and the hardcore metallic, industrial themes running through the film, including Dragon-eye's nemesis, Thunderbolt Buddha (Masatoshi Nagase). The first view of Thunderbolt is a side view as a shining metallic Buddha head gently swaying on a suburban train. The shot cuts to the train heading in the opposite direction, with a human head (Thunderbolt) sitting in the same position. Shortly later, in a rooftop scene Thunderbolt is seen in full, his face half-human, half-Buddha, as an old woman kneels and prays to him.

Drawing some parallels with Hitoshi Matsumoto's *Big Man Japan/Dai Nipponjin*, but unlike Matsumoto's subdued protagonist, Dragon-eye uses the power to increase his animal instincts, shown through a brief montage of scenes as a child where he learns how to fight, eventually reaching maturity as a powerful boxer. Crashing anime-style intertitles with a shouted voiceover and very little dialogue throughout the film. *Electric Dragon* still bears the hallmarks of an experimental film, its deliberate amateur-style part of its renegade charm.

The Girl on the Bridge/La fille sur le pont is a 1999 French film directed by Patrice Leconte, starring Vanessa Paradis as the impulsive waif, Adèle and Daniel Auteuil as her saviour and older lover, Gabor. The film opens with Adèle being interviewed, with the audience assuming that she is being questioned by a policewoman as other undefined characters (a jury, perhaps) are kept at a suitably blurred distance. In an eight-minute opening scene, Adèle confesses to a tempestuous, highly sexualized past, and as the camera moves closer, she begins to break, tears welling in her eyes and then running down her face. The film then cuts to scenes of Adèle on a high bridge in Paris, preparing to jump. The black and white gives these scenes a sense of noir cinema, accentuated by the appearance of Gabor in a trench coat. The binary of black water below and the reflections of lights along the riverbank tend to flatten out the dynamics of her location, and Gabor's moderated tone downplays the seriousness of Adèle's contemplated suicide.

> **Gabor**: You're too young to be so sad. Are you terminally ill? Do you not have a kidney, liver, legs?
> **Adèle** (*looks down at the river*): No, I just do not have courage. I'm afraid that it will be cold.

Gabor's engagement in the conversation has the desired effect of distracting her from her task. He tries to rouse her from her despondency with a comic metaphor, but she offers a quick rebuttal:

> **Gabor**: Do not throw out a good light bulb.
> **Adèle**: This one burned out a long time ago.

The Girl on the Bridge unfolds as a circus and casino-based drama, the black-and-white imagery highlighting the extremes, and the chaotic, high-intensity business of the backstage creating a (literal) blend of Bakhtin's carnivalesque and a de-colourized Vincente Minnelli epic. The binary perception of luck (good/bad, losing/winning) mirrors the black/white theme as Gabor mentors Adèle, first as his assistant in his theatrical knife-throwing stunts, and then as his muse, bravely risking their meagre earnings on games of roulette. Their relationship exists within an unrequited eroticism punctuated by a brief frisson, with Adèle often spurred on by Gabor to continue her casual sexual relations with other men. Gabor speaks of the existence of two planes: life and death, and illustrates by turning off the lights on their car at night, the scene switching from the brilliant glare (the white) of the car lights, to an enveloping blackness. Inevitably the sounds of a crash are heard, and in the blackness, Adèle speaks:

> **Adèle**: And what? We live?
> **Gabor**: No. Do you not feel that we are going to heaven?
> **Adèle**: This is not what I imagined.
> **Gabor**: That's because it is late. Everything is closed.

There is silence and the screen stays black for a moment, then opens on bright daylight with the car pointed into a ditch on the side of the road, an indicator of their pending change of fortune. The binary theme continues with together/apart, as the two head in different directions, different countries, but their dialogue continues presented as an unassuming telepathy.

The use of contrasting palettes in the post-Second World War drama *Frantz* (2016, dir. Francois Ozon) alternates between black-and-white imagery and colour at various times throughout the film. Opening with a landscape vista overlooking a small town, the foreground is framed through coloured footage of pink blossom and green trees, while the centre of the screen, the distant town low in a valley, is in black and white. The effect is surprising, our eyes drawn first to the colour of the blossom, before noting the drab grey in the background. Ozon's use of crisp black and white through many of the scenes set in the historic town of Quedlinburg in northern Germany reinforces the period of mourning for the Hoffmeister family, whose only son, the eponymous Frantz, was killed in battle in France. Also grieving is Anna (Paula Beer), the distraught young woman who was engaged to Frantz before his sojourn into war. The coloured fresco of the establishing shot gives way to a black-and-white, bleaker picture of Anna, dressed in black walking through the cobbled streets of the old town, bustling with street stalls, but with an air of despondency as an ominous bell tolls.

While much of the film is set in Germany, the narrative follows a visiting Frenchman, the dashingly handsome, moustachioed, Adrien (Pierre Niney), who had apparently befriended Frantz in Paris and has now sought out the Hoffmeisters to pass on his sympathies for their loss. The film returns briefly to a sepia-toned colour (reminiscent of hand-coloured black-and-white photographs) as Adrien reminisces about the time he spent with Frantz visiting the Louvre and dancing with girls. The scene cuts back to Germany and black and white, where, unable to bear the thought of entertaining a Frenchman, Frantz's father, Hans (Ernst Stötzner) stands outside the room where Adrien is telling his story. Colour reappears a short time later when Anna takes Adrien on a stroll beyond the edge of town. As they emerge from a rocky outcrop, colour seeps into the image, an indication of their burgeoning relationship and their distance from the town and all the grief it holds.

When looking at black-and-white films, our concern is not so much with those films that try to capture the technical abilities of an earlier era, such as Michel Hazanavicius's Oscar-winning *The Artist* (2011), which is a highly successful attempt to create, in many senses, a replica film of the silent film era. We are interested in those filmmakers who choose to avoid colour to create an aesthetic that helps to drive a film. Suzuki's reasons for shooting in black and white were partly enforced upon him; however, he was later to note that:

> Generally, a movie is composed of many elements that make a strong impression on the viewer. I call them tricks. I think colour is one of those tricks. (Mes 2001)

Suzuki's adherence to the simplicity of film, the honesty found in its base form also extended to the use of post-production effects, that he mostly avoided, despite the use of some CGI enhancement in his penultimate and final features (both in full colour), 2001's *Pistol Opera/Pisutoru Opera* and 2005's *Princess Raccoon*.

One of the more recent films to draw on monochromatic images is Sono Sion's enigmatic sci-fi, *The Whispering Star/Hiso Hiso Boshi*, one of his four features released in 2015. The film opens in a warm, sepia-toned black and white, and from the outset a titled dedication acknowledges the people still living in temporary housing units in areas impacted upon by the Tōhoku earthquake and subsequent nuclear disaster that struck Japan in 2011. Early scenes play on the concept of the housing unit as Yoko Suzuki (Megumi Kagurazaka) inhabits a prosaic domestic space, revealed as a traditional-looking one-room house, which also happens to be a spaceship floating silently in space. The house is driven by an on-board computer known as 6-7 MAH Em, which not only addresses Yoko via a whispered voice but also seems receptive to touch; when Yoko goes to clean the computer (that looks like a vintage radio unit) with a cloth, it giggles and says, 'Hey, that tickles!'. At the rear of the single room, netting divides a section that is filled with white cardboard packages. Yoko wanders up to the netting and gazes at the boxes.

The whispering of the title continues with Yoko, who does not directly speak, pulling a reel-to-reel tape player from a cupboard and playing excerpts from what can only be assumed as her (whispering) voice as an audio journal. She speaks about the house that she chose ten years before (although this does not confirm when the tapes were made, subsequent tapes she listens to state that more years have passed), noting the appeal of its retro styling and stating that 'It's ideal for my delivery work'. Listening back through the tapes it becomes apparent that 6-7 MAH Em has a malfunction that causes it to redirect course, instead of heading directly to its proposed destination. Within this scenario, the black and white begins to take on a more sinister tone, suggesting that the seemingly innocent computer may have Yoko drifting in space forever. Yoko's tapes also refer to her as a machine, but it is not until twenty-two minutes into the film that a comical 'change of batteries' occurs, confirming that she is android, not human.

A series of recurring shots of moths trapped in a light fitting contributes to *The Whispering Star*'s narrative, but also adds an unsettling element to the film, reminiscent of David Lynch's 1977 *Eraserhead*. The extended silence on board the 'house' (in a further comic turn, it is revealed as 'Rental Spaceship Z') is also used to enhance the claustrophobic effect, an obvious science-fiction trope, but its overly long use here seems to borrow directly from earlier sci-fi films, most notably Stanley Kubrick's *2001: A Space Odyssey* (1968) and Douglas Trumball's *Silent Running* (1972). Sion's narrative path is eventually given a rough end date of '11 years from now' when Yoko is expected to deliver her final package.

When Spaceship Z finally lands, on what certainly seems to be planet Earth, Yoko takes a package and carries it on foot through a bleak, damaged landscape (much like Sion used in *Himizu*) of scraggly trees, broken and disused roads and long stretches of power lines. From the inside of what appears to be an abandoned industrial building, Sion's camera looks out an opening across a landscape where waves can be seen breaking in the distance. As the shot moves forward towards a glassless window, the scene fades into full colour, and by the time the camera reaches the opening, Yoko can be seen marching determinedly towards the structure with the package that had earlier appeared to be white but is in fact bright yellow. Sion offers a brief moment of beauty, but when he cuts to an interior shot of Yoko and her package, the monochrome returns, and with it, a sense of despair. As Yoko looks around the abandoned room, broken windows, curtains billowing in the breeze, and in the distance, what looks to be a power station, Sion again brings the audience back to contemporary Japan and the remnants of the nuclear disaster. Days pass as Yoko waits with the package. She sits for a while but mostly stands near the doorway with the box. Eventually a man appears, with another male, presumably his adult son. He signs for the package, and with few words exchanged, departs. Yoko stays behind and gazes out the window, but no colour returns (Figure 3.5).

In her only vice, Yoko smokes cigarettes, adding a film noir touch to the film's other forms of retro imagery. Yoko returns to the spaceship, and the mundane nature, and for the first time is seen making a new recording, in which she ponders why humans still use courier services when they have teleportation at their disposal. Perhaps, she offers, 'it reflects humans' fading pride' at having created machines that can replace all human activity. Ever-curious, Yoko begins to peer into some of the boxes she is delivering, and here the stark monochrome accentuates the findings – a used cigarette butt, a lone pencil and a dented paper cup. These images lead to a long shot, back on Earth,

Figure 3.5 Devastation in *The Whispering Star* (2015).

looking down a deserted small-town shopping strip. The image, with a barely audible sound of the wind blowing, holds for a long time, intercut briefly with an image of a crushed beer can, building expectation that Yoko will appear. The sound of the can being stepped on introduces a new character in a fedora and trench coat (played by the late actor/musician Kenji Endo). Cutting back to the deserted streetscape, it is the new character that emerges from a side street some distance away, the can now stuck underneath his foot, and crunching with each second step as he makes his way towards us. Alone, the character, with one bandaged arm, stops to speak to a small tortoise, and then to a fibreglass dog standing sentinel at a railway station. As he wanders through the streets (and procuring an abandoned bicycle), Sion continues to remind the audience of the devastation of the tsunami as the man passes more evidence of destruction, overturned cars, a solitary surviving tree and overgrown fields littered with boats washed up onto dry land or smashed against buildings. Seemingly unperturbed, the man whistles as he rides and walks, the can still stuck under his shoe.

Sion's framing of the post-apocalyptic landscape is accentuated by the lack of colour. When Yoko is seen sitting on a chair, tying her bootlace, the chair is outside and propped up on a raised concrete block that sits in front of a two-storey concrete structure in ruins. The front half of a small, smashed boat is jammed up on the second level, the barely recognizable stern of a much larger ship sits between Yoko and the building, large chunks of it broken and splintered. The man speaks with Yoko, and as they speak, in a whisper, of course, Sion shoots from different angles (side, back and above) to show that they are surrounded by devastation.

The deliveries in *The Whispering Star* do not all neatly represent the after-effects of 2011, with a Bergman-esque scene when Yoko arrives on Planet Parass Zero to deliver a package to a home, only to find the intended recipient of the parcel is a chalked murder outline in a wealthy country estate. Among sheet-covered furniture, an old man sits with a young, blonde, Caucasian boy, both wearing suits, while opera plays on a record player. Yoko places the package on the table next to the man, hands him a pen and he silently signs for it. Yoko exits. The surrealism continues when Yoko returns to the place of her first delivery, and the landscape is littered with people, silently standing, upright with their arms by their sides and adjacent to ruins, or on the beach dotted with the washed-up refuse of buildings and ships. This framing of shots, especially with the use of cables and wires, is perhaps reminiscent of Fellini rather than Bergman.

Sion's film is one in which characters seldom question the way that things are. Although it contains many comic moments, the film is imbued with despondency. As they prepare to arrive at a new destination, Planet 62678, 'the last planet inhabited solely by humans', Yoko is informed by 6-7 MAH Em that she must abide by 'human protocol', and that 'Making sounds over 30 decibels is a crime'. As such noise 'could be lethal to the locals'.

As Yoko enters the planet she travels along a long corridor, lined with rice-paper walls behind which act as a frieze of silhouetted figures playing out idyllic scenes of human life: a father teaching his child how to throw a ball, an old couple bowing to each other, a birthday party, children skipping. The extended scene again works with the concept of black-and-white imagery, with the shadows blocking out details, in essence a binary representation of humankind. When Yoko arrives at her intended destination, the recipient of her parcel, a young mother, Ms Sori, walks towards the wall, but when she slides it back to greet Yoko, there is only blackness beyond the screen until an arm reaches through to sign for the delivery. Ms Sori retreats with her parcel as Yoko steps back. In silhouette, Ms Sori opens the package, but as Yoko watches, she sees that it only brings grief to Ms Sori and her family, while the other shadows around them carry on life as usual.

For what was to be Truffaut's final film, *Confidentially Yours/Vivement dimanche!* [lit. *Finally, Sunday!*] (1983), is presented as a black-and-white noir-fest that draws heavily on influences from Hitchcock. *Confidentially Yours* is based on the 1962 novel *The Long Saturday Night* by the American writer of 'hardboiled' fiction, Charles Williams. The murder mystery unfolds with real-estate agent secretary Barbara Becker (Fanny Ardant) dressed in high heels and a trench coat, presenting imagery of decades earlier, with few elements, mostly just the cars that are used, revealing the contemporary setting of the film. Even the monochromatic promotional images for the film harked back to early Hollywood and the *nouvelle vague*, with Truffaut clearly establishing the genre he wanted to depict. Becker's manager, Julien Vercel (Jean-Louis Trintignant), is suspected of murdering his wife's lover, and while Vercel holes up in the rear of his shop, Becker attends to the 'gumshoe' work, visiting back alleys and following various suspect people, all the while with Truffaut's use of black and white accentuating the shadows and austere lighting as Becker continues her investigations in their unnamed city and then down in Nice. The lack of colour renders the neon lights outside two identical nightclubs (one in each city) as bleak rather than vibrant. Ardant's thick dark hair effectively frames Becker's pale face and defines her high cheekbones in the true noir style of the femme fatale.

Truffaut's attention to detail in reconstructing the noir genre in *Confidentially Yours* includes rapid-fire exchanges of dialogue between characters. Impulsive behaviours, splashes of sudden violence and emphatic exclamations punctuate the entire film, bringing a melodramatic air that again fits the mould of cinema from decades before. Not without humour, Truffaut's film plays with French stereotypes when it features a bad guy being clobbered with a model *Tour Eiffel* before Becker and Vercel try to make their escape in an older model Citroën. When the car fails to start, and the police arrive on the scene, Becker drags Vercel into a darkened doorway and begins kissing him. When the police have gone and she releases her grip on him, he responds:

Vercel: What's got into you.
Becker: I saw it in a movie.

The comically self-referential nature of the scene reflects Truffaut's undoubted love of cinema and its ability to capture the dramas of life.

We shall finish this chapter by briefly looking at three other examples of very different French films shot in black and white for both formal and thematic reasons. The first, *Hate/La Haine* (1995), remains Mathieu Kassovitz's best-known film and continues to exert an iron grip on cinematic representations of the Paris suburbs (*banlieues*). Its mixture of urgent social commentary, emerging actors, virtuoso camerawork and enthralling hip-hop aesthetics introduced global audiences to a new style of French filmmaking that remains influential. The filming of *La Haine* was in fact done in colour and then printed in black and white; for Kassovitz, this decision 'bring[s] poetry into reality' (Aftab 2020) – the monochrome links the fictional world to the black-and-white television reportage of riots and police stand-offs that opens the film, it marks the film as something visually different to other *banlieue* films and it makes a bold artistic statement on behalf of Kassovitz (who would win the Best Director prize at Cannes that year). Placed alongside Ladj Ly's *Les Misérables* (2019), a similar *banlieue*-set film that problematizes notions of identity and youth assimilation while at the same time calling into question unchecked police power and brutality, Kassovitz's visual aesthetic seems austere and distancing. Compared to Ly's vivid, sun-drenched aesthetic – the opening scene of *Les Misérables* takes place in the aftermath of France's 2018 World Cup victory, in which countless red, white and blue flags are joyfully waved – *La Haine*'s noir stylings are rawer and disorienting. Jean-Luc Godard's *In Praise of Love/Éloge de l'amour* (2001) is divided into two halves: the first, set in present-day Paris; the second, set two years prior. Yet in a deliberate inversion of how the cinematic historical past is traditionally represented, Godard shoots the present day in 35mm black and white and the past on video, in hyper-saturated colour. For Godard, shooting in monochrome is not a stylistic default to be deployed when recounting the past but, instead, an ethical choice that requires us to re-evaluate the image itself, whether past, present or future. *Angel-A*, Luc Besson's 2005 fantasy adventure set in a black-and-white Paris, is a final reminder of black-and-white cinematography's seductiveness and its status as 'a meditation on reality [and] *a mediation of reality*' (Dixon 2015: 220). Paris – that most cinematically photographed of cities, frequently bathed in colour or refracted through digital enhancements – is here configured as a mysterious, romantic netherworld. Besson's earlier *Nikita* (1990) and *The Fifth Element* (1997) were drenched in colour, like radical pop art, baroque experiments in exaggeration, excess and hyperrealism. Angel-A embraces the limitations of black, white and grey to pay homage to a cinematic Paris that is as far away from *Amélie* or the opening montage of *Midnight in Paris* (2012) as possible, scaling back the visual glamour to hone in on the essence of the city's topography.

Conclusion

This chapter has listed examples of visual style, influence and exchange between French and Japanese cinema, and reminded us of the enduring principles of auteurism – the recognition of a particular visual and/or narrative style, and the tracing of coherence and consistency across a director's career. The likes of Michel Gondry remind us of the enduring plasticity and malleability of mise-en-scene and cinema's long connection to visual excess and theatricality in the search for purity. Our focus on monochrome in part pays a debt to the French *nouvelle vague* and the much-loved heritage of those films and shows how French and Japanese cinema continues to deploy black-and-white imagery across a range of genres as a stylistic convention, a marker of 'coolness', and a reminder of the textural possibilities of monochrome from a formal and a structural perspective.

4
Tora-san and the Monsieur Hulot influence

One of the rare opportunities for filmmakers, before the age of the multi-volume franchise films with a seeming different director at every turn, was the ability to create an on-screen character that captured the hearts and minds of the audience, so much so that the filmmaker would be rewarded with funding to continue the theme with a series of films. In this case, stylistic repetition was to be rewarded, not frowned upon, as the character carried the story, rather than necessarily advancing a complex narrative. The character himself (*sic*) need not necessarily be overwhelmingly likeable but at the very least needed to be interesting, offering the audience a degree of intrigue. In one instance, the thematic role of the outsider was well utilized in Japanese cinema in the episodic adventures of Yoji Yamada's 'lovable tramp' Tora-san (1969–95), played by established film and TV actor and comedian, Kiyoshi Atsumi. From the first film in 1969, *Otoko wa Tsurai yo*/*It's Tough Being a Man*, Atsumi played the hapless Kuruma Torajirō ('Tora-san') in a total of forty-eight films (all featured the same title, but with a subtitle to differentiate them), and several television spin-offs. The questionably 'lovable' Tora-san is an itinerant travelling salesman who, in most episodes, drops in unexpectedly on family or friends in search of a bed (or sofa) to stay on. He will generally outstay his welcome and get involved in family squabbles. Tora-san's iconic look includes a short-brimmed fedora, a wide cummerbund/girdle (a type of stomach warmer known as a *haramaki*) that he wears, visibly, under his jacket (not under his shirt or vest), and he often carries a small suitcase (Figure 4.1).

In many ways, the Tora-san series can be seen as influenced by Jacques Tati's Monsieur Hulot series of films that preceded Tora-san by more than a decade (1953–71), beginning with *Mr Hulot's Holiday*/*Les vacances de Monsieur Hulot* (1953), when the eponymous Hulot (played by Tati) first stumbles from

Figure 4.1 Tora-san in his hat and *haramaki* in the *Tora-san* series.

Figure 4.2 Monsieur Hulot in his hat and trench coat in *Playtime* (1967).

adventure to misadventure in his iconic hat, pipe and trench coat. Both Tora-san and Hulot carry themselves with an air of confidence, to the point of arrogance, despite their general incapacity to function in everyday situations. Both can be grumpy and impatient, and in Tora-san's case 'he vacillates all the time, failing to face up to inevitabilities until it is (almost) too late' (Ehrlich 1996: 7) (Figure 4.2).

Tati: choreographing meaning through movement

The dynamics of the Tati-Hulot interaction continue to exert a powerful influence, not just in a certain type of near-wordless screen humour, but in successive generations of screen comedians who have sought to explore the complexities, discombobulations and eccentricities of contemporary existence He is bracketed, rightly, alongside Charlie Chaplin and Buster Keaton as exemplifying how visual and sonic gags, distinctive body language and posture, and a befuddlement with modernity work together consistently and unobtrusively in ways that are both amusing and deeply troubling. Tati's meticulous involvement with all aspects of the film industry, and his fastidious attention to detail, accounted for him only producing six feature films across his career, beginning with *The Village Fair/Jour de fête* (1949), *Mr Hulot's Holiday/Les vacances de Monsieur Hulot* (1953), *My Uncle/Mon Oncle* (1958), *Playtime* (1967), *Traffic/Trafic* (1971) and *Parade* (1974). Each one, however, is a masterpiece. Tati began his career as a mime artist, and brought those gestures and poses, plus a radical commitment to sight gags, to his screen work. Sound also played a central part in his films, with its creative distortions and contortions lending a surreal veneer to his depictions of everyday. We recall the twanging sounds as a restaurant door elastically opens and closes in *Les vacances de Monsieur Hulot*, or the deafening click-clack of high heels as a character runs across the screen in *Mon Oncle* as much as the denseness of those films' mise-en- scene. As Jonathan Rosenbaum reminds us, Tati 'effectively directed each of his films twice – once when he shot them and then once again when he composed and recorded their soundtracks' (2014). Though he would go on to make other films – including *Playtime*, regarded by many as Tati's masterpiece – *Mon Oncle* was a commercial and critical success and remains for many Tati's crowning achievement. Tati once described Hulot as 'a character with a complete sense of independence, utterly unselfish, whose distraction, which is his main flaw, make him – in our functional times – a misfit' (Cauliez 1968: 107). Right from the start of *Mon Oncle*, this misfit status is codified through a highly dichotomised world in which values of nostalgia, community, and emotional attachment are placed in opposition to the inexorable shift to modernity, impersonality, and the new sterile and rigidly codified world of French suburbia that is perpetually ridiculed in the film for its pretentiousness and vacuity. Production design is an important part of Tati's narrative and aesthetic preoccupations. The opening credit sequence allegorizes the collision between the film's two worlds – Hulot's and the Arpels' – and their attendant designs and visual styles. The new world can be seen throughout the credits – high-rise skyscrapers are being constructed to the deafening sound of jackhammers and industrial machinery, and the names of individual technicians are layered onto signposts. It is only at the end, with the appearance of the title, that we switch locations, and enter the old France – 'Mon Oncle' is scrawled in chalk on a dilapidated wall. The rest of the film then investigates these two worlds, interrogating their differences and mining their idiosyncrasies for comic potential. Tati deploys Hulot as the figure capable of navigating these divergent spaces, and the scene in which he lovingly places a loose stone back into place on the crumbling wall that demarcates the two worlds highlights the very human presence within this fast-changing modern world. One of the film's most successful set pieces is the scene early on when Hulot ascends the staircase of his oddly rickety apartment. Tati films the action in an unbroken long shot – we periodically catch sight of Hulot through a window, lose him as he disappears behind a wall or around the back of a rooftop, and then finally see him enter his front door. Not only does the intricately built set here remind of similar designs from classic French films of the 1930s, such as those by Jean Renoir, Marcel Carné and Julien Duvivier that rely upon similarly constructed domestic apartments to reinforce values of solidarity and friendship that Tati here pays homage to, but it also underlines how much of Tati's humour derives from the interplay between individual and object, prop, or space. Shortly after entering his apartment, Hulot opens and closes a window to reflect sunlight onto a birdcage, causing the bird to sing 'in time' with each pivot. The chirping bird and Hulot's simple gestures here suggest innocence and playfulness, and also lay out the essence of much of Tati's comedic impulses. The prop here is a simple mechanism that makes a bird sing; not so the props in the ultra-modernist Arpel villa later on, full of impossibly engineered chairs (out of which Hulot topples), the iron backrests of chairs in the restaurant in *Playtime* (which ruin customers' suits), or a horse's reins in *Les vacances du Monsieur Hulot* (into which Hulot becomes entangled): these props cause havoc, reminding audiences of silent cinema, and the often fraught interplay between object and human that characterised the best work of Tati's idols, Buster Keaton and Mack Sennett. So it is not just exquisite blocking, choreography and body language that typifies Tati's work, but also the uses and misuses of things.

Icons from another era

It is not surprising that *Mon Oncle* is burdened with so strong a spirit of ambivalence towards modernity and progress. Taken as a whole, Tati's oeuvre 'foregrounds the interactions of human beings with contemporary consumer-oriented technology, and the ways in which such technologies alter human relationships and the fabric of lived experience' (Hilliker 1998: 59). These forces might be expressed as the effects of technology, mechanization, urban planning and design, and modernity at the level of human behaviour – a period, in the words of Kristin Ross (1995) – of 'fast cars and clean bodies'. Tati's two previous films, *Jour de fête* and *Les vacances de Monsieur Hulot*, as well as the later *Playtime*, all, to a greater or lesser degree, problematize the notion that technological progress is to be embraced and automatically succumbed to. In *Jour de fête* it was the tension between the leisurely postman's bicycle and the new Americanized system of accelerated postal delivery that suggested that post-war France was gradually being mechanized and 'improved' through faster, more efficient means. In the kitchen scene in *Mon Oncle*, Hulot is baffled by the new consumer goods and the odd sounds they make; later on, at Arpel's factory, Hulot is fascinated by the very modern plastic hoses that are being manufactured. Yet these technological advances do not necessarily equate to simplicity and efficiency in Tati's world. Rather, it is the 'old world'- the market place, the beach, the bicycle, the dogs running free in the streets – that offer respite from the relentless march of progress. In a famous BBC interview in 1976, Tati suggested that it is was not Hulot who was 'lost', but rather the people with whom he came into contact. Following this logic, Hulot's role in each film is to undermine the seeming certainty of the 'new', and to offer a radical break with modernity's insistence on forward motion, automation, and sterility.

So where does Tora-san fit in here? As we have already suggested, Tati's Hulot is cited as being influenced by the greats of Hollywood's silent era, especially Charlie Chaplin (whose 'Tramp' name in French, 'Charlot' was said to have influenced Tati's choice of name for his character) and Buster Keaton, and there are certainly elements of these forebears in the character of Tora-san, with Chaplin a popular figure in 1930s Japan to the extent that he spawned 'many local imitators' (Standish 2012: 6). Yet beneath Tora-san there is an underlying critique of Japanese culture, where the sense of exclusion represents an outlier in a collectivist society. Tora-san wanders around Japan, at times the passive observer, at times the active participant in parades, marches or arguments. As with Hulot, there are elements of Baudelaire's (and Benjamin's) *flâneur*, but Tora-san's purposes are not directly political, or so it seems, instead he is partaking of life as it happens, little is predetermined (Figure 4.3).

Figure 4.3 Hulot as passive, curious observer in *Monsieur Hulot's Holiday* (1953).

As was to become the case with the Tora-san character, Hulot/Tati 'is not a comedian in the sense of being the source and focus of the humor; he is, rather, an attitude, a signpost, a perspective that reveals humor in the world around him' (Cardullo 2013: 359). As with Hulot, Tora-san is 'causing chaos wherever he goes' (Regelman 1995), often creating the disturbance inadvertently, or deliberately, and then leaving the scene as the chaos unfolds (Figure 4.4).

Cardullo notes that Tati's keen eye as a director allows him to avoid the use of the obvious in setting up his comedic skits. His knowledge of cinematic techniques sees him 'refuse to use close-ups, emphatic camera angles, or montage to guide the audience to the humor in the images' (2013: 359); there is an intellectual pursuit required by the viewer, with often the unremarkable prop or action in a scene suddenly being called in to play. Cardullo cites the importance of the audience maintaining an 'innocence of vision' (360) that rewards with the comic payoff as Tati reaches his punchline.

Tora-san's comedy calls upon similar devices, and his humour has been traced back through Japanese theatre by Ehrlich where she finds its antecedents in *kyogen* performances 'based on skeletal plot scenarios and extemporized oral expositions' that drew on 'bawdy' dances, rustic folk music and comic narratives that were very distinct from 'the more stately *no* [*Noh*] theatre' (1996: 11). The appeal of *kyogen* was in its representation of the everyday, something we see extemporized in both Tora-san and Hulot. Tora-san's incredible freedom (partly imposed through his search for work, lodgings and even love) showed a playful

Figure 4.4 Tora-san oblivious to the chaos in *Tora-san: Our Lovable Tramp* (1969).

recklessness to Japanese audiences, with 'his ability to wander through the beautiful natural sites and towns in Japan' triggering for the audience 'a source of pleasure and envy' (Ehrlich 1996: 16), and adding to the rustic appeal of both the character and the film. Filmmaker Jun Ichikawa stresses the importance of Tora-san to Japanese society, regarding the first ten or so films in the series as the most important because at that time 'Tora-san might really have existed, that was in the Showa thirties and forties (1955–75), when types like him were still around, but now they don't exist anymore' (Schilling 1999: 104–5). Ichikawa discusses how this impacted on his own filmmaking, where '[j]ust like the Tora-san series, not much seems to be going on in the foreground of my character's lives, but in the background they are changing' (Schilling 1999: 104).

Once again, parallels can be seen between Tora-san and Hulot, the latter who is often 'personally . . . absent from the most comical of his gags, because he is nothing but the metaphysical incarnation of a disorder that continues long after his departure' (Cardullo 2013: 360). That Tora-san or Hulot is responsible for the disorder is the gag (a walking cane or suitcase left behind, a door or window left open), and, like Chaplin or even Rowan Atkinson's Mr Bean, the character's ignorance/innocence of what he has left behind helps to make him more endearing. As Tati explains, if the viewer 'expects tricks or gags from Hulot, he will undoubtedly be disappointed' (Cardullo 2013: 366). The creation of Hulot, as opposed to a Chaplin Chaplin-copy, was important to Tati, who maintained that there were 'no concessions' with Hulot, and that '[o]nce the gag is finished, matters don't go any further, the formula is not exploited' (Cardullo 2013: 367).

In terms of narrative structure, both Tora-san and Hulot follow a similar path through each of their films, yet their episodic nature (within each individual film) requires a degree of flexibility. As Cardullo notes of *Les vacances de Monsieur Hulot*, the film 'cannot be anything other than a succession of events at once wholly coherent and dramatically independent' (2013: 361). Embedded in Hulot's character is a sense of the passive, the often-curious observer, that Cardullo notes (in a 1980 interview with Tati) 'is the reversal of the traditional equation in comic films where you have a normal world confronted by a comical character – Chaplin for instance' (2013: 365). For Hulot, though, and we would argue, Tora-san, 'the world is made comical precisely because Hulot is not' (365). Hulot stumbles around France where he creates a bond with the audience that 'unleashes a return of the repressed, the abject, the excessive, the uncontrollable' (O'Donoghue 2015: 15).

Ambivalence to modernity (and love)

For the vagabond-like nature of both protagonists, time is largely immaterial and entirely fluid (Cardullo 2013: 361), a feature that is used to great effect to antagonize the audience, who may have the advantage of knowing or suspecting the consequences of each character's tardy behaviour. For Tora-san, much time is spent idly, often unemployed or unemployable, which Ehrlich relates back to the *Commedia dell'arte* and the character of the servant 'who does not do any real work' aside from messing in the affairs of his master's romance (1996: 12). His inability to abide by social codes is all the more remarkable (funny, or outrageous) because '[a]n individual in Japan is always part of something larger (the rare exceptions are considered to be bizarre loners)' (Buruma 2012: 183). Like Chaplin, Keaton and Harold Lloyd (whose iconic image of him hanging from the hands of a clock draws attention to the importance of time), both Hulot and Tora-san rely on the tensions created by split-second timing of a gag, through to the indication of poor timing as a sense of frustration for other characters and ultimately the audience. Together with the missteps and misbehaviours of both Hulot and Tora-san's (mis)adventures, time is employed to deliver the comedic goods, and in Cardullo's words, creates 'success as the result of cruel observation' (2013: 363).

Both Hulot and Tora-san establish appeals to nostalgia, Hulot, for instance, in his mockery of the technological age, and in Tora-san's unencumbered travels through rural and urban Japan where his character 'appeals to memories of simpler times, memories that seem to be of a time just a few years back, though unattainable' (Ehrlich 1996: 19). In both characters, there is a universal humanity at play that can only be realized when one is unlocked from the constraints of employment and the demands of family and society. The freedom to wander as a *flâneur*, at times wistfully ignorant and unrestrained can be found in both characters, celebrating what Ehrlich refers to as the 'ridiculous humanity of it all' (1996: 20). The Tora-san films also play a role in the Japanese calendar by being released (mostly) two times each year on the auspicious occasions of New Year (January) and the *O-Bon* festival of the dead (August), each new Tora-san appearance coinciding with moments of important religious significance, 'like an ancient festival god' (Buruma 2012: 210).

The ability to move freely across one's nation is another key theme in both the Tora-san and Hulot films. O'Donoghue (2015: 14) writes of how in Hulot's later films *Playtime* and *Trafic*, they are 'entirely set in those intermediary or transitory "nonplaces" that J.G. Ballard defined as central to late capitalism: hotels; airports, motorways, flyovers, streets, subways; boats, buses, cars . . .'. The unrestrained nature of citizenry afforded to both Hulot and Tora-san – alongside notions of gendered and racial privilege – free them up to exploratory adventures. They are rarely stopped by authorities or bound within the confines of the institutionalized societies of their respective countries.

Another feature of both film series is the seeming ageless characteristics of both leading protagonists (again something that is a feature in much comedy, from Chaplin to Bean). As Atsumi was approaching what was to be his final Tora-san film before his death in August 1996, it seemed 'the 67-year-old actor is constantly just about to turn 40' (Regelman 1995), an advantage of him in his earlier years taking on the persona of an older, grumpy or intolerant man as the Tora-san character was established. The same could be said of Tati in his role as Hulot, inhabiting a perennially late-middle-age. The introduction of younger characters in the form of Tora-san's nephew and his romantic interest, provide enough distractions to ensure that the audience does not grow tired of following the adventures of an old(er) man.

Despite the agelessness of the characters within the films, both the Tora-san and Hulot characters (and their films) are icons from another era. As O'Donoghue (2015: 14) notes, '[t]o claim Tati's fictions as historical documents or sociological artifacts does not mean that they do not bear the biases, absences and blind spots to which all such records are prone'. Viewed through the lens of the twenty-first century, O'Donoghue points to Tati's shortcomings when it came to the representation of women or people with non-Caucasian racial features. As with Tora-san, Hulot's treatment of women is often less than flattering, with leering advances and inappropriate objectifying of women based on appearance (especially weight-based). Tati only features three black characters across all his films; a boxer, a musician and a 'replica' Hulot, and his one Jewish character is heavily stereotyped as a financially obsessed slob (O'Donoghue 2015: 14–15). Tora-san's values also appear to be from another era, in one film he promises a dying friend that he will marry the man's widow to give her security once her husband has died. Tora-san makes preparations to settle down but realizes that his drifting lifestyle will prohibit him from being a good husband, so he reneges on the deal. As Buruma concludes though, episodes like this can add to the attractiveness of Tora-san (as an on-screen character) because 'the tragic fate of the outsider confirms how lucky we all are to lead such restricted, respectable and in most cases, perfectly harmless lives' (2012: 218). The success of the Tora-san series, however, is ultimately attributed to the charm of the man who played him, because 'as the irrepressible Tora-san, Atsumi Kiyoshi saved a studio and warmed the hearts of millions' (Schilling 1999: 121).

One area where there is a marked difference between Hulot and Tora-san is in the latter's complex nature where his ability to appear cruel or indifferent is countered by his propensity for regret. While Hulot is not one for reflection, Tora-san often muses on his life and the opportunities missed. At one point in *Otoko wa Tsurai yo: Torajiro aiaigasa/Tora-san Meets the Songstress Again* (1975, 'episode' 15) he finds himself in Hokkaido, reminiscing about his complex relationship with his sister, where he constantly sees himself as a disappointment to her, either through not being there for her or through his argumentative nature. In this episode, he sings:

> **Tora-san**: I'm a worthless brother. I know, my sister. Someday I want to be a brother you can be proud of. The hustle and my efforts [to settle down] never come together, and another sun . . . another sun sets with tears again. Another sun sets.

While Tora-san's melancholy mood seems to indicate change, his irascible nature and his inability to read other people's emotions continue to let him down. This becomes evident from the first film from 1969 (variously known as *Tora-san: Our Lovable Tramp, It's Tough Being a Man* or *Otoko wa Tsurai yo*), where his sister Sakuro (Chieko Baisho) is being romantically pursued by Hiroshi (Gin Maeda), an important worker in a nearby printing business. Across two crucial scenes, Tora-san shows his insensitivity, beginning with his visit to Hiroshi in the print shop, where Hiroshi is waiting for Tora-san who had been to visit Sakura at her office to find out if Sakura liked him. Tora-san strolls in:

> **Hiroshi** (*eager*): How was it?
> **Tora-san**: Nothing doing.
> **Hiroshi**: Huh?
> **Tora-san**: Give up. No hope.
> **Hiroshi**: Did you ask her?
> **Tora-san**: Sure thing. You're no talker, so I put it to her good.
> **Hiroshi**: That I want to marry her?
> **Tora-san**: Sure, but there's no chance.
> **Hiroshi** (*dejected*): I see.
> **Tora-san**: Cheer up. Let's go for a drink.

Throughout the exchange, Tora-san is without emotion to the point of being flippant. He turns to leave, but Hiroshi has more to say.

> **Hiroshi**: Have you ever been in love?

He turns away, overcome with emotion. Tora-san pats him on the back, more patronizing than comforting.

> **Tora-san**: I know. I know how you feel. Go ahead, cry. Have a good cry.

Tora-san turns around to admonish some of the workers who are watching their conversation. Hiroshi takes the opportunity to push past Tora-san and run out of the building, to go and see Sakura for himself. He finds her with her Aunt (Chieko Misaki) and her family (therefore Tora-san's relatives, too). Hiroshi pours his heart out to a startled Sakura, imploring that she stays happy, but that he must leave. He runs out the door, only to be replaced by Tora-san coming in, seemingly oblivious to the chaos he has created.

> **Tora-san**: What's going on? What did he come here to say?
> **Sakura**: Brother, what happened at the factory?
> **Tora-san**: Nothing. What did he say?
> **Aunt**: He said he's leaving!

Tora-san: What?
Sakura: Brother, wait a minute!

Hiroshi's boss runs in, castigating Tora-san for making him lose his vital employee, but Sakura interrupts them:

Sakura: Tell me what you said and did.
Tora-san: Nothing much. I just said to give up on you.
Sakura: Then when you came to my office . . . ?
Tora-san: Yes, you were cold.
Sakura (*breaking down*): I wasn't.

Some factory staff rush in to say that Hiroshi has left the premises. The boss runs out to try to stop Hiroshi.

Sakura (*to Tora-san*): You fool! You big fool!

Sakura runs out, while the family and workers all turn to look at Tora-san, but he merely turns away from them, indifferent. This scene again shows the complexity of the Tora-san character, his love for his sister seems apparent, but it is unclear whether he is trying to avert her possible marriage, or if he is unable to process the emotional depth of the situation. Sakura's initial response to talk of marriage was not 'cold' as Tora-san suggests but indicative of the suppression of emotion by young couples in courtship that plays an important role in Japanese cultural etiquette.

Sakura is able to catch Hiroshi, but in the meantime her family, joined by the now inebriated boss, grills Tora-san.

Aunt: Stop meddling!
Tora-san (*slaps the table*): What? Me meddle?
Aunt (*raising her voice*): Yes! If you hadn't, it would have turned out well!
Tora-san: Fool! What a joke! What lout can't even hold hands!
Boss (*drunk and angry*): Hiroshi is no lout. He's my chief engineer! We may fold up without him!
Tora-san: Good. More sunshine!

Tora-san's behaviour underscores the complexity of his character. Like Hulot, there are times when the audience may despise his conduct or be horrified at his/their rudeness. Aunt makes it clear that Tora-san's actions are reprehensible, and in a twist of blame, Tora-san turns things back to himself:

Tora-san: Kicking me out? It's the end if you say it! Okay. I'm the odd man here! I'll never come back! To think you'd say it!

The argument reaches its peak just as Sakura returns. She immediately goes to her brother and tells him that she is engaged to Hiroshi. In a moment, Tora-san shifts from a boorish loud-mouth to a caring sibling:

Sakura: You don't mind? Do you Brother?

Tora-san is too choked up to reply, fighting back tears of happiness. He turns away from the family to hide his emotions as Sakura says, to his back, 'Thank you for everything'. It is these moments of poignant melodrama that are a hallmark of the series.

As we have noted, both Yamada and Tati's works are strongly ambivalent towards modernity and progress. In one absurd scene in *Mon Oncle*, in which the extent to which technology has absurdly overtaken the Arpels' lives is laid bare, Tati shows how new-fangled gadgets imprison and terrify. After the Arpels find themselves trapped in their garage after the self-closing door mechanism fails, they first call on their dog to try and trigger the sensor, but to no avail. Next, they turn to their maid, Georgette:

Mrs. Arpel: We're locked in the garage.
Georgette: In the garage?
Mrs. Arpel: Georgette, listen. See the two lights?
Georgette: Yes, madame.
Mrs. Arpel: To open the door, just step through the beam of light.
Georgette: No, I can't! I'm terrified of electricity.
Mr. Arpel: There's absolutely no danger. Just walk in front of the electric eye.
Georgette: The electric what? I'll be electrocuted.

The scene is played broadly for laughs, and reminds of us the pomposity of the Arpels and how their 'keeping up with the Joneses' attitude serves only to highlight their ridiculousness. But it is a scene tinged with sadness – these citizens of an affluent, hyper-modern France are trapped in more than just a garage. Earlier, Mrs. Arpel had given her dinner party guests a tour of their home, reminding them all that in this domestic space, 'everything is connected'. Far from it, suggests Tati.

Such suspicions become even more apparent in *Playtime*, which is a culmination of many of Tati's ideas about the disquieting architectural principles that had emerged in France in the post-war period. In previous incarnations, Hulot seemed always comfortable in his environment, and part of the joy of the earlier films was seeing how he would prevail over the reigning confusion.

In *Playtime*, however, Hulot is herded along in contrast to the free passage he enjoyed in the earlier films: a passive onlooker rather than an active participant in the urban experience. In one scene, he leaves an apartment but becomes trapped behind the glass door as he seeks the exit into the street. When he finally escapes, the uncertainty remains, for Hulot continues to wander in a circle through a large car park and attempts to find his bearings within an increasingly destabilizing city. By this point, he is utterly lost (McCann 2008: 204–5).

Hulot's wanderings would continue in one more film – *Trafic/Traffic* (1971) – which sees him drive from Paris to Amsterdam to an automobile expo to show off his latest invention – a camper-car full of ingenious features and highly sophisticated gadgetry. Along the way, Tati trades in the usual sight and sound gags, and uses exaggerated gestures and postures to convey the sense of urban ennui and disconnection from modern life. A traffic accident appears to reanimate drivers, jerking them back to life like puppets on strings, while motorcycle cops move in complete robotic harmony. Modern life, as epitomised by the car, noted Tati in 1971, was becoming increasingly ridiculous: 'What they call comfort and new techniques have become so exaggerated . . . And when you become so remote from what's designed for you, the human connections between people start to go' (Rosenbaum 2022). For Tati, and for Hulot, human connections were all that mattered.

Conclusion

The links between Tora-san and Hulot suggest that the theme of the lone character has recognizable traits that struck a chord with both Tati and Yamada. Both filmmakers were able to capitalize on this by creating films that clearly resonated with French and Japanese audiences. Tora-san's fame is even parodied in a 2012 Japanese soft-drink commercial, where Hollywood actor Richard Gere, dressed as Tora-san, arrives at a small railway station in France, clutching an iconic Tora-san tattered brown suitcase. It is difficult to measure the impact that Tati may have had on Yamada, just as it is to assume the level of influence of Chaplin, Keating or Lloyd on both filmmakers. Wada-Marciano comments on the invaluable exchange between another European filmmaker, Ernst Lubitsch and his influence on Ozu, resulting in Ozu 'mastering the master' by overtly copying a scene from one of Lubitsch's earlier films in his 1934 *Woman of Tokyo/*

Tokyo no on'na (2008: 6). The impact of this early form of homage showed the maturation of the Japanese filmgoing public and

> created a sophisticated and distinctly modern form of spectatorship, wherein the viewers could relish the intertextual references to other films as well as the satire of their own experience as moviegoers. The spectatorial regime that such devices inculcated also had a postcolonial dimension: it mitigated the sense of shame over the hybrid origins of Japanese film culture and offered consolation through a modern sensibility that beckoned the viewer's participation. (Wada-Marciano 2008: 6)

Tora-san's on-screen arrival in the period just after the turmoil and protests of the late 1960s drew the attention of audiences back to a more benign sense of nationalism focused on the domestic trials of an individual character. The success of both Hulot and Tora-san in successive films indicates that through their respective French and Japanese cultural retellings of the wandering protagonist, universal values can be found.

Part Two

Themes, Ideas and Approaches

5

Unemployment and the isolating self

In Part One of this book, we traced the historical and stylistic paths of the French and Japanese cinema industries. Here, in Part Two, we draw our focus closer to the themes, ideas and approaches that are found in individual films and, as noted in our Introduction, explore how such films may veer from their national (or nationalistic) roots and instead 'expose universal truths about the human condition'. In the following chapters we analyze film structures, dialogue, characters, filmmakers and the industries themselves in search of the cinematic influences that work across the two nations. In this chapter we explore the ways that film serves to reflect the role of the individual in Japanese and French societies. We examine how the individual is placed within the 'collective' units of marriage, family, community and nation and how cinematic portrayals of employment (and unemployment) reflect changing social and gender roles across both nations.

The personal toll of unemployment

Politics was to play a decisive role in Japanese cinema from the 1920s with the suppression of left-wing ideals through severe censorship, the rise of the right, and influences from Europe finding their way into Japanese cinemas either through Western films or through a re-evaluation by Japanese filmmakers of the role of their films. Sato notes that 'propaganda films from the Soviet Union by directors such as Eisenstein or Pudovkin injected a far greater modernism than had hitherto been perceptible' (2008: 42), as Japan's filmmakers began to imitate and incorporate new narrative and technical styles into their films. In an almost serendipitous mirroring of influences, Eisenstein, who had spent time in Japan, acclaimed the power of kabuki theatre and Japanese aesthetics in general, and saw how film could be used to communicate ideological information to mass audiences. While the war years saw a focus on propaganda films right across the Northern hemisphere, the post-war period resulted in films with a more targeted focus on individual characters and their personal lives. Difficulties arising from the breakdown of family and social networks, and the impact of unemployment became staple themes for filmmakers in the push towards realism in cinema.

Kiyoshi Kurosawa's *Tōkyō Sonata* [*Tokyo Sonata*] was recognized at Cannes when it won the Jury Prize of the *Un Certain Regard* section. In *Tokyo Sonata*, Ryûhei Sasaki's (Teruyuki Kagawa) shame from losing his respectable-enough, upper-level *sararīman* [salaryman] job is no less of a 'crime' than that reflected in Mizoguchi's films of the 1940s and 1950s 'where an important leitmotif was that of a man living to atone for his crimes against a woman' (Sato 2008: 30). When Ryûhei unexpectedly finds himself laid off from his job, the sense of shame is so great that he cannot bring himself to tell his wife and children. The Japanese male is traditionally seen as the head of the household, and therefore expected to provide for his family, although even with a job, the salaryman can be plagued by 'a large element of self-doubt, and a frustration and nostalgia for lost autonomy' (Gill 2003: 3). Finding himself unemployed, Ryûhei has little choice then, but to queue up at the 'Hello Work' employment agency, teeth gritted as he stands in line. He is brought face-to-face with the agency clerk who offers him a job as a night-shift security guard. Ryûhei sighs deeply, but then brightens when the clerk changes tack, suggesting 'administrative work':

> **Ryûhei**: I'm much more suited to that.
> **Clerk**: Well, then, [reaching for a new folder] maybe this is more suitable for you?
> **Ryûhei**: Yes, please.
> **Clerk**: Manager at a Happy Mart store.

Ryûhei looks crestfallen.

> **Clerk** (*cont.*): Monday to Friday. 7am to 3pm, 850 yen (approx. US$10) an hour.
> **Ryûhei**: As I wrote it in the form you gave me, I used to be Administrative Director at Tanita [company].
> **Clerk**: There's no easy way to say this, but it'll be 100% impossible for you to match your former position.

The clerk dismissively turns from Ryûhei and presses the button calling the next person. The next scene shows a dejected Ryûhei ambling up the hill towards his home, a recurring scene where he meets his son as he rounds an intersection so that they can finish the journey home together. Inside, he hands a packet to his wife, Megumi (Kyôko Koizumi), telling her, 'Here's this month's salary'. She

Figure 5.1 Ryûhei by the riverbank in *Tokyo Sonata* (2008).

accepts in the culturally appropriate way, taking the package with both hands and bowing, not knowing that it is his final wage (as he waits on his severance pay).

Rather than face the ignominy of unemployment, Ryûhei dresses each day, packs his briefcase and as a ruse, leaves the house to spend the day under the freeway overpass, by the river, with other be-suited but laid-off workers and homeless men. He eats from a charity food kitchen to save money. He is further humiliated when forced to sing karaoke at a job interview, after jokingly stating it as one of the skills he possesses. His atonement is found later when he secretly begins work as a janitor in a shopping mall to ensure that he can continue to pay the family's bills (Figure 5.1).

Ryûhei's shame deepens, as he feels the janitor job is beneath him. Kurosawa's ability to portray Ryûhei's misfortune is achievable because 'his focus is on human personality; his characters often suffer because they learn too much about themselves' (Jacobs 2008: 144). Thus, when Megumi sees her husband down by the overpass one day, with the other homeless men, she does not confront him, as she understands how difficult the situation must be for him. Meanwhile, Ryûhei's eldest son, Takashi (Yū Koyanagi) wants to join the US military, through a new plan where non-US citizens can sign up. Takashi wants to protect his family, but Ryûhei forbids him from signing up, and they argue:

> **Ryûhei**: In this house, I protect you. That's how it works. You can't just do whatever you want . . .

> **Takashi**: I don't want your protection.
> **Ryûhei**: Get out, then. Get out. Get out!

Takashi goes to leave, but Megumi stops him and asks Ryûhei to reason with his son.

> **Ryûhei**: Takashi, if you want to leave home, fine, but not for America. Stay in Japan and do what you can here, understand?
> **Takashi**: What am I supposed to do? (pause) You say you're protecting us, Dad, but what do you do every day?

Ryûhei is forced into a stunned silence, while Megumi looks on, wondering what his answer will be. While this is significant to the audience (and Megumi) because of Ryûhei's unemployment, Takashi's comment has a greater relevance to Japan at the time of a decade-long recession, and its reliance on the economic support of the United States, and for the questionable worth of the salaryman and the futility of his daily toil. Historically, marriage in Japan comes with particular duties, not the least that it should be 'conceived of in terms of the provision of the next generation and not as a vehicle for the emotional fulfilment and sexual gratification of the individuals concerned' (Standish 2011: 80). Rosenbaum writes of the 'gap-widening society' (*kakusa shakai*) afflicting post-1990s Japan, and that *Tokyo Sonata* reflects the impact this has on families, rendering it 'important because it creates a cross-generational as well as cross-gender discourse which suggests that all aspects of contemporary Japanese society are affected by the social ramifications of a rapidly stratifying society' (2010: 119). Ryûhei's role is therefore less about him, than it is about what is required of him. Before Ryûhei can gather his thoughts to speak, Takashi responds:

> **Takashi** (*cont.*): You can't even answer me.

There is another prolonged silence, before Takashi excuses himself, and Ryûhei sits fuming, but helpless, shown in focused profile in the foreground as Megumi (slightly blurred through a low depth of field) looks across at him from the background. The selective focus pinpoints that the pain is his to bear. Ryûhei returns to the employment agency, this time suppressing his pride to take on the shopping-mall cleaning job.

The Sasaki family's difficulties do not end there. Their youngest son, Kenji (Kai Inowaki), a young teen, desperately wants to learn the piano, so he begins using his lunch money for secret lessons. He is a natural talent, and the piano instructor sends a letter to their home, suggesting he joins an exclusive music school. Ryûhei is (again) angry, and berates Kenji, with no feelings of hypocrisy as he says:

> **Ryûhei**: Going behind our backs, hoping you won't get caught. I hate that kind of cowardly attitude more than anything!

Kenji argues back, telling him that he will give up the piano, but Ryûhei angrily throws the boy against the wall. As if the emasculation of losing his job was not enough, Ryûhei's role as the family patriarch is also under threat. Kenji retaliates:

> **Kenji**: You're the liar, Dad.
> **Ryûhei**: What?

Again, Ryûhei is stunned into silence, concerned that his son knows about his unemployment situation. But Kenji continues:

> **Kenji**: You're lying when you say you'll listen if I talk. No matter how much I talk to you, you won't change your mind! . . . All you really want to do is lecture me and act tough!

Ryûhei slaps the boy across the face before Megumi steps in and shuffles him away for protection. Ryûhei, paces the room, and when challenged by Megumi as to why the boy should not play the piano, he argues that it would imply a back down, stating, 'It affects my authority as a parent . . . so I'm shoving my parental values down Kenji's throat if I have to!' Fellow filmmaker Juzo Itami (*Tampopo*) had noticed this social phenomenon some years earlier, and in a 1997 interview stated that the 'major problem with the younger generation, as I see it, is that the role of the father has become extremely weak', reasoning that '[b]ecause Japanese men fought the war and lost it, their value as a role model has really declined' (Schilling 1999: 79). This appears to be at the heart of *Tokyo Sonata*, where the parents' argument leads to a defiant Megumi, who finally confesses:

> **Megumi**: I saw you the other day. You were standing in the free food line at the park. (*Pause.*) You're unemployed, right?
> **Ryûhei**: (*Pause.*) You knew?
> **Megumi**: Yes, all along.
> **Ryûhei**: Why didn't you say anything?
> **Megumi**: Because if I had, your authority would be screwed. (pause) Screw your authority.

The ultimate shame comes when Ryûhei, in his orange janitor overalls at the mall, finds an envelope stuffed with cash in a toilet stall he is cleaning. The dilemma of whether to keep the money seems short-lived, as he rushes from the bathroom with the envelope out of sight, presumably in his overalls. In keeping with his run of bad luck, Ryûhei stumbles face-to-face into Megumi, who has wandered into the mall. He manages to blurt out, 'It's not . . . it's not what you think', before sprinting away. She watches him disappear into the distance. There is uncertainty about whether he is running to report the find or to escape. The scene then cuts back to three hours earlier, providing an explanation of why Megumi was in the mall at that exact time, an almost farcical coincidence, but one that provides a significant context for Megumi's lack of response to Ryûhei's running away.

Kurosawa often uses an observational directorial style, shooting the family's daily domesticity from outside their home, for instance, their images partly obscured by reflections on the window, or shot through a staircase. Teruyuki Kagawa's measured performance as Ryûhei sees him often framed to the side of a shot, head hung low as he tries to overcome the despondency that afflicts him. The growing isolation from his wife is accentuated as he questions his sense of worth. He runs from the mall, and keeps running, through the streets of Tokyo, into the night. He returns home after an eventful and almost tragic night. He sits with his wife and youngest child as they eat, silently, but with a sense that he has reached the bottom, and that somehow normalcy might resume in their household. Kurosawa's background in horror films can be seen to frame *Tokyo Sonata* in its portrayal of characters facing their fears. Rosenbaum sees this as a move where Kurosawa's '"coming out" of the metaphorical mode of expression [horror] into the realm of realism exemplifies the dire straits Japanese society finds itself in; there is no longer room for roundabout modes of expression' (2010: 123). In other words, Kurosawa's concern for the nation can no longer be shaded in the horror allegory but must be clearly spelt out to the audience.

The film's title takes its cues from Kenji's piano playing, and the eventual acceptance from his parents, who attend his recital, in an emotional finale to the film. Ryûhei's role as a parent seems to have come full circle, where he realizes that as long as he can provide for his family (he retains his cleaning job, and attends to it assiduously), he can fulfil his duties as a father. Thus, for Ryûhei, isolation proved to be a temporary state, a rite-of-passage for a new millennial salaryman, with a positive outcome.

Unemployment in France

In recent French cinema, unemployment is often shown 'as an alienating experience that often leads to the questioning of one's identity and place within a social class' (Grandena 2008: 111). A range of films have focused on the atomization of the working class, the pernicious effects of economic neoliberalism and globalization at the local level, and the increasing ideological gap between collectivism and individualism (e.g. *Time Out/L'Emploi du temps* [Laurent Cantet, 2001]; *The Measure of a Man/La loi du marché* [Stéphane Brizé, 2015]; *Those Who Work/Ceux qui travaillent* [Antoine Russbach, 2018]). Unemployment also plays a decisive role in Mia Hansen-Løve's debut feature, *All Is Forgiven/Tout est Pardonneé* (2007). Would-be novelist, Victor (Paul Blaine), has an Austrian wife, Annette (Marie-Christine Friedrich), and appears to be an attentive father to their young daughter, Pamela (played initially by Victoire Rousseau). Living in Austria to have proximity to Annette's family, Victor struggles with his writing and becomes increasingly despondent. A rift develops between the couple, and the unemployed Victor begins to spend more time away from his family, descending into alcohol and drug dependency. In one scene, it is Pamela's sixth birthday, and as she plays on the floor, Victor pours a drink for himself:

> **Annette**: You can't start drinking now.
> **Victor**: It's Happy Hour.
> **Annette**: It's 11am. You said not before 6pm.
> **Victor**: We need to celebrate Pamela's birthday.

His inability to fit into his wife's familial and social circles makes him increasingly obstinate and unreliable. Annette berates him for not bonding with her friends:

> **Annette**: He asked you what you do and you just sniggered instead of answering.
> **Victor**: Answering what?
> **Annette**: That you write.
> **Victor**: It's not a job.
> **Annette**: You could have said you teach French.
> **Victor**: I haven't in months.
> **Annette**: What's the difference? You'll start again. Why do you want everyone to think you're a loser?

She laughs softly, dismissing the conversation, but not convinced that he is willing to change his attitude. Frustrated, Annette arranges for them to move back to Paris under the impression that it will respark their marriage and Victor's motivations to write and teach (Figure 5.2).

Paris is, however, no stimulant for Victor who soon falls back in with old friends and with seemingly endless spare time, begins injecting drugs.

Figure 5.2 A developing rift in *All Is Forgiven* (2007).

Hansen-Løve's Victor seems to echo a Rohmer-esque protagonist; unfulfilled and mostly unlikeable, like the sulky Pierre (Pascal Greggory) in *Pauline at the Beach/Paulin á la plage* (1983), or the morose Remi (Tchéky Karyo) in *Full Moon in Paris/Les nuits de la pleine lune* (1984). Victor drops around to visit his sister, Martine (Carole Franck), and while she serves him food, he confesses:

> **Victor**: I can concentrate in the morning. I wake up strong, but lose my strength over the day. At night I stop writing, powerless. I'm another person. [pause] My conception of life: work in the morning, afternoon walks. And at night, I do drugs.
> **Martine**: It can't go on like this.
> **Victor**: I'm lacking in regularity and perseverance, I know. Sometimes I'm paralysed by anxiety.
> **Martine**: Give up the ascetic fantasy. Be practical. Fix yourself concrete goals you can reach. You can't change overnight.
> **Victor**: I sometimes wish I were someone else.

Despite Martine's seemingly helpful advice, Victor is too caught up in his own world. Martine extolls Annette's virtues, warning that Victor will lose her if he is unable to straighten out.

> **Victor**: She complains I don't make enough. She's right, but I don't have any ideas.
> **Martine**: Still reading manuscripts?
> **Victor**: No money in it.

> **Martine**: You still consider teaching? I mean at university.

Victor's negativity wins through; there always seems to be a response that will prevent him from changing, and he responds:

> **Victor**: I'd need a Masters. It's too late. I can't talk to kids. No interest.

Martine continues to try and encourage her brother:

> **Martine**: It'd be great if you could overcome your fear of work. It's not good to float around, totally self-absorbed.

Victor fails to take Martine's advice and soon descends even further into a spiral of hopelessness. But just when Victor seems to be written off as a failure, Hansen-Løve springs a twist by shifting the narrative forward by eleven years. Victor reemerges as clean, diligent and (mostly) employed. Through Martine, Victor reaches out to re-establish a relationship with Pamela (now played by Constance Rousseau), long since estranged from her father after Annette remarried. In this way Hansen-Løve has taken the cinematic motif of unemployment (and substance abuse) and cast it as a temporal state of being.

A more laissez-faire approach to employment is shown in *2 Autumns, 3 Winters* when Arman (Vincent Macaigne), with his lank hair and permanent three-day stubble confesses (to the camera) that at thirty-three years of age he has had a 'day of Revelation' where he decided to quit smoking, take up sport and realizes:

> **Arman**: I have to find a real job because right now my activity in life is going from one more or less interesting job to another. [pause] More 'less' than 'more' to be precise. Then I quit [his last job]. Right now, I'm in a . . . I'm in a long quitting phase at the moment.

Arman's lack of employment is made easier by his living rent-free in an apartment left behind by a friend who has relocated to the United States for an unknown length of time.

In *Rust and Bone/De rouille et d'os* (2012, dir. Jacques Audiard), Ali (Matthias Schoenaerts) is estranged from his wife, and arrives on his sister's doorstep, unemployed and with his young son in tow (Figure 5.3).

Ali does not seem too bright and is a keen no-rules fighter and kickboxer. While Ali's sister is working in a low-paid factory job, Ali asks around for work and soon lands an interview, which he conducts with little visible enthusiasm:

> **Employer**: What was your last job?
> **Ali**: Short time in an abattoir. It shut.

Figure 5.3 Precarity and uncertainty in *Rust and Bone* (2012).

> **Employer**: Never in security then?
> **Ali**: Yes, for six months I did work experience in a stadium as a night watchman. And in a parking lot, too.

The employer notes Ali's muscular physique and changes the topic.

> **Employer**: Ever done any contact sport?
> **Ali**: Boxing. For six years, and kickboxing for two.
> **Employer**: Can you prove it? Pictures? Boxing permit?
> **Ali**: I won a regional championship in Belgium. I have a belt.
> **Employer**: You quit?
> **Ali**: The coach did.
> **Employer**: Why?
> **Ali**: He died.

The employer then asks whether Ali smokes, drinks or does drugs, which Ali denies, but not very convincingly. The employer then fixes his gaze on Ali.

> **Employer**: Give me one good reason I should hire you.
> **Ali** (*pauses*): Trust me.

The scene soon cuts to Ali in front of a nightclub, radio earpiece in his ear and wearing a security jacket, visual proof that his interview had been successful.

Ali's story becomes entangled with Stéphanie (Marion Cotillard), a woman he met after saving her from a fight at the nightclub. While the potential for romance between the pair exists, Ali maintains a platonic distance from Stéphanie. When a severe accident leaves Stéphanie with a major disability, Ali's transient employment in different security-related jobs (mostly at night) means that he is readily available to help Stéphanie. The free time seems to eat at Ali, and he soon gets drawn into illegal, and savage, bare-knuckle fights, where he takes a cut of the cash raised through betting. When Ali gets involved with an illegal surveillance operation that results in his sister losing her job, they fight before Ali flees, heading north to a 'boot camp' for fighters. While the lack of secure employment is problematic for Ali, his inability to settle down with either work or relationships suggests that he prefers the excitement of not knowing what will come next.

In the French-Belgian co-production *Two Days, One Night/Deux jours, une nuit* (2014, dirs. Jean-Pierre and Luc Dardenne), Marion Cotillard takes on a different role, this time as the central protagonist Sandra Bya, a worker in a factory that makes solar panels. Sandra's employment is about to be terminated following a vote among her co-workers to decide whether to accept a bonus or keep Sandra employed, in an attempt to save money for the company. As a wife and mother of two children, Sandra and her caring husband, Manu (Fabrizio Rongione, in his fifth film directed by the Dardenne brothers), have bills to pay and a mortgage that is already putting them under financial stress. Underscoring the narrative is Sandra's struggle with mental illness and having just had time away from work on medical leave, is seen as no longer required at the factory by her boss, Mr Dumont (Baptiste Sornin). When Sandra's friend Juliette (Catherine Salée) confronts Dumont in his car to see if he will change his mind, Dumont is unmoved, and Sandra is gripped with fear, unable to speak. Finally, Juliette convinces him to hold a second ballot immediately following the weekend. Juliette tries to interrupt him, but he snaps back that he just wants to address Sandra, so she steps towards him.

> **Dumont**: It's nothing personal, but the recession and competition from Asia leave me no choice. See you on Monday.

He begins to drive off, but Juliette stops him. Gripped with anxiety, Sandra remains speechless, while Juliette further negotiates what time the ballot will be held. Dumont agrees, but adds:

> **Dumont**: But don't raise Mrs Bya's hopes. They almost all chose the bonus. It's their right.

He speeds off, and Juliette turns to find Sandra in the throes of a panic attack, clutching at her throat, unable to breathe or speak. Juliette gives her some water and Sandra recovers.

> **Sandra**: I don't know what happened. I couldn't speak. I wanted to say I'm well and ready to return to work, but I couldn't.

> **Juliette**: It's the emotion of being here and seeing Mr Dumont. Even if you said nothing, he gave in because you were here.
> **Sandra**: You think so?
> **Juliette**: I'm sure, and on Monday seeing you will make them think beyond their bonus.

This short scene, in the opening ten minutes of the film, establishes a number of themes. First, it shows the emotional engagement that individuals have with the notion of employment. While Sandra is obviously concerned with the financial impact of losing her job, underlying her situation is the sense of identity and confidence that being employed brings. A short time later, she explains to Manu that her co-workers' attitude was 'as if I didn't exist'. Manu tries to comfort her, but Sandra grows increasingly agitated.

> **Sandra**: They're right! I don't exist! I'm nothing, nothing at all.

She drops to the floor, crying and Manu immediately comes to her.

> **Manu**: You do exist, Sandra. I love you. You exist for them too. They hesitated before voting for the bonus.

Then, setting up the narrative drive for the rest of the film, he implores:

> **Manu**: That's why you must see them one by one this weekend.

Sandra disagrees, suggesting that she sees them on Monday before the vote, but Manu persists.

> **Manu** (*cont.*): Tell them you want your job, you need your salary and to be with them, not alone on the dole.
> **Sandra**: It will look like I'm begging.
> **Manu**: No, it won't. . . . It's not your fault they lose their bonus if you stay. Your boss decided that, not you.

This leads to the second point raised in *Two Days, One Night*: that is, its clear commentary on the pressures of capitalism and an increasingly global industrial system that can impact anyone, anywhere and at any time. Sandra's situation is not exclusive to her as an individual but speaks to broader, universal concerns around precarity and identity.

As Sandra embarks on her quest to convince her co-workers to support her, she encounters them as just a range of people facing similarly difficult financial circumstances. When she meets Willy (Alain Eloy), he tries to justify his actions, while his wife (Lara Persain) stands by his side.

> **Willy**: I didn't vote against you. I voted for my bonus. Dumont put one against the other, not me.
> **Sandra**: I know. It's sick forcing you to choose. But I don't want to lose my job. Without my salary we can't get by.
> **Willy**: I can't. I need my bonus. Our eldest is at uni. That's 500 Euros a month.
> **Willy's wife**: 600, if you count her bills.

Willy indicates that he might reconsider, but his wife interrupts:

> **Willy's wife**: What is there to think about? We can't.

She turns to Sandra.

> **Willy's wife** (cont.): I wish we could help, but I've been on the dole for months. We salvage [bathroom and flooring] tiles to make ends meet.

Again, the broader issues of global capitalism are brought to the fore, this time highlighting the challenges of low wages and the need for double incomes for economic survival.

The observational, realist mode of *Two Days, One Night* (there is no musical score apart from occasional diegetic bursts of music) captures Sandra's determination and her constant struggle to overcome the fears of what she sees as a personal failure by not being able to hold down her job. Despite the often-bleak scenarios being played out, *Two Days, One Night* closes on a more positive note, not because of any structural changes, but because of Sandra's individual acceptance of her situation.

Isolation

Isolation takes a different form in Yôjirô Takita's 2008 *Departures/Okuribito* (winner of the Best Foreign Language Film at the 2009 Academy Awards), when cellist Daigo Kobayashi (Masahiro Motoki) moves back to his hometown following the dispersal of the financially ruined orchestra that paid his salary. One of the many films to feature 'the relationship that exists between local geographical contexts and global processes' (Ortiz-Moya and Moreno 2016: 881), *Departures* highlights the problems of Japan's ageing demographic that has hollowed out the nation's smaller towns and villages. Other films such as Kore-eda's *Our Little Sister*, Sion's *Himizu* and *Dear Doctor/Dia Dokutâ* (2009, dir. Miwa Nishikawa) all attest to the 'imbalanced geographical system' created by global capitalism in the late twentieth century, where '[o]n the one hand, peripheral and rural regions aged due to the exodus of young populations moving to the megalopolis; and on the other hand, the inflow of immigrants supported the fast urban growth of the core urban regions' (Otiz-Moya and Moreno 2016: 884). So, when Daigo finds himself back in his hometown, the dearth of people willing to take up the unsavoury job of preparing the dead for their funeral ritual (encoffinment, or *nokan*, casketing), coupled with his need for employment for financial survival, means that he must accept the job, even though he came across it through a misunderstanding (that has a link to the film's title). The act of accepting the position entrenches Daigo's loneliness when his wife, Mika (pop star Ryōko Hirosue), leaves him because of her horror that he works in an industry where he touches dead bodies.

Departures opens in the present time, with Daigo driving through the snow-covered countryside, and a voiceover stating that it has been two months since he left Tokyo and that this had been 'an awkward time'. The action then cuts to a home where a funeral is in progress, and where Daigo and his boss, the elder Sasaki (veteran actor Tsutomu Yamazaki, from films including *Tampopo* and *A Taxing Woman*) begin to prepare a young woman's body for placing in a coffin (and later, in traditional Japanese culture, cremated), all under the watchful eye of the gathered mourners. Not all goes to plan though, as Takita lightens the mood with a comic moment, before the film's titles appear and the action cuts to a large symphony orchestra and choir performing, Daigo's soon-to-be disbanded place of work. Daigo and Mika leave Tokyo, and it is apparent that Daigo internalizes his worries, having hidden the enormous cost of his newly purchased cello from Mika. He is forced to sell the instrument, and they head to his hometown to live in the house he inherited from his late mother. Daigo's insularity is driven by his need for acceptance, so, realizing that Mika is hurt that he did not initially inform her of the cost of his cello, he again hides the truth about where he is working. In the more traditional and superstitious parts of Japanese society, there is a general fear of anything or anyone to do with death, burial or cremation (Mullins 2010: 103), and Daigo's new employment, which involves touching the dead, would only revolt Mika. When Daigo clutches Mika in a fit of desperation, she clings to him, unaware of the shame that he feels for not only accepting the position and its sometimes-humiliating aspects (e.g. dressing up as a corpse for a promotional video) but also for hiding the truth from his wife.

The personal isolation between Daigo and Mika in *Departures* is also reflected in Daigo's own sense of isolation from his now-deceased mother, in whose fully furnished house they now live, a constant reminder of her and of Daigo's father who left them when he was a young child and is now just a blurred memory for Daigo. Takita's film draws heavily on metaphor, so Daigo's musing on the lives of salmon swimming upstream, to their inevitable death, leads to a conversation with an old man on the futility of life. Daigo states, 'Sad, isn't it. Coming all this way just to die. It doesn't seem worth it.' The old man replies, 'They want to come home, back to where they were born', before wandering off, leaving Daigo to his thoughts. Daigo's pain, it seems, is long-entrenched, with the old lady who runs the local bathhouse, Mrs Yamashita (Kazuko Yoshiyuki), confessing to Mika about Daigo:

> **Mrs Yamashita**: He takes it all on himself. When his folks split up, he'd never cry in front of his mother. [*pause*] But he would when he was alone in that bath. The poor little thing, his shoulders shaking . . .

Takita also draws attention to Mika's loneliness, and her inability to get Daigo to open up to her. In one brief scene, Daigo attends to a dead body in the middle of the night; as he sneaks out, Takita shows a sleeping Mika in bed, from a low Ozu-like angle, looking like a corpse from an earlier scene, the bedding flattened across her like a shroud. The camera then cuts to a closer shot, angled from above, where the sheen on Mika's face again looks like a corpse; however, she slowly opens her eyes, indicating her awareness and suspicion of why her husband is leaving the house at that hour.

Although not yet a parent, Daigo's situation places him within the crisis of masculinity, emphasized earlier in this chapter through *Tokyo Sonata,* that faces the unemployed man in Japanese society and began to impact on representations of the employed male/father as Japan's economy weakened through the 1990s. As Iles notes, once seen as 'a driving force of moral guidance, now the salaryman-as-father is an object of satirical ridicule' (2008: 204). In relation to *Departures*, Takita shows how a hierarchy of employment types exists, which also impacts on one's social standing. Daigo leaves Tokyo because he does not see himself fitting the salaryman lifestyle. In his hometown, he is berated by an old classmate (who refuses to introduce Daigo to his wife and daughter), who tells him, 'Get yourself a proper job!' Mika eventually discovers what Daigo is doing, and also berates him, again in an Ozu-style scene where both characters are kneeling in their tatami-style living room.

> **Mika**: Aren't you ashamed having a job like that?
> **Daigo**: What's to be ashamed of? Touching dead people?
> **Mika**: Just get a normal job.
> **Daigo**: (*Getting angry*) 'Normal!' Everyone dies. I'll die, and so will you. (pause) Death is normal.

Figure 5.4 Mika and Daigo kneeling in *Departures* (2008).

Mika: Spare me the word games! I want you to quit. Please [See Figure 5.4].

Mika then pleads with him, confessing that she was 'broken up' over them having to sell the cello and leave Tokyo. She gives him an ultimatum, but he hesitates.

Mika: I'm going home. Come see me when you quit.

She stands to leave and he reaches out to stop her.

MIka: Don't touch me! You're unclean!

Mika rushes from the room, and a stunned Daigo remains frozen, in his kneeling position. The scene cuts to Mika standing beside her suitcase at the snow-covered train station, indicating that the limits of her distaste have been reached.

Takita's film ends on a more positive note than Daigo being deserted, but the film nevertheless reinforces the social and cultural change that have taken place in Japan. One of the corpses that Daigo attends to has been dead for some time, an increasingly common feature of isolation within Japanese society where 'the awareness of lonely death has arisen in the context of twenty-first-century Japan, contributing to an unease over not only economic decline but shrinking population and troubled sociality' (Allison 2015: 48).

The sense of isolation is not limited to men in film, of course. In Chapter 1 we outlined the (female) character of Tony in *Mon Roi/My King*, and her quest for happiness. Tony's self-referential questioning of her life at first appears to be as a result of her accident, but as the film unfolds, a more destructive, nihilistic streak appears. In one scene, Tony is presenting during a debate among her legal peers, in her speech under the title of 'Must You Ruin Everything?', some of it in voiceover as she enjoys a day at the horse races with her boyfriend Georgio, she is representing the opposing argument. She begins by asking the gathered audience the topic question:

> **Tony**: Must you ruin everything? As if the world were new? As if it were the first morning? As if it were still dawn? . . . The truth . . . is that what has already been ruined, our founding disillusion, is our freedom.

The speech is interrupted by an audio drop to match the vision on screen as Tony squeals with delight as her backed horse wins a race. The audio then moves back to her speech, then takes on a much more positive tone (in line with her brief to oppose the topic).

> **Tony**: You must have nothing to lose to love heart and soul. You must eclipse the giddiest heights to dare to plunge headlong. You must endure the fall of empires and the greatest storms, to be together in that moment. You must have lived, you must have lost over and again, to triumph with you.

These words appear against images of Emmanuelle Bercot's Tony and Vincent Cassel's charming, cheeky and at times irascible, Georgio cementing their devotion to each other, buying jewellery and embracing in overt, and very public showings of their affection. But underpinning all of this is a sense of foreboding, both in the audience's knowledge that things will change, but also in the soundtrack where the rich score contains a droning minor key, and in the monologue that cannot help but anchor the positive with the negative. The action cuts back to Tony giving the speech, watched by Georgio.

> **Tony**: Love is nothing when it's new, clean and pure. Love before the storm is not a decision. It's a decree. When the event, accident or opportunity occurs, be there. Standing. Find the word, action or look. Yes, my love, in that moment, rely on me. I won't go missing. At that minute [she turns to Georgio] I'll be there.

Tony's speech receives enthusiastic applause, and later in a restaurant, her friends gently chide her about the soppiness of the speech, but Georgio springs to her defence, saying, 'It's beautiful, she gave of herself. She took a risk in life!'

The first thirty minutes or so of *Mon Roi* build a complex rendering of Tony, and eventually, a scene (perhaps further into the future than the story has ventured so far) features Tony on the phone with her child, in a conversation that shows that she and Georgio are no longer together. A pairing of shots, one after the other, shows the pain and isolation that Tony is feeling. In the first, a medium-long shot, she sits on a step in full, late afternoon sun, staring out across a beach. Other recuperating patients pass by, and she sits, unsmiling, with her crutches beside her with her leg extended in a brace as a clear indication of her physical pain. The shot cuts closer, with the camera now swung around behind her, as she clutches her mobile phone, then drops her head in despair. Director Maïwenn then overlaps the scene with happier times, the laughter-filled wedding of Tony and Georgio.

The title of *Mon Roi* (*My King*) could be seen as a cynical take on the idea of marriage: the sense that the elevation of the other partner in the relationship (in this case, Georgio) can only be destined for a crashing realization that the relationship is built on an uneven power structure or, to push the analogy, that the monarch holds sway over the (his) subject. Thus, when Tony finds herself with the upper hand at times during their relationship, including gaining custody of their child, Georgio is unable to accept what he sees as a challenge to his authority.

The use of film to highlight the ways that individuals are treated in society has a long thematic history, as shown in Chapter 4 through the Hulot and Tora-san characters. Large-scale events can lead to a renewed focus on the individual in the societal or familial setting, the May 1968 strikes and protests providing a touchstone for French filmmakers, including Truffaut, Godard and Claude Chabrol, in the immediate aftermath and for decades after. In Japan, the March 2011 Tōhoku earthquake, tsunami, and subsequent Fukushima nuclear disaster framed films such as Sono Sion's *Himizu* and *The Land of Hope/Kibō no Kuni* (2012), and Ryoichi Kimizuka's *Reunion/Itai: Asu e no Tōkakan* (2012). The disaster reinforced the vulnerability of a Japan that was still emerging from a decade of economic decline, creating 'a precariousness felt by everyone and not just those (precariat, unemployed, socially solitary or withdrawn) on the underside of a bipolarized, divided society' (Allison 2015: 50-51).

In Yaguchi's *Survival Family* (2016), a different sense of isolation occurs when a mysterious but complete power outage (affecting all electronics and magnetics, including batteries) renders Tokyo uninhabitable. With no communications, the family sets out (along with a large portion of the Tokyo population) on foot to find if there is power anywhere else in Japan. A comedy-drama, *Survival Family* tackles the post-apocalyptic road movie with a light touch (certainly far removed from the horrors of the adaptation of Cormac McCarthy's *The Road*, directed by John Hillcoat in 2009), although the real-life events of the Fukushima nuclear disaster of 2011 serve as a sobering backdrop for Japanese audiences. It is the father, Yoshiyuki Suzuki (Fumiyo Kohinata) that must, reluctantly, take on the role of strength, at times reaching for a long-suppressed humility in order to gain the respect of his wife and children. The film opens with a look at the everyday lives of the Suzuki family, adhering mostly to stereotyped characters, from Yoshiyuki the inept dad, with his mundane salaryman job, to the banalities of their domestic lives as the domesticated mother prepares the evening meal. Underlying these early scenes, however, are images of the facile indulgences and vanities of twenty-first-century life writ large in the Suzuki's gender-balanced nuclear family; the daughter's false eyelashes, Yoshiyuki's toupee, the son's constant disengagement through his wireless headphones and his easy access to fast food rather than eating his mother's home-cooked meals.

The Suzukis wake up one morning to find that all power is off and suffer minor inconveniences in getting ready for their day, including having to take the twenty floors of stairs to leave their apartment complex. The family, like those around them, attempt to keep to their usual routines. The son, a college student, Kenji (Yuki Izumisawa), cycles to university, and the daughter, schoolgirl Yui (Wakana Aoi), meets with her friends, all mortified at the inability to communicate through their mobile devices. The mother, Mitsue (Eri Fukatsu), wanders around a darkened supermarket, grabbing what she thinks they'll need for a day or so without power. All transport is ground to a halt, so Yoshiyuki makes his way to work on foot, only to find that nobody can get in because the electronic doors are unable to be opened. In a reference to the loyalty of the salaryman, the workers smash the doors and optimistically make their way up to their offices, ready to begin their day's work, but with no power to their computers and no way to communicate with other divisions, they can merely sit and chat with each other. By day three, Yoshiyuki's boss declares there is no work to be done, and he packs his bag to join his family as they leave Tokyo to head for the mountains. Water becomes scarce, the banks cut off any access to cash, and litter begins piling up in the streets, creating a situation where the normal modes of politeness disappear, in what is generally seen as a collectivist society – each individual's pursuit takes on a grave importance. The remaining residents of the apartment block meet to decide whether to evenly divide provisions between everyone, but this merely unearths old resentments.

The *Survival Family* provides an acerbic look at commercialism, through the meaningless nature of commodities such as the uselessness of the mobile phone without power. The Suzukis finally decide to leave Tokyo, on two bicycles and a large tricycle that is barely big enough for Yoshiyuki to share with his wife. The shortage of clean water leads enterprising hawkers to begin selling it at rapidly inflating prices, with the Suzuki's scoffing at one bidder selling bottles of water for 1,000 yen (about ten times the usual price), only to find a short while later, as they move through the suburbs on their way out of the city that it is now selling for 2,500 yen. Later, a man offers a lady his Rolex watch, and then his car in exchange for a freshly caught fish, but she sends him away, telling him such things are now worthless. By the sixteenth day, the family camp in the shadows of Mt Fuji, fast running out of water and necessities such as matches. Yoshiyuki, the patriarch who tries to exude an assertive nature even though he is mostly clumsy and incompetent, declares that everything will be fine: 'You can light a fire without matches', he confidently tells his son. 'Cavemen could do it, of course we can, too.' When Kenji asks him how it is done, Yoshiyuki simply replies, 'I'll show you when the time comes.' A short time later, Yoshiyuki can be seen desperately rubbing sticks to try to start a fire, with no success.

The family continues on their journey, the husband's comically disastrous attempts at leadership posing a challenge to his masculinity and causing friction with his wife as they head vaguely West towards Mizue's hometown, thousands of kilometres away. In an episodic manner, they cycle along the mostly empty freeways, littered with immovable cars, but running desperately low on supplies. The map that Kenji has taken from a disused bookstore is from a children's atlas and fails to provide the type of detailed information they need. When they stumble across the camp of a small group of professional-looking cyclists, they watch with envy as the cyclists use their functional camping gear to prepare a meal. The cyclists assist the family and ride alongside them for a while. A passing troop of army soldiers, marching on foot, mentions that there are provisions in Osaka, so the Suzukis alter their plans only to find Osaka mostly deserted and without power. The inference is that even Japan's army, the defender of the nation, is unable to be effective when it has no way of communicating.

By Day 67, the family are once again in the countryside, starving and near exhaustion, when they spy a pig in a field. They capture the pig, whose keeper, a farmer, arrives just as they are working out how to dissect it. Although far from friendly, the farmer takes them in and gives them food, shelter and water.

The rural community is able to sustain itself, with water drawn from wells with manual hand pumps and a barter system between neighbours of homegrown fruits, vegetables, meats and dairy produce. The farmer insists that the Suzukis help him to slaughter the pig, then slice and salt all the meat, a job the city-based family find nauseating. When he offers them the opportunity to stay and help on the farm, the family decide to ride on to Mizue's hometown to be with her parents. Fed and rested, they set out on their journey, only to find their way blocked by a large river. This time, Yoshiyuki takes the lead, immediately gathering things to make a raft to get them all across. Just when it seems that Yoshiyuki has proven himself as a father and husband, the raft falls apart midstream, and the film takes a darker turn, with the toupee, that until this point has been a running comic motif, now cast in a more sombre tone.

Survival Family explores the precarity of employment and what this means for a family. It critiques mankind's reliance on technology, and the ways that nature and tradition offer a site for survival. As a comedy-drama, the film returns to a light-hearted conclusion, but with a sense of change, an apprehension about the trappings of technology.

Conclusion

The films analysed in this chapter remind us how cinema reflects the structural aspects of contemporary society in Japan and France. They highlight the importance (especially in the more traditionally male-dominated households) of permanent employment as ontologically both economic and psychological imperatives for survival. These films all illustrate the range of universal factors that sit alongside the individual need for employment in the contemporary age. In both Japan and France, we see the link between employment and identity, and the serious mental and physical toll that unemployment can wreak on individuals, their families and society more broadly. Unemployment can lead to poverty, ill-health and even violence. Likewise, precarious employment (and other social and economic changes) can lead to isolation and the geo-spatial requirements that demand individuals relocate in order to ensure employment. In a 2019 interview with Marta Bałaga, director Robert Guédiguian, whose film *Gloria Mundi* examines the debilitating effects of the gig economy and the ongoing erosion of France's socialist ideals by modern market forces, was characteristically outspoken:

I believe that a precarious lifestyle is becoming more and more prevalent, at least in France, where I live. People constantly worry about their jobs, and they don't go to vote any more. The outskirts and the suburbs are becoming more and more detached. These people are completely cut off, with their main concern being how to make ends meet. It feels like war sometimes, with each of us against all the others. There is no solidarity any more, no brotherhood, and even family ties suffer because people tend to compete so much – just like in the film. Global capitalism makes us all very selfish and narcissistic. The only solution to how to survive is very individual, as this idea of being part of a community or a collective group is no longer valid. It's everyone for themselves.

The transformation of work under the guise of neoliberalism remains a fundamental aspect of the cinema of precarity in France and Japan, especially post-2008, and explains how many of these films evoke a nostalgia for meaningful employment, class solidarity and a coordinated push-back (in most cases unsuccessfully) against the neoliberal order.

6

Location and the sense of place

François Truffaut's *The 400 Blows/Les Quatre Cents Coups* (1959) famously opens with a roaming montage of the streets and landmarks of Paris, with views of the iconic Eiffel Tower from street-level, obscured then released as Truffaut gives the audience a grittier, monochromatic look at Paris than simply circling the tower in a postcard-type montage. The film therefore unmistakably situates the viewer in France: for the foreign viewer, hinting at the exotic architecture of France, and for the French viewer, a real-life sense of the nation's capital. The film's musical score begins over these scenes somewhere between grand and playful, before pulling back to a more austere, simple, plucking of a violin's strings as the tower suddenly looms large, right there in front of us, before, just as quickly, the camera pulls away, as if in a speeding car. As the tower recedes into the distance, the string-plucking slows to a funereal tempo, before the screen fades to black, and the film begins. The use of location in *The 400 Blows* is crucial to the narrative development of the film: the city that seems to offer everything is exposed as a harsh environment, until the film's young protagonist is packed off and sent to a juvenile home in the countryside. Here too, there is no salvation, at least until the boy escapes and runs to the seaside in the film's famous, sudden and dramatic freeze-frame ending. Through this young protagonist, Truffaut lays bare the human condition with the harsh physical environment of firstly, the bleak urban streets of Paris, and then the confines of the boys' home, impacting on the life and development of the child. Without the support of his family, he is aimless, without roots in an unforgiving world.

The use of a location such as Paris in Truffaut's film provides an audience with a recognizable context that can help to establish a story through understandings (or challenges to understandings) of the geographical, political, economic, social or cultural significance of a place. As Tweedie (2013: 80) writes, the cinematic neorealism 'revived' by the *nouvelle vague* filmmakers in their 'elaborate Parisian city films' created representations of 'gratuitous, virtually unmotivated images

Figure 6.1 Establishing a sense of place and mood in *The 400 Blows* (1959).

of architecture and urban space – sometimes flipped through like snapshots from a summer vacation, sometimes subjected to an ethnographic gaze – [that] reproduce the atmosphere of a city' (Figure 6.1).

An extension of this in-cinema experience is that film has created new interests in locations as a destination for film fans to explore. Although the concept has been around for generations (exemplified by the myriad location-based bus tours around the Hollywood/LA region) it has more recently been coined 'contents tourism' or 'film-induced tourism' (Beeton 2005). The Japanese government's use of the term 'contents tourism' (*kontentsu tsūrizumu*) reflects the type of pilgrimage-like visitations that have a long history in Japan, noted from the late 1600s onwards where people were said to have trekked to places made famous by the renowned poet and haiku master, Bashō Matsuo (Seaton and Yamamura 2015: 2). The 'contents tourism' term has been adopted by Seaton and Yamamura who see it as inclusively capturing 'the plurality of contents (narratives, characters, locations, music and so on) that may drive touristic behaviour' (2015: 9, n. 2).

Other films operate using locations in a different, but no less effective way. Ozu's *Tokyo Story*, for instance, opens not with a view of the eponymous city, but with a harbourside village, and an old couple planning their trip to the capital, (with a passing stop in Osaka). The first view of Tokyo that Ozu presents is not of an iconic landmark but a suggestion, a line of smoking industrial chimneys, accompanied by the hypnotic hum of machinery, a technique used earlier in Ozu's first sound film, *Only Son/Hiroi Musuko* (1936) (Burch 1979: 178–9). The old couple in *Tokyo Story* are grandparents visiting their daughter in Tokyo, and Ozu uses quick establishing shots of a suburban railway station, a sign 'Dr Hirayama

– Internal Medicine and Children's Diseases', and a family's washing drying on bamboo poles, before quickly settling into his famous floor-level tatami-mat scenes, with his methodical framing of shots from a low-angle (giving each shot, what Tadao Sato called a 'ceremonial quality'), inside the house. Fumiko (Kuniko Miyake), the doctor's wife and mother to their two young and insolent boys, is performing her domestic duties in preparation for the arrival of her husband's parents. The only confirmation that this city is Tokyo is given through dialogue, first when widowed daughter-in-law Noriko (Setsuko Hara) greets the old couple with 'Welcome to Tokyo', and then when Grandmother Tomi (Chieko Higashiyama) states, 'It's like a dream being in Tokyo', even though there has been no evidence that they have seen much of the city. Ozu creates the impression of the city, an imaginary, idealized construct, rather than seeing the need for direct, iconic visual representation. Grandmother continues, 'I'm glad I've lived to this day. The world has changed so', hinting that Tokyo represents change, but the vastness of the city is referred to later when she admits that she has no idea what part of Tokyo they are in, and her husband can only respond that they are in the suburbs somewhere. She replies, not too impressed, 'It was a long ride from the station', implying that unlike the prestige of the inner city, their son's status is less impressive as he lives only on the outskirts of Tokyo.

But Ozu does not completely hide Tokyo from the viewer. At thirty-seven minutes into the film, the viewer accompanies Noriko and the grandparents on a brief guided bus tour of the city, complete with a narrated history and views from the bus window. Thus, Truffaut's hurried glimpses of Paris may have been influenced by Ozu's earlier work with the framing of shots through the bus window limiting the viewer's access to the city, as Truffaut was to do with his glimpses of *la Tour Eiffel*. As Noriko and the grandparents enjoy their sightseeing, Ozu keeps the viewer constrained as we see their backs as they look from a high vantage point, iron railings suggesting they are looking down from the Tokyo Tower, but without the use (or expense) of an actual location shot (Figure 6.2).

In Tokyo, the family struggle to find the time to devote to looking after their parents, so they send them off to a spa in a seaside village. The grandparents realize that they are a burden on their busy children (who are themselves not willing to go to much trouble to host the old couple), and decide that they 'have seen Tokyo', so should now return home. Tokyo, it seems, has created a heartless environment for their children, a site for the disassembling of 'social concepts of patriarchal authority, and the concomitant disintegration of the traditional

Figure 6.2 Tightly framed views of Tokyo in *Tokyo Story* (1953).

family' (Standish 2006: 180). As the old couple look to fill in time until they can return home, they look out over Tokyo and remark that the city is so big that if they got lost, they would never be able to find one another again. For them, the city is a place of isolation and a threat to their unity.

For Ozu, *Tokyo Story* does not need to be completely set in Tokyo, and later scenes take place on the train out of Tokyo as the old couple return to Osaka, and then onto their home village. Tokyo, however, remains the key reference point for the film, both geographically and as a centre where change takes place. The film could easily have been titled Hirayama Story, given its forensic examination of the lives of the family members where the 'generational rift is focused on the materialistic attitude of the children' (Standish 2006: 208). Instead, Ozu draws attention to the dehumanizing city with its grand sights and monuments, an aspirational point for sons and daughters to make good of their lives at the expense of their relationship with their rural-dwelling parents. Ozu's narrative sees the city in a troubling way and does not shy away from the idea of thwarted ambition and the lack of filial piety among the young. Even the grandfather expresses disappointment in his son's ability to only rise to the level of a suburban doctor. So, while the city offers opportunity and employment, it also creates barriers and new points of conflict between the family.

One of the few iconic shots Ozu uses is a brief establishing shot of Osaka Castle, in anticipation of the couple again transiting through the city, catching a short meeting with their other son, Keizo (Shirō Ōsaka) at the train station. Feeling ill, the grandmother and her husband instead leave the train at Osaka to stay with their son overnight, something that Ozu does not show but instead relates back through the young son telling his work colleague what has happened. They return to their village, but the grandmother's illness is serious, and the family must meet their sense of duty and leave Tokyo to keep vigil at her bedside.

As the grandmother lays dying, her husband questions, 'Did the trip to Tokyo cause this?', but his elder daughter snaps back, defending the city: 'She was so lively in Tokyo. Wasn't she?'. Ozu's steady-shot composition ensures that the focus remains on the actors or the central image of each shot. In some of the film's final shots, as Noriko takes the train back to Tokyo, Ozu cuts from the noisy industrial clamour of the train (signifying Tokyo) to the tranquil harbour and the serenity of the village, as the grandfather prepares for the loneliness of widowed life.

Tokyo also features in Kiarostami's *Like Someone in Love*, as reluctant sex worker Akiko (Rin Takanashi) is placed in a taxi to be driven to a client, Professor Watanabe (Tadashi Okuno), late one night. In an extended series of scenes, Kiarostami shifts the focus from the driver to Akiko, with the bright lights of Tokyo's shopping strips clearly visible through the car windows around them. The scene then shifts to Akiko's pov as she gazes out the window listening to voicemail messages from her grandmother who is briefly visiting Tokyo. For several minutes, shots shift from interior to exterior (with shop lights brightly reflected in the taxi windows), from Akiko's pov then back to watching Akiko. When Akiko's messages get to the point where her grandmother tells her she is waiting under the statue at the station, Akiko instructs the driver to divert to the station. As they drive past the statue, Akiko sees her grandmother waiting there, but instead of asking the driver to stop, she asks that they go around again. As they circle the statue for the second time, Akiko gets a clearer view of the solitary figure of her grandmother. The circular motion of the taxi gives a restrictive view out of the window, showing a limited view of Tokyo just as Truffaut teased the audience with his glimpses of Paris.

The use of location is highly valued in Masayuki Suo's 2014 musical comedy, *Lady Maiko/Maiko wa Redi*, a film about a young country girl, Haruko (Mone Kamishiraishi) arriving in the former capital city of Kyoto to study how to become a *maiko* (an apprentice geisha). With most exterior scenes shot on location in the historic city, the film contrasts contemporary Japan with traditional. Haruko's strong regional dialect is a mixture of rural accents from the far north and far south of Japan, rendering her as a yokel who could never (it seems) become refined enough to take on the role of a *maiko*. In a nod to *My Fair Lady* (1964, dir. George Cukor), the film charts a course of cultural renewal for the hapless Haruko, with Kyoto fulfilling its role as a centre of culture and refinement. In many ways *Lady Maiko* differs from the Hollywood version of the musical, offering instead a more whimsical approach to its songs, almost as an afterthought for the characters rather than as the film's raison d'être.

In a similar way, this time in a French musical, Paris is used as the backdrop to *Beloved/Les Bien-aimés* (2011, dir. Christophe Honoré), where songs perform a contemplative, often introspective role for the characters, again a long way removed from the all-singing, all-dancing repertoire of the Hollywood musical. These songs allow the protagonists to stroll through the streets of the city, past landmarks and the iconic architecture across several decades, from the 1960s through to the 2000s. *Beloved* (aka *The Beloved*) follows the lives of the young Madeleine (Ludivine Sagnier), in the 1960s and 1970s, an assistant in a fashionable women's shoe store and her relationships with an impetuous Czechoslovakian doctor Jaromil (Radivoje Bukvic/Rasha Bukvik), who becomes her first husband, and an unexciting gendarme, François Gouriot (Guillaume Denaiffe), who becomes her second. The young Madeleine becomes pregnant to Jaromil, but he returns to Prague. The film skips ahead to 1968 and Madeleine has a daughter, Vera (Clara Couste). Madeleine travels to Prague to try to lure Jaromil back, but he avoids her. By 1978, Madeleine has married Gouriot so that Vera can have a secure family around her, but Jaromil returns and declares that Madeleine and Vera should leave Gouriot to live with him elsewhere in Paris. Things do not go as planned, and Vera runs to the banks of the River Seine to attempt to figure things out. A song ensues, and in the course of the song Honoré sets up for a time shift to 1997 by cutting back and forth between the fourteen-year-old Vera (Couste), and her older, adult self, played by Chiara Mastroianni. She/they wander along the river bank and across its iconic bridges. Late in the song Madeleine appears, and again Honoré links the two eras with early Madeleine (Sagnier) intercut with the senior Madeleine, played by veteran actor Catherine Deneuve.

While musicals are relatively rare in Japanese cinema, 2014 also saw the release of Sono Sion's urban-based *Tokyo Tribe/Tōkyō Toraibu*, a gang-war film with almost all dialogue delivered through the medium of rap, and based on a manga series 'Tokyo Tribes'. While the film does feature several shots of recognizable Tokyo locations such as the neon-infused Akihabara district, it mostly relies on a futuristic, dystopian rendering of the city with its neon-lit laneways and nightclubs, overtaken by the lawless 'tribes' of the title, described by one rapper as a 'shaking city that never closes its eyes'.

Similarly, the recreation of the recognizable landscape of Paris is featured throughout Jeunet's *Amélie*, a film that 'mythologises Montmartre at least as much as it captures its reality, resorting to elusive truth, selective fragmentation and cosmetic changes' (Vanderschelden 2007: 69). Rather than present a realist view of contemporary Paris, Jeunet prefers to create 'an idealised representation of Montmartre as a clean, non-threatening version of Paris' (Vanderschelden 2007: 69). Jeunet engages the audience so that 'the artificial recycling of virtual past atmospheres and individual memories encourages nostalgia' (71). Using projectors, filters and backlighting, and props in vibrant colours, Jeunet ensured that '90 per cent of the lighting effects were achieved during the main photography' (Vanderschelden 2007: 53), adding to the sense that the audience is experiencing an accurate vision of Paris.

Amélie's success with local and international audiences could be seen as a direct result of the creation of images that 'resuscitate a past imagery rendered familiar', as in the photographs of Robert Doisneau, so that Jeunet '(re)constructs a timeless Paris' (Vanderschelden 2007: 69). This timelessness is 'driven by the authenticity of location shooting and an anchoring into daily routine', while simultaneously putting the locations 'through a stylisation process facilitated by colour manipulation and the introduction of special effects'(69). A similar technique is also applied to the inauthentic Paris presented in Baz Luhrmann's *Moulin Rouge!* (also released in 2001), a film shot almost exclusively in Australia (and some later scenes shot in Spain). As with Luhrmann's work, *Amélie* plays with notions of time and space, 'using accelerated shots, which symbolically enhances the compression of time and history' (Vanderschelden 2007: 71). In a sense, Jeunet could be harking back to the days of the *nouvelle vague* that 'staged its drama in a space at once far more dynamic and enduring than any studio set' (Tweedie 2013: 53). As with the use of recognizable locales in *Amelie*, the cinema of that time 'was the record of a series of encounters among a range of artists, including the director, but also the stars and the crew, and the space of the city' (53).

Paris also serves as the setting for a whirlwind romance in the Japanese film, *I Have to Buy New Shoes/Atarashii Kutsu wo Kawanakucha* (2012, directed by

Eriko Kitagawa). The plot device of a Japanese photographer, Sen Yagami (Osamu Mukai), arriving in Paris for a three-day visit with his younger sister (who soon deserts him) allows for a plethora of scenic views of the city. The tourist premise allows Sen to practice his art while falling in love with Aoi Teshigahara (Miho Nakayama), a freelance writer living in Paris, after an accidental meeting. The screenplay appears to have been based on the multi-talented actress and singer, Nakayama, who, at the time of shooting, had lived in Paris for almost a decade. Landmarks such as the Eiffel Tower and the River Seine feature heavily as Kitagawa builds on the iconic city's reputation as a romantic destination.

A final notable intersection between France and Japan occurs in the aptly titled *Paris I Love You/Paris je t'aime* (2006), a portmanteau film in which eighteen international directors each shot a five-minute segment addressing a particular aspect of life in Paris. Using the romantic vicissitudes and dislocations of urban life as an ongoing structuring device, eighteen of the city's twenty *arrondissements* are visited in a random order, with events in each one gradually uncovering Paris's diversity and heterogeneity. Nobuhiro Suwa's entry is 'Place des Victoires', a meditation on maternal grief with Juliette Binoche as a mother grieving the loss of her son and Willem Dafoe as an imaginary cowboy the dead son idolized. The multiple themes in *Paris je t'aime* that emerge from the film's starting point – racism, grief, class conflict, lost love, found love, cultural difference – exemplify contemporary sociopolitical realities in the city. Suwa's entry – generally regarded as one of the most accomplished by critics who were otherwise disappointed by the whimsical and shallow treatment of the city – sits within a broader consideration of the city's mobile cultures and global flows, its engagement with French and non-French directors, and the crossovers with national boundaries.

Imagining the nation through rural–urban divides

The cinematic separation of urban and rural spaces is a popular motif in Japanese cinema, through Ozu Yasujirô's *The Only Son/Hitori Musuko* (1936), where a young man leaves 'the defined locale of his village for the undefined urban spaces of Tokyo' (Standish 2012: 8), or through Seijun Suzuki's *Tokyo Drifter/Tôkyô Nagaremono* (1966), as on-the-run gangster 'Phoenix' Tetsu (Tetsuya Watari) traverses the nation to escape various hitmen and the law. This mobility can be tied to notions of Japanese tradition and a form of masculinity where mobility can be found in 'wandering mendicant monks and pilgrims, roaming leaderless warriors, and travelling actors' (Gill 2003: 1). The urban–rural divide is also found through Tora-san's (mis)adventures as he travels across Japan (see Chapter 4), through Takeshi Kitano's *Hana-Bi/Fireworks* (1997), and Yôjirô Takita's *Departures*, all films in which the rural–urban divide is presented at different moments as a dichotomous space of good/evil, innocence/corruption. Even the comedic fantasy of *Assassination Classroom/Ansatsu Kyôshitsu* (2015 Eiichirô Hasumi) features a rural-based high school that privileges experts from Tokyo as the most effective solution for saving them from death at the hands of their alien teacher, a CGI smiley-faced shape-shifter who has threatened to destroy Earth. While the manga and anime-based *Assassination Classroom* rests on a somewhat absurd scenario, the students are separated from their (presumably) city-bound parents. The film therefore utilizes the framework of the urban–rural dichotomy and 'highlights the spatial disembedding of kinship relationships' (Standish 2012: 8) that takes place within the 'rupture' of the 'pre-modern' country and the urban's 'conflicting forces of "empty space" and alienation ... and the allure of excitement of perceived opportunities' (10).

Kôji Fukada's 2013 comedy-drama, *Goodbye to the Summer/Au Revoir L'Été/ Hotori no Sakuko* [lit. *Neighbouring Sakuko*, or *Sakuko on the Margins*], is said to be an ode to Eric Rohmer's *A Summer's Tale/Conte d'été* (1996), with much promotion of the film favouring its French title. The film quickly shifts location from the city as a young would-be university student, the titular Sakuko, fails an entrance exam and decides to retreat with her aunt to her seaside hometown. Sakuko is played by Fumi Nikaido, fresh from two Sono Sion films; her powerhouse performance in *Why Don't You Play in Hell?* and a darker performance as an abused daughter in *Himizu*, and Fukada casts her as an innocent among the natural settings of the harbour and nearby forests. Fukada privileges this rural setting as a backdrop to a series of entangled relationship dramas, with the wide-eyed Sakuko (often used as a light-hearted comic foil) watching her older aunt and relatives negotiate various romances. There is no shortage of slightly odd characters in the village, especially when Sakuko first arrives, suggesting the orderly nature of the city versus the parameter-less boundaries of village life. Sakuko finds herself toying with a relationship with a young man, Takashi (Taiga Nakano, later to star in Fukada's *Harmonium*), who has fled the radiation leaks from nearby Fukushima, adding an element of historical drama to proceedings. There is certainly an element of Rohmer's style, with Fukada perhaps also tipping his hat to Jeunet's *Amélie*, with frequent close-ups of the round, all-too-cute visage of Sakuko, much as Jeunet did with Audrey Tautou's character.

Kiyoshi Kurosawa is not only a filmmaker but also a critic, academic and screenwriter with a career featuring a succession of successful thriller and horror genre films. His 2001 *Pulse* (with similarities to the technology-based horror of *Ringu*) was screened at Cannes and later adapted for a US feature with a screenplay co-written by *Nightmare on Elm Street* creator, Wes Craven. The US remake proved to be a moderate box-office success, despite a very harsh critical reception. When shifting his sights to France for *Daguerreotype*, Kurosawa stated that he 'wanted a mix of European horror and classic Japanese horror', where ghosts are present from the beginning of the film, and then (in the traditional *kaidan* way), following the death of the main character (*Japan Times*). Kurosawa was careful to make the delineation between making a film in France, and a French film, stating that 'I thought I should let French directors be responsible for that and instead I'd use French material to create fiction' (*Japan Times*).

In 2001, the Luc Besson written and produced feature, *Wasabi*, was filmed on location in Tokyo, directed by Gérard Krawczyk. An action-comedy, it stars in-demand actor Jean Reno and young TV star, actress Ryōko Hirosue (who went on to great critical acclaim in *Departures*). Reno plays the protector role to the diminutive Hirosue but is culturally ignorant in the decidedly foreign Tokyo.

Tokyo features as the location in *Fear and Trembling/Stupeur et Tremblements* (2003) from a book of the same name by Amélie Nothomb (1999), a semi-autobiographical account of her life. Directed by Alain Corneau, the narrative follows a young Belgian woman, Amélie (Sylvie Testud) returning to Japan to work, after living there up until the age of five. Amélie's attempts to merge into Japanese society prove difficult as her cultural misunderstandings see her successively demoted from her prestigious role as a translator down to a bathroom attendant. The theme is extended with *Tokyo Fiancée* (2014), directed by Stefan Liberski that is again based on a semi-autobiographical novel by Nothomb, *Ni d'Ève ni d'Adam*, featuring a young Belgian woman and first published in 2007. The central character, Amélie (this time played by Pauline Etienne) again returns to Japan after leaving as a child. Amélie wants to follow her dream of not just becoming 'a real Japanese', but of becoming 'a venerable Japanese writer'. On arrival in Paris, Amélie throws open her curtains each morning, her voiceover narration exclaiming:

> In Tokyo I awoke each day filled with inexplicable happiness. The simple happiness of being alive . . . The rooftops, streets, temples, bikes, pedestrians, cats, passengers . . . they all said they'd been waiting for me, that they'd missed me, that order had been restored, and that my reign would last 10,000 years.

Amélie claims the city for herself, with Liberski filling the screen with images of Japanese daily life, for instance, bringing a tourist's simple delight to the otherwise banal activity of catching the train.

Amélie's rediscovery of Japan in *Tokyo Fiancée* allows Liberski the freedom to deliver tourist-style images of Tokyo's streets, from neon-lit night drives to *koi* ponds and leafy gardens. Her involvement tutoring Rinri (Taichi Inoue) in French, also gives the opportunity to see inside the house of his parents, a wealthy Japanese family, stereotyping urban Japan and its obsession with the latest kitchen gadgets, robotics and odd beauty products such as face rollers (mirroring Hulot's fascination with the modern house in *Mon Oncle*). Amélie even admits in one voiceover as they cycle the city's streets, that her French lessons with Rinri have simply 'morphed into a guided tour of Tokyo. Rinri's Tokyo, always somewhat baffling'. The cultural exchange reflects Japan's place in the globalized world, with Rinri drinking Coca-Cola and cooking Swiss Fondue, and soon the two begin a romantic relationship, but she struggles with the cultural formalities of Japan (Figure 6.3).

Where Liberski's Tokyo is initially presented as a welcoming place as Amélie acclimated herself, later she becomes unsure of the relationship and the city

Figure 6.3 Confusion and displacement in *Tokyo Fiancée* (2014).

takes on a less inviting form as she leaves a karaoke bar. In a close follow-shot, she wanders the busy night-time streets, and in a voiceover says:

> **Amélie**: Leaving the bar, I lost Rinri in the Shinjuku throng. I don't know why, I suddenly felt unhappy.

Liberski keeps the camera tight on Amélie's face as she becomes agitated, panicked.

> **Amélie**: Abandoned. Ridiculous.

Rinri finds her and they hug. While their relationship continues, Amélie's uncertainty remains, and she retreats to nature (the mountains) to figure things out. This again gives Liberski the opportunity to present a tourist-infused image of Japan as Amélie treks through bamboo forests and snow-covered mountains, confessing:

> **Amélie**: I mean, Japanese mountains represented a sort of pinnacle for me.

But as with Japanese culture, the mountains prove impenetrable to Amélie, and again, a feeling of displacement settles in, and she becomes lost. The seemingly endless beauty of her surroundings takes on a sinister tone. Forced to spend the night in an empty temple, she awakens the next morning to discover a breathtaking view of Mt Fuji and begins her trek anew.

> **Amélie**: That night, I died. I died of the cold. I'm convinced it was the splendour of Mt Fuji that brought me back to life. Just in time.

Amélie's bodily survival therefore takes on a metaphysical link to the seemingly magical powers of the Japanese landscape.

Films such as *Tokyo Fiancée* may seem to sit beyond the realm of French cinema due to either their setting or the nationality of their director, such as the US-born Schnabel's *The Diving Bell and the* Butterfly/*Le Scaphandre et le Papillon* (2007) or, as noted, esteemed Iranian director Abbas Kiarostami's 2012 *Like Someone in Love*, a French/Japanese co-production. Kiarostami's film takes place entirely in Tokyo, in a country where he noted, 'It was the only country where, even before going there, I felt a special emotional connection to the place' (Criterion Collection 2014). Kiarostami's Japanese influence was also made overt in *Five/Panj*, also known as *Five Dedicated to Ozu*, a 2003 film shot in Iran but consisting of only five, static long takes in homage to Ozu.

Harmonium/Fuchi ni tatsu 2016 by Kôji Fukada is based in Japan, but a production of the Paris-based Comme des Cinémas, the company that has a history of working with highly regarded Japanese filmmakers. Other films that had the support of Comme des Cinémas included Shôhei Imamura's final feature, the fantasy-based *Warm Water Under a Red Bridge/Akai Hashi no Shita no Nurui Mizu* (2001, entered in competition at Cannes), a film with some thematic parallels with Ron Howard's 1984 *Splash*, although with a bizarre sexual twist involving bodily fluids. Kiyoshi Kurosawa also teamed with Comme des Cinémas on *Journey to the Shore/Kishibe no Tabi* (screened in *Un Certain Regard* 2015), a romantic tale of love and death, which also has parallels with Hollywood films such as Jerry Zucker's *Ghost* (1990) or Alejandro Agresti's 2006 *The Lake House*, a remake of the Korean hit *Siworae/Il Mare/The Sea* (2000, dir. Lee Hyun-seung). More recently, Comme des Cinémas joined a second production with Naomi Kawase on 2017's *Radiance*, as noted in Chapter 1, the romance based on an ageing photographer with failing eyesight and the love he finds with a younger woman who writes audio descriptions of films for the sight-impaired. Kawase is noted for her use of her home prefecture of Nara as a location for her films, where her 'style has remained close to documentary, using location shooting and natural light, and eschewing melodramatic incident or convoluted narrative' (Jacobs 2008: 105).

The use of smaller rural towns and coastal areas as locations to offer a sharp contrast to the suffocating bustle of Japan's megacities is found in many films. Hirokazu Kore-eda is one filmmaker who often looks for the gentle side of humanity in his films and therefore, as in *Our Little Sister/Umimachi Diary* [lit. *Seaside Diary*] (2015), chooses to set many of his films beyond the busy confines of the major cities. *Our Little Sister* is again a film based on a serialized manga. The tranquil seaside town of Kamakura is the hometown of three sisters in their twenties who must look after their young teenage stepsister following the death of their philandering father. Kore-eda directs the film with acute attention to the details of nature, or the quiet artisan activities of the town, the cinematography at times reminiscent of the muted-pastel palette anime that features in the work of the Studio Ghibli artists. The everyday setting of *Our Little Sister* allows Kore-eda to explore his key themes of 'isolation, loss, death, memory and the search for meaning; his excellence lies in his ability to anchor these philosophical concerns in the concrete realities of daily life and individual emotion' (Jacobs 2008: 125), so the use of the quiet village enhances, rather than detracts from, the lives of his protagonists.

The controversial *Black Snow/Kuroi Yuki* (1965, dir. Tetsuji Takechi) featured overt sexuality resulting in its battle with censors in the early to mid-1960s

(Alexander 2003), but it is perhaps also prescient in its telling of the failure of capitalism, when the near-deserted motel under the deafening flight path of a US-controlled air force base is used primarily for prostitution. The use of location shooting replicated the move towards noir in the US and French cinema that had begun to favour the grittiness of urban streetscapes (Turim 2016: 63). In their examination of *Sketches of Kaitan City* (2010), Ortiz-Moya and Moreno note that in Japan, the 'restructuring of capital entails the disposal of the low-profit elements of the production system; it can be the buildings, which become unused or underused, as they could not hold the economic functions of the new emerging system, or even the workers' (2016: 892). Although writing about Japan in the contemporary era, the picture is nevertheless mimetic of the 1960s and the crime-riddled motel (sex, gambling, violence) found in *Black Snow* (Figure 6.4).

Michel Gondry (*Mood Indigo*) uses the urban–rural divide as a narrative device in *Microbe and Gasoline/Microbe et Gasoil* when the titular characters, two young teenage boys, build a makeshift car to ferry them out of the city (Versaille) to the countryside. In Gondry's imaginative style, the boys, Daniel (nicknamed Microbe because he is smaller than his classmates), played by Ange Dargent, and Theo (Gasoline, because of his hobby of playing with motors), played by Théophile Baquet, build the car to look like a wooden house, so that they can avoid registering it as a car. When they stop by the side of the road, wooden rails drop down to hide the wheels, a slightly absurd attempt at camouflage. The boys share a range of episodic adventures as they travel through the country, gradually losing almost all of their possessions, and the car. Gondry's penchant

Figure 6.4 Isolated motel in *Black Snow* (1965).

for the absurd is reflected when the boys win an aeroplane trip back to their home city, but odd things happen, including the plane coming in to land tail first (courtesy of reversed footage). Ultimately though, the city is presented as both a place to escape from, and as a sanctuary to return to.

The urban and suburban streets, temples, apartments and shops of Tokyo are the setting for the entirety of the appropriately named *Adrift in Tokyo/Tenten* (2007, dir. Satoshi Miki) as renegade debt-collector Fukuhara (Tomokazu Miura) and his reluctant companion, slacker college student (now in his eighth year) Takemura (Joe Odagiri) trek across the city for the purpose of Fukuhara turning himself in to the police for a murder he has committed. The two use the opportunity to visit places from their past, and as they stand looking at a cleared lot at a site where Takemura grew up, Fukuhara wistfully concedes, 'Half the memorable places in Tokyo have become coin parking lots'. Takemura though, lacks Fukuhara's sentimentality, stating that he hates memories and that he had burnt all of his childhood photos. The city therefore holds no special hold on him, despite his obviously intimate knowledge that he shows while navigating the streets, ending up in Shinjuku after becoming separated from Fukuhara, allowing Miki to show the city's streetscapes in daylight, sunset and night-time views.

Adrift in Tokyo, based on a novel of the same name by Yoshinaga Fujita, meanders along (adrift, as the title suggests), through its comic, episodic-style narrative, intercut with flashbacks that show the lives of both protagonists beyond their current circumstance. As noted, Fukuhara is the more nostalgic of the two, and relates a story back to Takemura as they wander the streets late into the night:

> **Fukuhara**: I sometimes rode the last bus on Sunday with my wife.
> **Takemura**: What for?
> **Fukuhara**: To be lonely.
> **Takemura**: You're so weird.

The scene cuts to a flashback of Fukuhara and his wife as the only passengers on a night-time bus.

> **Fukuhara** (v/o): The last bus on Sunday is so lonely. When you're lonely, you grow fond of the other person. We lived together only by our love for each other. But love can wear out. That's why.

The bus 'stop' button lights up, and the shot returns to Fukuhara dozing, sitting alone (apart from another passenger, either drunk or asleep, across the aisle), his wife now gone. He wakes with a start, to see his wife outside the window, in the rain and waving goodbye.

>   **Fukuhara** (v/o): It would've been different if we'd had a son.

He scrambles to the back seat of the bus, but she continues to wave as the bus pulls away. The scene cuts to the men, now in bathrobes at a Tatami Inn, but the conversation continues:

>   **Takemura**: Why did she suddenly leave the bus?
>   **Fukuhara**: Maybe it was some sudden impulse.

The discussion then turns to each other's ability to control their emotions. Fukuhara's story illustrates the relationship between not only himself and his wife but also the sense that Tokyo is not always the vibrant city that much of the film shows. While the film features many views of Tokyo, Miki avoids iconic sites that may be rendered cliched or too deliberately 'touristy' (Tokyo Tower, Shibuya Crossing), rather focusing on lesser-known areas or using alternate angles that add a more down-to-earth view of its streetscapes.

Country living in French cinema

Just as Tokyo does not feature in all Japanese films, not all French films take place in Paris. Films take place at the beach, in the suburbs, in former colonial outposts, in smaller urban centres, in nondescript towns and villages and in the countryside. As far as the latter is concerned, an underlying ideological aspect of much of contemporary French cinema is that life in the countryside pivots between a hard-scrabble struggle to maintain a traditional way of life (which, often ironically, is considered an asset in a globalized, connected world of uncertainty and fragmented community) and a romanticized refuge far from the urban centre (often, though not always, Paris) in which community bonds are strong, resistance to the forces of modernization and modern capitalist practices is resolute, and nostalgia for a previous era is reactivated via familiar stereotypes.

Graeme Harper and Jonathan Rayner note that cinematic landscapes draw not only on the literal, but also on the metonymic and the metaphoric, and 'can articulate the unconscious as well as the conscious [and] can therefore be landscapes of the mind offering displaced representations of desires and values, so that these can be expressed by the filmmakers and shared by audiences' (2010:

21). In a move that dates back at least to the early 1980s, and the emergence of the 'heritage' film tradition (a popular genre that told stories about French history and constructed particular notions of French national identity for domestic and international audiences through the deployment of grand sets, meticulous period costumes and luscious cinematography that drew attention to France's bucolic beauty), films set in the countryside will often contain soaring shots and pans of the landscape to accentuate its pictorial beauty. These shots function, in Harper and Rayner's terms, as both conscious and unconscious representations of a rapidly evolving France, reminding audiences of how France used to be before the onslaught of unrelenting progress.

Within the borders of France, an emerging corpus of 'rural films' (several of which use the making of wine as a backdrop) have looked at the complex professional and personal dynamics that play out in areas far from the city. Diverse examples here include Agnès Varda's *Vagabond/Sans toit ni loi* [lit. With neither shelter nor law], from 1985, or the Belgian duo Gustave Kervern and Benoît Delépine's road movie *Saint-Amour* (2016), with Gérard Depardieu and Benoît Poelvoorde as an estranged father and son who travel from Beaujolais to Burgundy, the Rhone valley, Bordeaux and the Loire. In *A Tale of Autumn/Conte d'automne* (1998), Eric Rohmer places great emphasis on the relationship between the main character Magali – a widowed winemaker – and the earthy environment in which she works. It is set in Saint-Paul-Trois-Châteaux, in the southern Rhone valley, where Magali views her winemaking as a craft and not a trade. She declines to use pesticides on her grapes unlike the neighbouring vineyard owner, whose use of chemicals makes his land more efficient and productive but spoils the taste of the wine. Indeed, many 'wine films' explore these tensions – between artisanal craftsmanship and mass-produced, industrialized manufacture – and thus allegorize wider concerns, in France in particular, about globalization and the effects of the European Union's Common Agricultural Policy.

These, and many other films, also redraw the contours of the Hexagon (the geographically determined nickname for France) by proposing an alternative, more nuanced account of cinematic France that shifts away from Paris towards the distinctive qualities of the rural and the non-urban. Directors now draw attention to the ways in which the unique combinations of geography, climate and civic attitudes shape the representation of these rural parts of France. Regions like Alsace, Languedoc, Rhône and Beaujolais, so often neglected by French filmmakers in favour of the big urban centres, are now showcased for their picturesque landscapes, slower pace of life and an emphasis on tight community networks.

Watched alongside *Adrift in Tokyo*, Varda's *Vagabond* offers a far less glamorous view of the countryside as her long tracking shots follow the ultimately tragic wanderings of Mona Bergeron (Sandrine Bonnaire) through Southern France. Shot in a part-documentary style with occasional voiceovers and direct-to-camera interviews with 'witnesses', Varda tracks the young Mona (in her late teens or early twenties) as she ambles through the harsh winter climes of the wine-growing districts in the south. Mona takes on some itinerant work, but refuses to commit to employment, relationships and even, it seems, to life itself. Varda exploits the landscape from the opening scene of a barren, windswept vineyard, a solitary tractor raising a cloud of dust as it ploughs the soil between the rows of empty vines. The overcast sky and an abrasive screech of (non-diegetic) violins give the scene a particular bleakness as the camera moves from a long shot to finally direct the focus towards a heavily clothed farmworker collecting pruned branches in the cold, hostile environment.

Soon after these opening scenes and the discovery of Mona's frozen body in a ditch, a new scene opens against vision showing sunlight highlighting ripples across sand in a view of what could be a desert. A voiceover (by Varda) begins, preempting the tragic tale about to unfold. The camera begins to move, eventually tilting upwards to reveal a pleasant-looking beach, where a young, naked woman (presumably Mona) steps easily from the water, refreshed and vibrant. Varda cuts immediately to a view of postcards of naked women on beaches, as a young man gazes at them, before selecting one. The postcards are a direct match with the previous shot, both of which reinforce the literal picture-postcard beauty of the French coast. In just a few minutes, Varda has moved from the austere winter vines and the tragic find of Mona's body, to what could be called an idyllic retreat. But Varda's *Vagabond* is no idyllic film, and once Mona hitches a ride with a passing trucker, the remainder of the film drops any pretence at promoting a beautiful France. In the truck, Mona observes row after row of holiday accommodation buildings and comments on their ugliness. The driver explains:

> **Driver**: The summer's better. Wall to wall people. 90,000 in the summer. Only 3,000 in the winter.
> **Mona**: That leaves 87,000 empty beds.

Mona soon parts ways with the driver and begins her episodic journey, wandering through ploughed fields, finding shelter in disused houses, in a small cottage run by a beatnik goat-herding couple and a crumbling chateau. The bleakness is only interrupted by Mona's brief encounter with a friendly academic who extends the hand of friendship, allowing Mona to sleep in her car. But the restless Mona soon leaves, the dissonant musical score again rising as a foretelling of what is to come.

Varda's use of land and village scapes unfolds as her horizontal tracking shots follow alongside Mona and her large backpack. Varda's camera, though, sometimes leaps ahead of her protagonist or drops back as she disappears from view leaving us with a static view of a weathered wall or a pile of discarded wooden pallets. It is as if Varda is critiquing the built environment, lingering on its ruin and disrepair, or even on nature itself, with human life a transient, temporal invasion of that space. Varda's interiors are close, cramped and over-furnished rooms that suggest maybe they too are no place for refuge. Mona's penultimate night sees her seek shelter in a plastic hothouse at a vineyard. She shivers the night through yet returns the following evening only to befall a tragic accident. Mona's final moments are spent in a ditch, in the dirt, perhaps, Varda is saying, the closest to nature we can get.

Counter to the bleak landscapes and barren vineyards presented in *Vagabond*, *Back to Burgundy/Ce qui nous lie* [lit. What binds us] (2017, dir. Cédric Klapisch) opens (literally), with the drawing apart of blue curtains by a young boy (the young Jean, later played as an adult by Pio Marmaï) who then gazes out the window as a voiceover describes:

> **Jean** (v/o): When I was little, every morning I would look out the window and I'd think . . .

The shot switches to what the boy sees; he is overlooking lush verdant vines stretching off into the far distance.

> **Jean** (*cont.*): . . . every morning it changes.

As he utters these words the green vines morph into autumnal browns and yellows, as the same scene (in an edited time lapse), rolls through the various seasons. Each time though, the beauty remains, and unlike Varda's use of an almost atonal score, Klapisch uses a gentle folk-pop song to underscore the softness of the landscape. The fullness of the screen captures the rolling hills in the background, sometimes snow-covered, sometimes green and lush. The black pillar-box masking of the screen suddenly moves upwards from the bottom of the screen, to allow the cast and crew credits to appear, the lettering appearing as cut-outs that allow the image of the fields to be seen behind them. Soon the images, still moving through their seasonal cycles, are divided into composite shots across the screen and time-lapse segments show grape pickers moving through the vines and clouds passing over the hills. These opening scenes last almost two minutes, until the scene cuts back to the window; this time, the boy has grown, and the adult Jean sullenly gazes out.

> **Jean** (v/o): Yeah. When I was a kid, I thought every day was different. And it would always be like that. It would always keep changing.

The shot moves back to the interior of the house, Jean slumped against the window frame with the vineyard in the distance.

> **Jean**: But then I realised that, here, nothing ever changes.

Throughout *Back to Burgundy*, Klapisch examines in forensic detail the practices of winemaking (soils, labelling, picking, tasting, selling, bottling . . .) and charts the mythic connection between winemaker/director and the land. To establish the changing rhythms of the Burgundy countryside throughout a twelve-month cycle, he hired a photographer to take a picture of the same tree every day at 3.00 pm for one year. Klapisch uses the rituals of the Beaune *vendange* to make broader comments on the importance of friendship: a mutual common purpose becomes the adhesive that bonds together disparate social and cultural groups. Many of Klapisch's films feature notable scenes of eating, drinking, chatting in bars and in streets, visiting famous monuments, listening to music and making wine. These are not solitary activities but become shared, reciprocal experiences that deepen and evolve over time.

Films about wine in particular tap into deep historical resonances within French national culture, inspiring patriotic sentiments with its representations rooted in the essentialist concept of the nation, and it remains a powerful symbol of cultural continuity in the face of the changing relationship between global, national and regional identities in France. Wine forms a significant part of that idealized representation. Indeed, we can link this filmic treatment of wine – and the regions that produce it – back to French cinema's ongoing fascination with the *cinéma d'héritage*.

Like many French productions, *Back to Burgundy* and *Vagabond* feature the names of regional shooting locations prominently in their opening credits. In

Back to Burgundy, the final moment before the young Jean opens the curtains features the words *la région: Bourgogne-Franche-Comté*, while Varda's film presents a list of locations thanking *'les habitants des villages'*, no doubt in honour for their hospitality, but also in recognition of those non-actors who appear throughout her film as either characters or extras, before another credit is given thanking *la municipalité de Nîmes*. This acknowledgement at the beginning of each film shows the importance of location (as noted in Chapter 2) as a narrative setting, and also (often) its importance in acquiring state or regional funding.

French colonialism

Many of France's most powerful films take place far from the *arrondissements* of Paris, instead set in those war-torn or poverty-stricken nations that have been subject to varying periods of French colonial power. Any thoughts that the *nouvelle vague* opened a new chapter of French self-reflection can be countered, for instance, by the knowledge that:

> [T]he period's obsession with cars and cleanliness, with speed and suburbanization, with neat structuralist models for language and society and equally tidy cities, masks a failure to acknowledge the nation's continued participation in a dirty colonial conflict in Algeria, a war whose underlying nationalist rationale belied the ubiquitous claim that France had launched a new era in its history. (Tweedie 2013: 47)

In other words, if audiences were looking to new wave filmmakers to stage the counter-revolution against the nation's colonial project, they would have to wait a while yet.

When considering films that do question colonization, the African-based films of Claire Denis (*Chocolat*, *White Material*) immediately come to mind, along with Godard's *The Little Soldier/Le petit soldat*, released in 1963 after a lengthy ban due to its controversial torture scenes, or the more recent *Intimate Enemies/L'Ennemi intime* (2007, dir. Florent Emilio Siri), set during the Algerian war. But equally important are those set in Polynesia or parts of Asia (Régis Warnier's 1992 *Indochine*, or Pierre Schoendoerffer's 1992 *Dien Bien Phu*). But the importance of the conflict in Algeria is never far away, with a spate of films in recent years that focus not on Algeria itself but are set in contemporary France and are populated with (mostly white) characters that are dealing with the psychological aftermath of the war. Three films that were released in 2020 seem to follow a similar pattern of families that have an older patriarch who has harboured anxieties and violent thoughts since the war. Yamina Benguigui's *Sisters/Soeurs*, Lucas Belvaux's *Home Front/Des Hommes* and Maïwenn's *DNA/ADN*, each feature characters that have been affected, leaving the next generations to try to find peace.

French colonialism also provides a disturbing undercurrent rather than being directly addressed in Mahamat Saleh Haroun's *A Season in France/Une Saison en France* (2017). Haroun's personal background as an émigré from the former French colony of Chad in Central Africa underscores the migrant experience at the heart of *A Season in France*. Despite the tantalizingly cheerful title, *A Season in France* shows that any form of French-language history or culture makes little to no difference when it comes to legal migration. A widowed father of two, Abbas (Eriq Ebouaney), is working in Paris after fleeing his homeland in the former colony of the Central African Republic. His wife was killed as they fled, but Abbas, his two children, a boy, Yacine (Ibrahim Burama Darboe), and a younger girl, Asma (Aalayna Lys), and Abbas's brother Etienne (Bibi Tanga) were able to eventually make their way to France without passports or any official migration documents. While race is never overtly mentioned in the film, the underlying sentiment suggests that if Abbas and his family were white, their circumstances would be different.

Haroun sets up a number of false visuals in the early parts of *A Season in France*; Abbas has a job in a fresh-produce market and he and the children are nicely settled in a modern, spacious and new apartment, while Etienne carries himself with the air of an erudite academic. Both men have romantic partners and seem fairly settled in Paris. Things soon unravel, though, when it is revealed that Abbas is on his last chance appeal for any kind of visa status in France and faces deportation with his children. The owner of the apartment that he has loaned to Abbas is returning and they have to find somewhere else to live. Etienne is revealed as having only a temporary casual job as a security guard outside a pharmacy, and lives in a crudely constructed shanty alongside a canal, sneaking a shower every now and then at a local swimming pool. Their circumstances are a constant threat to their dignity and pride. Late in the film, Abbas has lost his job and is unable to pay the rent on the decrepit temporary accommodation he and his children have recently moved into. The landlord tells him they have to leave. Always desperate to keep his children positive, Abbas sits with them and unfolds a map of the world.

> **Abbas**: Let's pick a country.
> **Asma**: A country where they won't throw us out.
> **Yacine**: What about school? Do we stop going? I'd like to finish the year.
> **Asma**: Papa, the North Pole! It's good there. There's snow and polar bears, too.
> **Yacine**: There's no one there. Australia's better. It's by the sea, too.
> **Asma**: Chad. Bangui [their former home] is just below it.
> **Yacine**: Brazil, with the Rio Carnival.

Yacine swings his arms, dancing in appreciation of the Carnival, and ignoring the possibility of returning to Africa.

> **Asma**: Argentina, where they make Chica Vampiro [a teen TV show].
> **Abbas**: Or Morocco. It's sunny. Or Spain.

Abbas has lost interest in the map, increasingly despairing of their plight as he begins to stand and move away from the children.

> **Asma**: Uh, uh. Not Spain. The USA. New York.
> **Yacine**: Alaska.
> **Asma** (o/s): Canada?
> **Yacine** (o/s): Are there Mongols in Mongolia?

Abbas wanders over to stare out the window. It is, of course, all an artifice. Without documents or money, Abbas knows he is not free to choose a destination and resettle.

Evicted from their apartment, Abbas and the children are able to shelter at the house of his girlfriend, Carole (played by *Vagabond*'s Sandrine Bonnaire). Tragedy strikes, though, as Etienne dies in horrific circumstances that highlight the pain and frustration facing undocumented immigrants. Even in death, there can be no permanency, as Yacine (in a voiceover as the camera travels across the gravestones of other émigrés) tells of how Etienne's grave is only temporary, and that, 'After 5 years, we'll need to find him another grave, if not, he'll be cremated'.

While Abbas's fate seems to be sealed, Carole urges him to seek one last chance through the administrative court. 'Have faith' [*foi quoi!*], she tells him, 'have faith'. But Abbas and the children disappear, leaving a simple note for Carole. Against footage of Carole desperately searching for the family, Abbas's voice is heard reading the letter:

> **Abbas** (v/o): To feel undesirable is a horrible thing. Carole, I'm leaving to give my children a peaceful future, far from this Europe that has become a Tower

of Babel. . . . For me, every man is capable of writing his own story. Mine was made invisible, impossible to tell. But someone will tell it, one day . . .

The harsh realities of unflinching bureaucratic migration systems and the failure of past historical links through colonization are clearly highlighted in Haroun's *A Season in France*. The temporal nature of one's existence is shown as dependent not only on physical survival, but also on the ability to settle and create a 'home'. The film ends with a final shot, reminiscent of the final shot in *The 400 Blows*, of Carole, standing on a windswept plane where a refugee camp has been razed to the ground. Her last forlorn hope at tracking Abbas has failed, and as she slowly turns, her eyes lock onto the camera, as if she is pleading to the audience, to us, to appeal to our humanity.

As with *A Season in France*, the earlier film *Samba* (2014, dir. Olivier Nakache and Éric Toledano) centres on the theme of migration and the difficulties faced by a long-term émigré from a former French colony in Africa. In *Samba*, the eponymous character (played by Omar Sy) has finally run out of time and (most) avenues to gain legal residency in France. He is assigned help through a volunteer refugee support group and begins a personal relationship with Alice (Charlotte Gainsbourg), a businesswoman with no experience in the legal processes of the migration system. Samba's skills in commercial kitchens – 'I'm almost a qualified chef', he tries to explain at one stage – are no use to him without official residency papers, and he is forced to take on any type of casual work he can find, including as a security guard, always with one eye cast for police or immigration officials, like Abbas is later to do in *A Season in France*. Based on the novel, Samba pour la France, by filmmaker Delphine Coulin, *Samba* again explores the racial and ethnic divides that reflect contemporary French society.

While Samba and his uncle, Lamouna (Youngar Fall), have the advantage of fluent French-language abilities, their status pits them against the same challenges as those who are from other cultures and linguistic groups, as shown in the refugee centre where volunteers do their best to interpret for Eastern European or Asian emigrants. When Samba's application for residency fails and he becomes 'officially' an illegal immigrant, Lamouna instructs him on how to avoid detection from the authorities:

> **Lamouna**: From now on you have to dress differently. European-style! Jacket, pants and a briefcase like a businessman. Slip a magazine under your arm. And dump your jeans and your awful old shoes. Be quiet and discreet like I taught you. And don't go out drunk!

Samba: I don't drink! That only happened once...

Lamouna: Let me finish. Avoid train stations and big metro stations. After 6pm take the bus. Finally, never cheat in the metro, some have been deported for that.

Samba stares intently at his uncle, as if sceptical of the old man's words. The scene then cuts to the inside of a train carriage with Samba dressed in a coat and tie, clutching a magazine, seemingly successful in taking on the disguise that is needed. As he makes his way down the carriage, he feels all eyes on him as the (all white) passengers each turn to look at him, judging and accusing, and increasing his feelings of paranoia. A later formal meeting with Alice, in her volunteer capacity, only accentuates the position he finds himself in, and he begins shouting at her. Alice is, however, feeling vulnerable and shouts back at him, only later to confess that she is recovering from a breakdown due to the demands and stresses of her life as a businesswoman where, she explains, she worked 'Like a slave'. So, while Samba's life is filled with uncertainties and challenges that will ultimately affect his future, Alice can see that her stress-related problems are minor compared to Samba's predicament.

Reflections of Japan as colonizer

The colonization issue, it seems, is a more sensitive issue in Japanese cinema. Few contemporary filmmakers delve head-on into Japan's colonization and forceful attempts at takeovers in Korea, Taiwan, parts of China and various islands in the Pacific and the South China Sea. Japan's regional involvement in colonization and military confrontation is reasonably well documented in the cinemas of Korea (*My Way/Maiwei* 2011, dir. Kang Je-gyu; *The Battleship Island/Gunhamdo* 2017, dir. Ryoo Seung-wan; and the 'comfort women' based *Spirit's Homecoming/Gwihyang*, 2016, dir. Cho Jung-rae) and China (*Little Soldier Zhang Ga/Xiao Bing Zhang Ga*, 1963, dir. Wei Cui; *Red Sorghum/Hóng gāoliáng*, 1987 dir. Zhang Yimou; *The Tokyo Trial/Dōngjīng Shěnpàn*, 2006, dir. Gao Qunshu; *The Flowers of War/Jīnlíng shísān chāi*, 2011, dir. Zhang Yimou; *The Eight Hundred/Bābǎi*, 2020, dir. Guan Hu). Facing up to past events is often a painful experience that requires sensitivity and deft handling of the topic to avoid prompting new hostilities. Historically, Japan's early entry into filmmaking was recognized by its leaders who 'dispatched newsreel cameramen to film the Russo-Japanese War' in 1904, to have them capture on celluloid 'Japan's well-trained modern infantry and navy using the latest technology to fight and beat the Russian army' (Baskett 2008: 7).

While filmmaking was swept up in the propaganda waves leading up to, and throughout the Second World War, it was after the war that a number of 'imperial era' filmmakers produced films 'that were critical of the war but benignly sympathetic to the imperial impulses that motivated it' (Baskett 2008: 10). Michael Baskett refers to the historical regimes of Japanese filmmaking in its colonial outposts in the 1920s and 1930s, noting that it established 'formal' markets in Taiwan and Korea, but Manchuria provided the opportunity for a 'new semicolonial style of imperial film market' in which the US-trained filmmaker 'Henry' Kotani 'brought Manchuria into reach for mainstream Japanese audiences in much the same way that John Ford popularised the American West' (2008: 28).

A number of contemporary films such as *Riding the Breeze/Nanpū* (lit. *Southern Wind*, 2014, dir. Kōji Hagiuda) present an arms-length version of the relations between former colony Taiwan and Japan through heartwarming tales of friendship across cultural (rather than political) divides. When fashion editor and journalist Aiko (Mei Kurokawa) arrives in Taiwan to cover a cycling event, she befriends another young woman, Tonton (US-born Teresa Daley), and their lives become entwined as they journey around the island together. Another film to address Japan's relationship with Taiwan was *Cape No. 7/Hǎijiǎo Qī Hào* (2008, dir. Wei Te-sheng), a film chosen as Taiwan's entry for Best Foreign Language Film at the 2009 Academy Awards (but was not nominated).

The strategy of addressing Japan's role in the Second World War through more personal or romantic narratives has appeared in a number of films including Shintō Kaneda's *Postcard/Ichimai no hagaki* (2010) and Kiyoshi Kurosawa's *Wife of a Spy/Supai no tsuma* (2020). In *Postcard*, middle-aged conscript Sadazo Morikawa (Naomasa Musaka) writes a postcard to be delivered to his wife, Tomoko (Shinobu Otake), in case of his death. When he is killed, his friend Keita Matsuyama (Etsushi Toyokawa) is tasked with delivering the postcard to the grieving Tomoko. While *Postcard* is not directly critical of the Japanese government, it is very much a film that questions the futility of war and the resultant personal tragedies it brings.

Kurosawa's *Wife of a Spy* (winner of the Silver Lion at the 2020 Venice International Film Festival) similarly offers a thinly veiled dig at the futility of war. Using a restrained tone throughout the film, Kurosawa's story unfolds gently, letting the drama reveal itself slowly and, as Gerow points out replicates Kurosawa's established style of 'eliminating much that comes between events and using editing to suggest narrative trajectories' (2016: 349). This elliptical style is found in his films regardless of the genre; a war film, a French mystery, a gruesome horror film, or even in his oddball sci-fi comedy, 2017's *Before We Vanish*/*Sanpo Suru Shinryakusha* [lit. Strolling invaders]. Even in *Before We Vanish*, Kurosawa is toying with the idea of 'war' through an invasion narrative of aliens infiltrating the everyday bodies and lives of suburban Japanese. Ultimately, Kurosawa's film works on a metaphysical level where the aliens stop their invasion once they are able to 'conceptualise' the idea of love. With almost no hi-tech dramatic invasion scenes, *Before We Vanish* reflects notions of passivity, a nation being subsumed by a non-militaristic 'alien' force that could easily be seen as Kurosawa's private commentary on Japan's non-aggression pact in the post–Second World War era.

Absences

Austrian filmmaker Michael Haneke's body of 'French films', made in France, in French and with a rollcall of famous French actors, released *Code inconnu: récit incomplet de divers voyages* / *Code Unknown: Incomplete Tales of Several Journeys* in 2000. *Code Unknown* features a cross-threading of narratives that sees one character leave France, Maria (Luminița Gheorghiu) through deportation to Romania, although she manages to get smuggled back into France, and one character just returned to France from a photographic assignment during the Balkans War. Upon his return to Paris, Georges (Thierry Neuvic) seems to struggle to find inspiration in the banalities of everyday life, including with his actress partner, Anne (Juliette Binoche). In one of the film's many long-take scenes, Georges is pushing a shopping trolley as he and Anne are shopping in a supermarket, perhaps the ultimate in banal activities. Anne relates to Georges her experiences of hearing a child's screams when she is alone in their apartment, during his long absences. She tells him she has received a mysterious handwritten note about the child, and its possible abuse, that deepens the mystery. Georges offers some possible solutions that Anne immediately counters, so he remains detached.

Anne: You don't care, do you?
Georges: I do. But you got the letter. Not me. I can't decide for you.

> **Anne** (*yelling*): You could fucking help! (*calm*) It's too easy just to wash your hands of it.
> **Georges**: I never hear her crying. I don't even know her. I don't know her parents.... Not my problem. Can you get that into your head?

They walk towards the camera, Georges pushing the trolley. Anne stops in front of him to place some bottled water in the trolley.

> **Anne** (*hissing*): It's never your problem. When there's trouble, you're gone.
> **Georges** (*sarcastically*): Of course, you're right.
> **Anne**: Aren't I?

Georges walks on with the trolley until Anne catches up to him and he turns.

> **Georges**: Why don't you grow up and stop letting others decide for you.
> **Anne**: And you never run away?

Anne's resentment towards Georges's continued absences is constant, and she attributes his detachment to his failure to relish everyday life. As they continue through the supermarket, Anne suddenly confesses to Georges:

> **Anne**: I am pregnant.

Georges stops, stunned.

> **Anne** (*cont.*): What if I was pregnant?
> **Georges**: Is this a joke?
> **Anne**: No, it's not a joke.

Georges remains standing, a puzzled look on his face before Anne again refers to his absence.

> **Anne** (*cont.*): I aborted while you were away.
> **Georges**: Did you?
> **Anne**: You decide.

Another shopper walks by, momentarily disrupting their conversation.

> **Georges**: What is this? Do you expect me to take you seriously?
> **Anne**: No, I don't.

When Georges walks off, shortly afterwards, Anne chases after him giving the impression that she is going to attack him. But rather than enact violence, she wraps her arms around him and they kiss hungrily, a desperation to their affection, mimetic of lovers who are meeting for the first time after a long period apart.

In *Wife of a Spy,* absences take on a more suspicious tone, when Yūsaku Fukuhara (Issey Takahashi) leaves home on regular business trips into Manchuria, at that time under precarious Japanese control. His wife, Satoko (Yū Aoi), an amateur actor for her nephew's aspirational filmmaking, becomes alerted to her husband's mysterious actions when a young woman who travelled to Manchuria with Satoko's husband, is murdered. When Satoko confronts Yūsaku, insisting he tells her what happened, he confesses, but she appears unconvinced by his words:

> **Yūsaku**: From Busan, we took the train and headed to Manchuria. The capital was bustling. I felt a type of hope that I can't feel in Japan anymore. We received permission to visit Kwantung Army's research lab. I wanted to procure medicine. We occasionally saw mounds from the car. First, I thought they were disposed farm crops. Up close, I could see many hands and feet sticking out. Smoke was coming out. Corpses were being burned.

He moves towards Satoko as if his physical immediacy will stress the importance of his words.

> **Yūsaku**: Corpses of plague victims.

He suddenly turns and walks away from her, and almost flippantly adds:

> **Yūsaku**: We ended up saving one woman's life. Yes, Hiroke Kusakabe [the murdered woman]. A nurse and the military doctor's lover. She told us the plague epidemic was caused by the Kwantung Army's biological weapon.

Yūsaku's monologue seems to convince Satoko, but when he suggests that the biological weapon is part of a plan to draw the United States into the war and that he wants to make this public, she questions his devotion to the nation. His absences from Japan, in her eyes, have made him less of a patriot.

Conclusion

The concept of film or 'contents' tourism noted earlier is a way to increase the economic capacity of a film beyond mere screening. The Japanese government's 'increasing role in the promotion of popular culture' (Seaton and Yamamura 2015: 6) has extended beyond the use of film locations purely for the production of a film, but for interest in a location to be maintained beyond the release of a film. The push into creative industries through the 'Cool Japan' campaign in the early 2000s (inspired in part by the UK's 'Cool Britannia' foray into monetizing the creative industries in the 1990s) resulted in publications such as the *Japan anime tourism guide* and the *Japan anime map* in the early 2010s to try to capitalize on fan tourism (Seaton and Yamamura 2015: 7). The rise of globally connected websites furthered the availability of details of particular film locations, such as *JW Web Magazine*, which lists eight famous locations from foreign films that have been set in Japan including *Babel* (2006), *Kill Bill Parts 1 and 2* (2003), *Memoirs of a Geisha* (2005) and *The Wolverine* (2013). *Tsunagu Japan* (2016) lists a combination of sites from Japanese films (including *Godzilla/Gojira*, 1954, dir. Ishirô Honda; *Death Note/Desu Nōto*, 2006, dir. Shūsuke Kaneko; *Departures*, 2008; *Thermae Romae* I and II, 2012 and 2014, dir. Hideki Takeuchi), foreign films (*You Only Live Twice*, 1967, dir. Lewis Gilbert; *Black Rain*, 1989, dir. Ridley Scott), and anime (Hayao Miyazaki's *My Neighbor Totoro/Tonari no Totoro*, 1988 and *Spirited Away/Sen to Chihiro no kamikakushi*, 2001), complete with links to regional tourism association homepages.

When asked if one of his films was shot overseas, Seijun Suzuki once quipped that in his films 'time and place are nonsense, so there's no need to film abroad' (Mes 2001). In the same interview, Suzuki was asked about an upcoming shoot scheduled for Paris and replied that he was invited to be a director for a short sequence in an omnibus film (presumably for the concept pitched by Tristan Carné that was eventually released as *Paris, je t'aime* in 2006, with Suzuki listed with a 'personal thanks' in the film's credits). When pressed on why he accepted the project, Suzuki responded, 'Because my producer forced me to do it! (laughs)', perhaps confirming his earlier thoughts that there was really no need to shoot abroad (Mes 2001).

The importance of location shows in the many cinematic exchanges between France and Japan. Films such as *Hiroshima, Mon amour*, which reappears in the narrative of Nobuhiro Suwa's 2001, *H Story*, where Beatrice Dalle stars as an unnamed actress struggling with her role in a remake of Alain Resnais's classic film. Suwa was also to use Paris as a location in *The Perfect Couple/Un couple parfait* (2005), and in *Yuki and Nina/Yuki to Nina* (2009), co-directed with French filmmaker and actor, Hippolyte Girardot. The importance of Tokyo as a setting is seen in numerous films throughout this book, perhaps none as overt as the triptych *Tokyo!* (2008), a collection of short film 'segments' directed by Michel Gondry, Leos Carax and Korea's Bong Joon Ho.

7

Confrontational cinema

Filmmakers from both France and Japan have long used the medium to represent the real world (through a variety of realist or formalist interpretations), a space populated by idiosyncratic characters who are subject to the social forces around them. The myriad influences that cross between the two national cinemas can be further revealed in their attitudes towards portraying scenes of overt sexual imagery, nudity, drug-taking and violence. Japan's reputation as a base for producing films that shock has been, in part, due to its respect for the art of cinema, and a refusal to impose heavily punitive restrictions on filmmakers. Internationally, controversies have arisen because of 'the increased flow of Japanese cultural materials that are treated differently by various viewer-ratings systems' (McLelland 2017: 6), where a film given a cautionary rating in Japan may be banned or classified 18+ in a foreign country thereby restricting its possible audience reach. In a similar mode, French film has also been able to move far beyond the morally restrictive confines of, say, the United States and its regulatory environment. Nevertheless, film continues to challenge and shock audiences with such hyper-realist films as Gaspar Noé's confronting rape-based backward-narrative, *Irréversible/Irreversible* (2002) and Bruno Dumont's equally savage *Twentynine Palms* (2003), where:

> In the age of the jaded spectator, the cynical cinéphile, this brutal intimacy model is a test case for film's continued potential to inspire, shock and bewilder – raw, unmediated reaction. (Palmer 2006: 22)

For Japanese cinema, provoking these raw reactions through 'brutal intimacy' have been synonymous with the works of some filmmakers, from the explicit sexual encounters in Nagisa Ōshima's 1976 *In the Realm of the Senses/Ai no Korîda* to the more absurdist (but no less shocking) violence and torture in Takashi Miike's 2001, *Ichi the Killer/Koroshiya 1*, and gratuitous bloodshed in Sono Sion's 2015 *Tag/Riaru Onigokko* [lit. A Real Game of Tag]. Is it, as Palmer suggests, that the filmmakers seek a 'raised artistic profile' (2006: 23) through confrontation? For Japan, these filmmakers are not on the periphery, but are a firm part of the film industry, perhaps in contrast to other nations where 'avant-garde filmmakers make a living as teachers, technicians within the film industry or through other day-jobs' (Smith 2000: 11).

Eroticism and sexploitation

The open nature and respect for artistic integrity in Japan provide filmmakers with wide parameters in which to operate. This is not to say that Japan is free of restrictions, on the contrary, Ōshima was charged with obscenity for a book of photographs and script notes from *In the Realm of the Senses*, (he was later acquitted in 1982), and before him, Tetsuji Takechi had been charged with obscenity for 1965's *Black Snow* (Alexander 2003), a film that had run into trouble 'from the script stage onward, and the first edited version submitted [to EIRIN] had to be recut' (Zahlten 2017: 44–5). Ōshima was able to effectively bypass Japanese obscenity laws by having the film stock developed in France, wary of such laws in the Criminal Code dating back many decades that prohibited 'the display of genitalia and pubic hair'. As the esteemed critic of Japanese film Donald Richie once exclaimed, '[i]n this hypocritical land, one hair and you are out!' (Burnett 1980: 182). This code remained in place until the 1990s when a loosening of regulations resulted in the 'much-heralded "liberation of hair" (*hea no kaiki*)' (Cather 2009: 61), in which the wording added the qualifying '*in principle* the pubic hair and sex organ should not be exposed' (italics added, Alexander 2003: 156, n. 32). When Ōshima's film was eventually released in Japan, almost one-third of the film had been removed or airbrushed out, a total of 'forty-nine objectionable scenes' (Alexander 2003: 152).

But France, too, has long nurtured a hands-off approach to cinema, where it often seemed to lead Europe (or at least, fell into line with liberal Scandinavian countries) in creating institutional support for the avant-garde, and a laissez-faire approach to on-screen sex, nudity and violence. The concept of a cinema that challenges the audience, can be seen through the lens of the early avant-garde filmmakers that dared move beyond modernism and its 'formal innovation in the arts', to a position in film where it 'implies something more radical, namely an attack on the very institutions and definitions of established practice' (Smith 2000: 15). This 'attack' could be found in French cinema's Surrealist movement beginning in the 1920s, with Germaine Dulac's 1928, *The Seashell and the Clergyman/La Coquille et le Clergyman*, cited as the most widely recognized French example of this cinematic form. In the post–Second World War era, this grounding was to create a sphere in which 'international art cinema' could thrive, led by not only younger French and European filmmakers such as Godard, Jean-Marie Straub and Danièle Huillet, or the seemingly unleashed Rainer Werner Fassbinder, but also in Japan through the work of Ōshima (Smith 2000: 17).

The sexploitation and fantasy oeuvre of Jean Rollin is an example of French horror cinema that has challenged censors and public morality. *The Rape of the Vampire/Le Viol du vampire* (1967) established new levels of extreme sexuality and graphic violence that capitalized on relaxing French censorship laws and the emergence of pornography into mainstream culture and indicated how previously marginalized voices were, post-May 1968, incorporating subversive gender ideologies into an aesthetic of excess. Indeed, the fusing of sex and violence in Rollin's vampire series (*The Nude Vampire/La Vampire nue* [1970], *Requiem for a Vampire/Vierges et vampires* [1971] and *The Shiver of the Vampires/Le Frisson des vampires* [1971]) should not be dismissed as pulp genre horror, but as a direct link back to the early surrealism of Franju, Buñuel and Gaston Leroux and the 'cinema of attractions' of Feuillade.

Often overlooked in Ōshima's films are his radical political views, such as in *Night and Fog in Japan/Nihon no Yoru to Kiri* (1960), where he stood against his nation's security treaty with the United States by creating a film that seemed to privilege anarchy and revolt. To emphasize his point, Ōshima drew on an accentuated theatrical 'stylized tableaux and an intricate flashback structure to explore conflict among different generations of protestors' (Smith 2000: 19). Venturing into propaganda-style techniques, Ōshima's film was confronting in its vitriolic rendering of patriotic fervour, and the stultifying environment of the studio system resulted in his leaving the relative security of Shōchiku studios to work as an independent.

The importance of Japan's confrontational cinema in the 1960s and 1970s is not to be underestimated as this was an era where filmmakers in particular 'challenged the socio-political basis of Japan's post-war economic prosperity through a stylistic assault on realism, and thematically through an attack on social mores' (Standish 2006: 331). The notion of an orderly post-war Japanese society was being turned on its head as Imamura, Ōshima, Suzuki and other filmmakers sought to employ allegory and metaphor to explain the changes wrought on their now passive nation over successive decades. Despite concerns by some that the increase in sexually explicit and sexually violent films would have an impact on social behaviour in Japan, there was no corresponding increase in the number of reported sex crimes (Alexander 2003: 153). Films continued to push boundaries as filmmakers sought to capture the idiosyncratic cultures of contemporary Japan, where 'even the most horrifying violence, as long as it is not real, can be judged purely aesthetically' (Buruma 2012: 223). The appropriation of eroticism and nudity into the subgenre of *pinku* films created an 'industrial genre', by which 'Pink Film paradoxically supported, and was indeed integral to, the [studio] system that ostensibly shunned it' (Zahlten 2017: 27).

More recently, filmmakers such as Mak P. Forever (aka Makku P. Fōevā) have continued the line of sexploitation (and deliberately titillating rip-offs of existing film titles) in films such as *Strip Mahjong: Battle Royale/Datsui-mâjan batoru rowaiaru* (2011) and sequels including *Strip Mahjong Idol: Warring States (Naked) Battle Royale/Datsui-mâjan Idol Sengoku jidai batoru rowaiaru* (2015). These films are produced independently or by smaller studios and production companies, unable to attract funding commitments from major studios. Other films are made as live-action adaptations of existing *ecchi* (sexualized) or pornographic manga or anime, such as the Sundome series of high school-based films, originally directed by Daigo Udagawa with *Sundome* (2007) and sequels *Sundome 2* and *Sundome 3* (2008) (respectively) and then by Kazuhiro Yokoyama with *Sundome New* and *Sundome New 2*.

A confrontational style is also the hallmark of French directors like Catherine Breillat. *Fat Girl/A ma soeur!* [lit. 'To My Sister!'] (2001) and *Romance* (1999) were compelling, if violent and troublesome, examinations of female sexuality, and even the deeply divisive *Anatomy of Hell/Anatomie de l'enfer* (2004), a study of blandly incessant sexual mores that was criticized by many as deliberately provocative, can be read as a provocative text 'that disrupts the comfort of both the pornographic and clinical gaze, while actively contemplating what it is to be female in a phallocentric and patriarchal society' (Foster 2016). As noted earlier, Gaspar Noé's films are also renowned for their often-confrontational style. In *Enter the Void* (2009), Noé set (and shot) the film in Tokyo, although as an English-language film, it mostly follows the exploits of ex-patriot Americans Oscar (Nathaniel Brown) and his sister, Linda (Paz de la Huerta) as they engage in a riot of hedonistic behaviours centred on illegal drug-taking and sex. The film's experimental style of constant motion camera work, neon-infused lighting and droning soundtrack mimic the hallucinatory trips that Oscar is continually embarking on. Flashbacks to Oscar's childhood and a tragic car accident that killed their parents have forever scarred Oscar and Linda, with Noé returning to the grisly, traumatic accident and its repercussions multiple times throughout the film. The Tokyo setting provides a *Blade Runner*-esque dystopian feel to the film, and Oscar and Linda's foreignness adds to their outsider status where their circle of friends are mostly expats (French, English) that are involved in the drug trades or sex industries.

Following a rapid barrage of titles flashing on the screen in a variety of fonts and colours, underscored by a rhythmic electronic soundtrack that sounds more than a little like the assault of noise from a Japanese pachinko parlour, the titles stop on the word ENTER. The film takes us immediately to Oscar's pov, complete with momentary 'blackouts' as he blinks. Oscar stands on his balcony looking out over the streets of downtown Tokyo and is joined by Linda, before she leaves, and Oscar is left alone in the crowded apartment. Soon, still from Oscar's pov, he begins lighting up a form of hallucinatory drug, and after a seemingly interminable number of attempts, begins to achieve the high he was seeking. As he does so the screen begins to fill with an array of kaleidoscopic shapes and colours, and the camera momentarily shifts from his pov to show us Oscar laying back on his bed experiencing the high and continuing to light his drug pipe. As happens throughout the entire film, the camera remains in motion, often spinning in aerial views above the protagonists or the cityscape with an underlying electro-industrial noise droning in the background.

Oscar's drug-induced fantasy of colours is finally interrupted (after almost four minutes of screen time) by a phone ringing, and the scene returns to his pov before he answers. Although Oscar was briefly shown from above, momentarily, it is not until he makes his way, groggily, to the bathroom and he sees himself reflected in the mirror that the audience really gets to see him, a young man with a crew-cut, barely out of his teens. The film remains from Oscar's pov for around twenty-five minutes as he joins his friend Alex (Cyril Roy) on a drug run, until he is fatally shot in a bathroom by Tokyo police while trying to dispose of the drugs that he was about to sell. In a shot that shifts from looking at Oscar's still, bloodied hands, the screen blurs before fading to black. When 'normal' vision returns, after a number of cryptic visual scenes of bathroom walls and bright lights, it is to an overhead shot looking down on Oscar's lifeless body draped around the (squat) toilet where he was shot. The scene is highly reminiscent of Danny Boyle's 1996 *Trainspotting* and its infamous toilet scene, where Ewan McGregor's Renton (Oscar is dressed almost identically in an olive-green t-shirt) dives into a toilet to retrieve his opiate suppositories. Noé's camera spirals down, excruciatingly slow towards Oscar's prostrate form, lingering slowly as it nears, before pulling upwards again as the police move in and drag his body out.

While all these visions create a bleak picture in *Enter the Void*, Noé intersperses his film with his trademark explicitly overt images of sexuality. Most of these images are of nudity centred around the nightclub where Linda performs her erotic dances, but often this extends into the dressing rooms and offices where casual sex frequently takes place (Figure 7.1).

The constant camera movements, the use of flashing light and constant drops in and out of focus all add to the surreal overlay of the film where glimpses of flesh and body parts are only transient. Later in the film, Noé increases the number of sexual acts shown, this time with glowing lights emanating from the genitals of anyone involved in some kind of sexual activity (including fellatio and cunnilingus) and ethereal wisps of light, or perhaps they are tendrils of smoke suggesting the intensity of the activity. Noé includes the vision of an abortion taking place, and eventually a view of intercourse from inside a vagina (presumably Linda's), with the head of a penis (presumably Alex's) thrusting towards the camera until it achieves its desired aim of ejaculation.

While these scenes suggest Noé is intent on gratuitous visions (a critique of many of his films), this up-close act of copulation sets off the film's denouement, with footage of sperm, now taking on a central pov (throwing up more uncertainties – is this a flashback to Oscar's conception, or is it a 'new' Oscar?) as it searches towards an egg and eventual fertilization. Soon a baby is born, and again from the baby's pov, there are blurry images of Linda, the new mother,

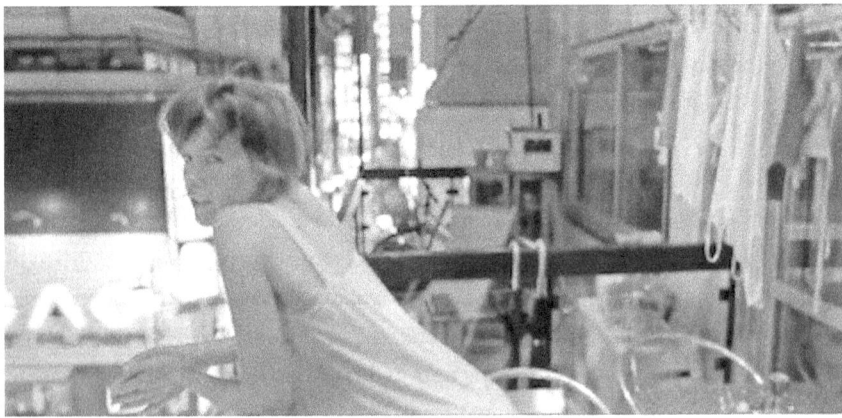

Figure 7.1 The calm before the storm in *Enter the Void* (2009).

slowly coming into focus as the baby reaches her breast and suckles for the first time. The baby watches and then cries as the umbilical cord is cut, before being carried out to a crib and the end titles erupt onto the screen with the words THE and then VOID, the companion-piece ending to the opening ENTER of the film. Like most of Noé's films, *Enter the Void* is confronting, illusive and at times, infuriating. His use of sometimes cryptic narrative structures, hardcore imagery and industrial-charged sounds are both innovative and derivative (of experimental cinema). By setting *Enter the Void* in Tokyo, Noé utilizes the constant twenty-four-hour-a-day movement of the city and its neon intensities, to frame both the narrative and visual aesthetics of the film.

Violence

A prolific filmmaker and writer (directing twenty-one feature films in the period 2007–17), Sono Sion is unafraid to challenge audiences with savage imagery, such as in *Guilty of Romance/Koi no Tsumi* (2011), which opens with detectives discovering a gruesome murder where bodies have been mutilated then the different body parts sewn back on other bodies. With the release of *Tag* in 2015, Sion went even further in his opening scenes of a school bus excursion, with a convoy of buses filled with jubilant schoolgirls being dissected by a mysterious razor-like wind. The drivers are decapitated and the girls (all except one, Mitsuko – played by Reina Triendl – who was bending down at an opportune time) have their torsos severed from the lower half of their bodies, leaving a pulsing, bloodied mess of lower bodies, still seated, on the now roofless buses. A dazed Mitsuko runs from the carnage and soon turns up at another school, only to find herself the only survivor (again) when her classroom is blasted apart by a machine-gun-wielding teacher. The violence is sudden and barely restrained, as the film lurches through a range of increasingly bizarre scenarios. Sion's film contains some confronting, hyper-violent moments, perhaps as Smith (2000: 12) notes of avant-garde cinema, '[a]n evening of avant-garde films ought to be thought-provoking and stimulating but offers no guarantee of being pleasurable or beautiful in the conventional senses' (Figure 7.2).

Violence of a different form appeared in an earlier high school-based splatterfest, the now-iconic *Battle Royale/Batoru Rowaiaru* (2000 Kinji Fukasaku), and its 2003 sequel *Battle Royale 2: Requiem/Batoru rowaiaru II: Chinkonka* (Kinji Fukasaku and Kenta Fukasaku). Similarities in the use of

Figure 7.2 Schoolgirl carnage in *Tag* (2015).

violence in *Tag* can also be directly drawn back to the *Battle Royale* films where 'the impact of competitive social relations are played out on the body' (Standish 2006: 338). In fact, the opening school bus scene in *Tag* is a direct homage to an opening scene in *Battle Royale*, only with a more violent outcome. Rather than presenting each incredible and bloodied death count in the Battle Royale films as a form of banal violence, it was said that Kinji Fukasaku wanted to reflect his own anger at the way Japan had taken on a subservient role to the United States when he was young (Standish 2011: 1). It was such a mood that had led to Japan's *New Wave* of filmmakers in the 1960s much as the French *nouvelle vague* of the 1950s captured the national mood in France. Japan's 1960s saw the rise of 'a dissentient group of *avant garde* filmmakers who created a counter-cinema that addressed a newly constituted, politically conscious audience' (Standish 2011: 1). Standish suggests that the *Requiem* reference in the title of the final *Battle Royale* film was not just an ode to the elder, recently deceased, Fukasaku (who died before the film's premiere), but a signal of the passing of the baton from the *New Wave* filmmakers of the 1960s to the young generation of the new millennium (including his son) 'to carry on the struggles of idealism in an increasingly utilitarian global geopolitical world order' (2011: 146). This may explain the global success of the Battle Royale films and their ongoing notoriety as essential films in the contemporary Japanese canon.

The Battle Royale films and *Tag* are also reminiscent of Miike Takashi's films where 'there is no redemptive humanism because his films form part of a postmodernist sensibility' that, to draw on Eagleton, portrays 'a world in which indeed there is no salvation, but on the other hand nothing to be saved' (Standish 2006: 338). The violence and torture in Miike's groundbreaking *Ichi the Killer/Koroshiya 1* (2001), based on the manga of the same name, are intense and unrelenting, as the savage Ichi (Nao Ōmori) becomes caught up in a *yakuza* (gangster) battle. Miike infuses the film with wry comic scenes and violence of such ridiculousness, that the film operates on a number of levels. The bloodthirsty, sadomasochistic yakuza boss, Kakihara (Tadanobu Asano), sees himself as the cruellest of them all, but when he discovers Ichi, he realizes that it is possible to be even more depraved. The violence in *Ichi the Killer* comes in all forms; guns are rarely fired as knives, blades and skewers are seen as more effective and damaging weapons. The film was released internationally in various versions, ranging from 129 minutes to 110 minutes, depending on the number of violent scenes that needed to be cut to satisfy local censors, but its comic-book style, over-the-top violence allowed it some freedom to be screened. It was later banned in Norway, Malaysia and Germany, but has generally survived as a cult film in art-house cinemas and on DVD and streaming channels. Excesses of violent imagery such as those in *Ichi the Killer* are seen as (or excused as) a part of Japanese entertainment that operates as a form of release, where it is seen as a form of recreation, or play, that 'often functions as a ritualised breaking of taboos, which are sacrosanct in daily life' (Buruma 2012: 222).

Released in 2013, comedian Hitoshi Matsumoto's *R100* (the title refers to the intended rating age for the audience – a comic nod to the idea of NC15 or R18) offers the promise of confrontation but is a generally light-hearted (and occasionally odd) foray into the world of sadomasochism, with a B-story about a filmmaker creating a film that will only achieve an R100 rating. While the film avoids nudity and graphic sex, even at the level of the soft-porn found in *pinku* films, it does question the environment that governs the film industry and the application of moral standards. Matsumoto's film applies a comic touch to a sensitive issue in Japan, where the vision of the artist/auteur should be given free rein. For Standish, this was perhaps first explored in the mid-1960s with the overt sexuality and miscegenation in *Black Snow* and with Imamura's *The Pornographers*, a film that questioned the 'conflict between spontaneous "animal" sexuality and contemporary morality' (2011: 101). Matsumoto's *R100* toys with the ways that institutional structures are put in place to 'protect' the audience, but with little regard for the aims of the artist.

Censorship codes in Japan have not only impacted upon local films but have also had to be re-thought when being applied to foreign films and, as noted, proved detrimental to the Japanese release of *In the Realm of the Senses*. Questions arose around whether Western standards regarding obscene material should be upheld, with Alexander providing a possibly difficult scenario:

> an 'art film' cast in a French setting, reflecting French (rather than Japanese) cultural values, and expressed in the nuances of the French language, would be difficult for Japanese officials to edit without totally losing the 'artistic meaning' of the film. (2003: 156)

This resulted in many foreign films (except those that breached the visual code relating to 'pubic hair and sex organs') entering Japan in unedited form, with, by the 1970s, some commercial successes such as the French series of soft-core films *Emmanuelle* (beginning in 1974, dir. Just Jaeckin) and *The Story of O/Histoire d'O* (beginning in 1975, also directed by Just Jaeckin).

Preceding this international rush of films, Yoshida's *Eros + Massacre* was controversial in 1969 not just as a three-hour epic but for its partial adherence to the *pinku* films of the era, with sex and nudity, and a scene that features Eiko Sokutai (played by Toshiko Ii) masturbating in the shower (with a carefully placed reflection of light obscuring her genitals), a scene that begins with images of men playing rugby as Eiko's panting breath is the only sound heard. The shot then cuts to the shower, in what looks to be homage to Hitchcock's *Psycho*, although Yoshida's camera continues to pan slowly down Eiko's naked body, whereas Hitchcock's film cuts away to more murderous images. A later scene, perhaps even more controversially, features an incestuous moment of lovemaking between a brother and sister (one of Sakae's lovers, in the flashback sequences), an act caught by the brother's wife.

While sex is a contentious area for those charged with monitoring and categorizing films, violence can also be difficult to clearly define. With its sporadic bursts of savage violence set against moments of peace and serenity (nature, stills of artworks, beach walks and the solemnity of dealing with chronic disease), Takeshi Kitano's *Fireworks/Hana-Bi* shook international audiences. Here was Kitano, the household-name TV comedian, shooting contemporary Japan in a way that 'shrewdly inserts' Kitano the filmmaker into 'an unorthodox, atypical nationality that suits the transcultural forms international festivals celebrate' (Davis 2001: 51). Kitano's portrayal as Yoshitaka Nishi, a *Dirty Harry*-style, good-cop-gone-bad, clearly resonated with audiences in Japan and overseas, serving as a standout example of 'the discourses of the "new violence" of the 1990s [where] good versus evil is displaced onto the dominator and the dominated' (Standish 2006: 326). Nishi's brutality is countered by his concern for his ailing wife, Miyuki (Kayoko Kishimoto) and his deeply troubled, wheelchair-bound partner Horibe (Ren Osugi). The film's denouement manages to capture these emotional binaries in one short, tragic moment that occurs off-screen; Kitano, for a change, sparing the audience from what would be a visibly gruesome event.

Kitano's directing career has continued apace as he traverses genres from twisted autobiography in *Takeshis'* (2005), *Glory to the Filmmaker/Kantoku: Banzai!* (2007) and *Achilles and the Tortoise/Akiresu to Kame* (2008) to comedy such as the (*yakuza*-based) *Ryuzo and the Seven Henchmen/Ryûzô to 7 nin no kobun tachi* (2015) to violent *yakuza* dramas such as *Outrage/Autoreiji* (2010) and its sequels *Outrage Beyond/Autoreiji: Biyondo* (2012, sometimes listed as *Beyond Outrage*) and *Outrage Coda/Autoreiji sai Shūshō* (2017). The line between actor and filmmaker is often blurred (as explored in his somewhat surreal autobiographical works listed earlier, or even his performance in *Battle Royale* where he retains his name as Kitano-*sensei* – Teacher Kitano), where he presents 'not narratives that offer any essential truths or ideals; rather we are offered a transcendence of boundaries that is open to multiple readings' (Taylor-Jones 2013: 106). The *Outrage* series of films feature a complex web of hyper-masculine characters (there are few women in the trilogy), gangsters (including bosses and 'underbosses'), corrupt cops, corrupt politicians and corrupt businessmen. Each film is set out in a procedural narrative, with each containing a suspenseful 'slow burn' approach, with violence just a hair-trigger away. Kitano (listed in credits as Beat Takeshi) stars in each of the films as Otomo, placing himself in a supporting role as a loyal, cold-blooded *yakuza* henchman around whom each story unfolds. The longevity of this type of gangster genre appears to be because 'the *yakuza* world with its *giri* [sense of honour and duty], its emotional conflicts, and its social suffering, is a stylized microcosm of Japanese society' (Buruma 2012: 182). While the style and narrative structures of *yakuza-eiga* remain the same as films from forty or fifty years ago, the *yakuza* films of today still shine a light on contemporary Japan.

Many Japanese films from the 1990s and early 2000s resulted in 'the increasing drift towards greater visceral appeals through the spectacularization of violence encouraged in the digital age [that] has further shifted the emphasis away from violence as a performative language of morality or justice to the display of phallic power as the endpoint' (Standish 2006: 326). Thus, the *Battle Royale* films appeared to be the denouement of this, a blood-filled epitaph to a decade of on-screen violence, that filmmakers like Sono Sion seemed keen to return to less than a decade later. In Kitano's case, the first *Outrage* film sees Kitano's Otama end up in a high-security prison. In *Outrage Beyond*, when the troublemaking, smug, and extremely corrupt Detective Kataoka (Fumiyo Kohinata – *Survival Family*'s hapless dad, in a more sinister role) springs for Otama's parole, Otama suggests that he is not worthy of parole, as he slashed the face of another inmate. Kataoka, who is plotting and dealing with several gangs at once, has an ulterior motive for Otama's release, and dismisses the knife attack:

> **Kataoka**: Win some, lose some. All's fair, yakuza-style.
> **Otomo**: Even a yakuza has principles which he lives by.

Otama is like many of Kitano's quick-tempered characters that hark back to the great samurai and warlord performances by Toshiro Mifune (including *Throne of Blood* and *Seven Samurai*), rapidly escalating from almost whispered dialogue to loudly barked orders (usually telling a subordinate to kill an adversary), but in a way involving a clench-jawed yelling, often while seated. The stillness of the character emphasizes the rising volume and dramatic impact of their words. The ambitious Underboss Ishihara (former young acting heartthrob, Ryō Kase) exemplifies this method, flying into rage in an instant. When one of Ishihara's henchmen returns from a failed mission to assassinate Otama, Ishihara, seated behind his desk, admonishes his underlings. Standing in front of Ishihara are Okamoto (Shun Sugata) and his son, the failed assassin; others fill the room, including Gomi (Ken Mitsuishi) and Shiroyama (Tatsuo Nadaka), all of whom are older than Ishihara, but in disregard to Japanese etiquette, he shows no deference to their age. Ishihara begins: (capitals to indicate the fluctuating pitch and his rising anger):

> **Ishihara**: You said he's good, BUT HE'S USELESS!
> **Failed Assassin**: I shot him, but the elevator was small.
> **Ishihara**: DID YOU HEAR ME? I ASKED IF YOU KILLED HIM!
> **Failed Assassin**: I'm pretty sure the bullets hit his belly.
> **Ishihara** (turning to Okamoto): What's wrong with YOUR FAMILY? YOU CAN'T KILL ONE LOUSY PUNK? OKAMOTO! WHAT KIND OF EXAMPLE ARE YOU SETTING?
> **Okamoto** (*bowing*): Sorry.

Ishihara: Shiroyama and Gomi. (*They stand.*) Are you just going to sit around watching?
Shiroyama and Gomi: No.
Ishihara: We don't provide FOR INCOMPETENTS LIKE YOU! I'll have your turfs seized at the NEXT EXECUTIVE MEETING!

The delivery of dialogue in angry tones, littered with threats to the physical safety of anyone not in support of their aligned yakuza clan, is soon followed up by acts of violence (Figure 7.3).

Point-blank shootings and a bitten-off finger (an inventive twist on the practice of *yubitsume* – slicing off the tip of a finger as a form of torture or sacrifice, usually done with a sword or knife) pale in comparison to later incidents, first escalated by Otama himself (who is very restrained for the first hour of the film), when he reaches for a power drill. Later, in one of Kitano's trademark understatements, he (as Otama) invites Ishihara to play baseball with him. The following scene features an automated baseball pitcher that adds an almost comical element to an extremely violent and repetitive act that is soon followed by mass shootings and a stabbing in slow-motion that emphasizes the horrifically wet sounds of each knife plunge. *Outrage Beyond* reflects Kitano's desire to confront audiences with surprising amounts of violence, delivered as sudden punctuating points throughout his films, often through the use of 'static compositional shots that frame, rather than support and interact, with the action' (Taylor-Jones 2013: 111). The viewer is left with a strange sense of physical detachment from the violence in Kitano's films, which does not detract

Figure 7.3 Angry Ishihara in *Outrage Beyond* (2012).

from their impact, but in many ways adds to their power. While other directors may use fast edits and multi-angle close-ups to reinforce a violent act, Kitano pulls back or uses the static framing of his shots to ensure that all the action takes place through the movements of his protagonists.

Where Kitano's films are situated in the oeuvre of Japanese cinema is perhaps hard to determine. The definition of 'art house' seems most apt, but as Standish notes, art-house cinema 'has historically defined and distinguished itself in opposition to its commercial counterpart, [and] aspires to "high" culture status, but in reality, occupies an often-indeterminate position between these two polarities' (2011: 5). The original *Outrage* had the sixty-first highest box office take in 2010, with US$8 million. As its sequel, *Outrage Beyond* took a reasonable US$16.9 million at the Japanese box office in 2012, ranking forty-third, suggesting that commercial success is not out of the reach of such a film. The supposedly final part of what has become a trilogy, *Outrage Coda*, ranked fortieth in 2017, but with a much smaller take of just over US$11 million.

While Kitano's films often seem to feature violence for its own sake, earlier filmmakers such as Imamura and Ōshima dared to question the formalities of institutionalized Japan and the sanctity of marriage, and for Imamura, 'the characters in the marginalized societies depicted in his films come together as a result of spontaneous (sometimes violent) sexual unions' (Standish 2011: 81). The institution of marriage may be sacrosanct, as featured strongly in both *Tokyo Story* and *Tokyo Sonata*, but Japan's filmmakers have long taken risks in exploring what is beyond marriage. Even Sono Sion's *Guilty of Romance* operates around a theme of unfulfilling marriage when the bored housewife, Izumi (Megumi Kagurazaka), begins looking to explore her sexuality and becomes more and more adventurous, a theme that returns later in the film when, disguised, she is forced to have sex with her unsuspecting husband, Yukio (Kanji Tsuda), in a sleazy love hotel. The film's plot shifts between a murder investigation and the questionable act of infidelity, against a '*Clockwork Orange*-style of violence, sado-masochism, prostitution and murder' (Pugsley 2015: 105). Such imagery serves to reinforce the belief that 'contemporary Japanese taboos against various forms of "sexuality", and definitions of "obscenity" represent a bastardization of an original indigenous Japanese erotics' (Standish 2011: 101). The films of Imamura in the 1960s, for instance, created a platform where 'female sexuality is renegotiated through reinvented "nativist" traditions that ostensibly predate Japan's modernization and . . . still linger beneath the surface of contemporary Japanese society' (2011: 82). In other words, Japanese filmmakers willing to push societal taboos through their films could be said to be tapping into the 'real' Japan, where sexuality was not taboo, certainly not in art. Standish looks to Donald Richie's appraisals of the works of Ozu and Imamura as two ends of the spectrum: Ozu's 'official' Japan with its beauty, its hierarchies and its forms of loyalty and devotion, and Imamura's 'real' Japan populated by the 'selfish, lusty, amoral, innocent, [and] natural' (2011: 82–3). It is this latter category that contemporary filmmakers such as Takashi Miike and Sono Sion are often labelled. While this may be the case for a number of these filmmakers' works, they reflect an awareness of the former category and present films or sections within their films that draw from this 'official' image of Japan. Sion's *Himizu/Mole*, for instance, is infused with an underlying narrative about loyalty (or the lack thereof) between parents and their children. The addition of a catastrophe (the Fukushima tsunami) means that the protagonists, reclusive teenager Sumida (Shota Sometani) and adventurous Keiko (Fumi Nikaido), need to be self-reliant as they avoid Sumida's violent father and Keiko's destructive mother. Sion avoids the overly graphic violence of *Guilty of Romance*, and his later *Tag*, in *Himizu*, instead of focusing on the ways that the young Japanese are caught between passive acceptance and actively seeking a positive future.

Each of these films reflects the sensitive elements of Japanese society where, as Alexander maintains, '[t]ransgressions of social mores are shocking to the public consciousness because they intrude on the expected level of public quietude' (2003: 161). With time and repetition, though, levels of offence or revulsion to those transgressions may lessen 'as the objects of revulsion, such as graphic depictions of sexuality or sexual violence, appear more commonly in public discourse' (Alexander 2003: 161). Such attitudes may explain films such as *Dawn of the Felines/Mesunekotachi* (2017, dir. Kazuya Shiraishi), a sometimes-lighthearted film with frequent sexual imagery and underlying social commentary about the everyday lives of a trio of sex workers in Tokyo. The quotidian aspects of the women's lives include not only the boring waiting for clients to call their agency, 'Young Wives' Paradise', but also their childcare responsibilities, or their discomfort with their escort service employing a driver who asks personal questions about their sexual activities. The film structures individual narratives for each of the women and their clients, highlighting the psychological exchange that takes place beyond the physical. Rie (played by Michie) offers comfort to an old widower, but becomes emotionally attached to him, Yui (Satsuki Maue) is an abusive single mother, whose favourite customer is a stage comedian with a penchant for bondage. Masako (Juri Ihata) meets with a wealthy young man, a *hikikomori* (a 'shut-in', or recluse) who trades online and observes the world through his computer screen, he has all his food delivered (what looks to be a diet entirely of pizza) and sees no need to leave his apartment. The film's presentation of transgressions to social mores therefore acts as a loose framework rather than a focused theme throughout the film.

Part of a commemorative series of five films commissioned by Nikkatsu for the forty-fifth anniversary of its famous 'Roman Porno' *pinku* (soft pornography) films, *Dawn of the Felines* can be seen as a more realist, poignant portrayal of contemporary Japan than the earlier films that eschewed strong narratives for opportunities to feature nudity and sex. The film name-checks its 1972 predecessor, *Night of the Felines*, but attempts to create a more complex storyline. The requirement that the films in this series require a sex scene every ten minutes, prohibits *Dawn of the Felines* from establishing an intimate link between the audience and its characters. Instead, the film presents societal 'transgressions' not necessarily through the career path of the women but in other ways such as the fine line between sadomasochism as a form of entertainment in an adult bar and a more animalistic use in a private setting, where the lines between consensual and non-consensual sex are blurred.

Regardless of which medium is being used, the line between the erotic and the pornographic is highly subjective, and Alexander uses a French example to illustrate how *In the Realm of the Senses* could be seen as non-pornographic. He points to the trial of the Marquis de Sade and the finding that 'while the writings of de Sade were offensive to the average man's sense of modesty and in opposition to proper concepts of sexual morality, they did not (effectively) appeal to sexual passion and therefore could not be considered obscene' under Article 175 of French law at that time (2003: 165, n. 71). The distancing of fantasy from reality has long been accepted in Japanese society, where '[a]s long as the *tatemae* (façade) of hierarchy, etiquette and propriety is upheld, the frustrated company man can look at pictures of tied-up women as much as he likes' (Buruma 2012: 224). In other words, what counts as offensive may, for the most part, be in the eye of the beholder.

France and Japan both feature heavily in Olivier Assayas's *Demonlover* (2002), a tale of corporate greed and mistrust centred on the production of pornographic anime and 3D animation for a global market. Critic-turned-filmmaker Assayas (also the son of noted screenwriter and director, Jacques Rémy) has a long association with Asian cinema, including his work with Hong Kong actor Maggie Cheung (leading to a brief marriage with her), and a feature-length TV documentary on Taiwanese director Hou Hsiao-Hsien for the *Cinéma de notre temps* (*Cinema of Our Times*) series on French public television. *Demonlover* charts the rising importance of the adult online film market, and the lucrative trade deals that provide distribution networks for animation produced in Japan for global audiences. The ambitious Diane (played by Denmark's Connie Nielsen, fresh from a major role in Ridley Scott's 2000 *Gladiator*) ruthlessly climbs her way to a senior position in a company licensing Japanese adult films. Working with, or against the equally ambitious Hervé (Charles Berling), Diane becomes caught in a web of complex double-crosses as she negotiates with competing firms to angle for control of the market. The Japanese links trail off (apart from a later dinner in a Japanese restaurant in Paris), as the film takes a decidedly darker, more violent turn. In a sense, Japan's importance in the film wanes as it becomes evident that it is a stable and constant source of animated material. *Demonlover* explores further, though, with the discovery of links in a partner company to torture-porn sites. Assayas closes the film with an acerbic comment on the creation of the torture sites to merely satisfy teenage boys around the world, surreptitiously using their parents' credit cards.

While the portrayal of violence can make for engrossing (if not disturbing) action scenes, at times it is the aftermath of violence that has a more lasting effect. Bruno Dumont's 1999 film, *Humanity/L'humanité* (sometimes listed as simply *Humanité*) is one such film where in the opening minutes, after a potentially tragic scene where a man running across fields, trips and lands face down in mud (reminiscent of the tragic ending of Varda's *Vagabond*). The man's face is slightly moved to one side, so one eye is visible, but his stillness suggests that he is dead, or at the very least, unconscious. Suddenly he moves, and shortly after he returns to his car and it is revealed that he is a policeman, a low-ranking Superintendent, Pharaon de Winter (Emmanuel Schotté). Pharaon (as he is casually referred to by most characters throughout the film) seems stunned, and when he receives a call on his radio, he answers slowly before we see his car (even more slowly) drive away down the country lane. The relatively tranquil shot then switches to a graphic shot of a woman's, or girl's, hairless vagina, bloodied and bruised, followed by more shots establishing the damaged body of the girl/woman, dirt-smeared and covered with ants, lying in long grass. The shot moves to a longer view, the girl's lifeless upper body stretching away from the camera down a ditch, obscuring any identifying features about her age, or who she might be. In these short glimpses into the grotesque remnants of past violence, Dumont sets the tone for the film.

Despite the fact that he had never acted before, Schotté won the Best Actor award at Cannes for his performance as Pharaon. It is a complex portrayal, where it is difficult to understand whether he is some kind of idiot savant, or someone deeply traumatized by past events. There are many scenes and performances in the film that recall the discomfiting style of David Lynch, with even the startling opening discovery reminiscent of Jeffrey Beaumont's (Kyle MacLachlan) unearthing of a severed human ear in *Blue Velvet*. As with Lynch's film, the violent act that has been committed is an inciting incident that hangs over every action from that point forward. Dumont's unsettling long takes of characters silently staring, with close-ups of perspiring necks or windblown hair, seems to make every male character, including Pharaon, into a suspect; as if the silence presupposes guilt. In a review of the film, Roger Ebert wrote, 'We wait for something to happen and then realize that something is happening – this is happening' (2000). Late in the film, Pharaon travels to England as part of his investigation. While in a high building he sees a fight happening on the street below, but even though the violence is real, he simply turns away from the window disinterested, detached from the immediacy of life and the events that occur before him.

Conclusion

The overt use of violent and sexual imagery in both French and Japanese films reflects the desire for filmmakers to present narratives imbued with heightened human emotions. In Japan, there were few female directors during the height of the *pinku* phase in the 1960s and 1970s, or few who owned up to working in that industry, with some changing their name to a more masculine form, as '[a] female director's name would have disturbed the appearance of totalised male subjectivity' (Zahlten 2017: 68). Even today, it seems only filmmakers like Mika Ninagawa with her 2012 film *Helter Skelter/Herutā Sukerutā*, a live-action adaptation of a heavily sexualized and violent manga of the same name, appear to be willing to take risks. In France, Catherine Breillat has boldly pushed forward with sexually charged films, as has Julia Ducournau (*Raw/Grave* [2016] and *Titanium/Titane* [2021]), who has, more recently, looked unflinchingly at body horror, trauma and cannibalism(Figure 7.4).

From another direction, a number of contemporary male directors in Japan appear to thrive on films that push the boundaries between eroticism and outright

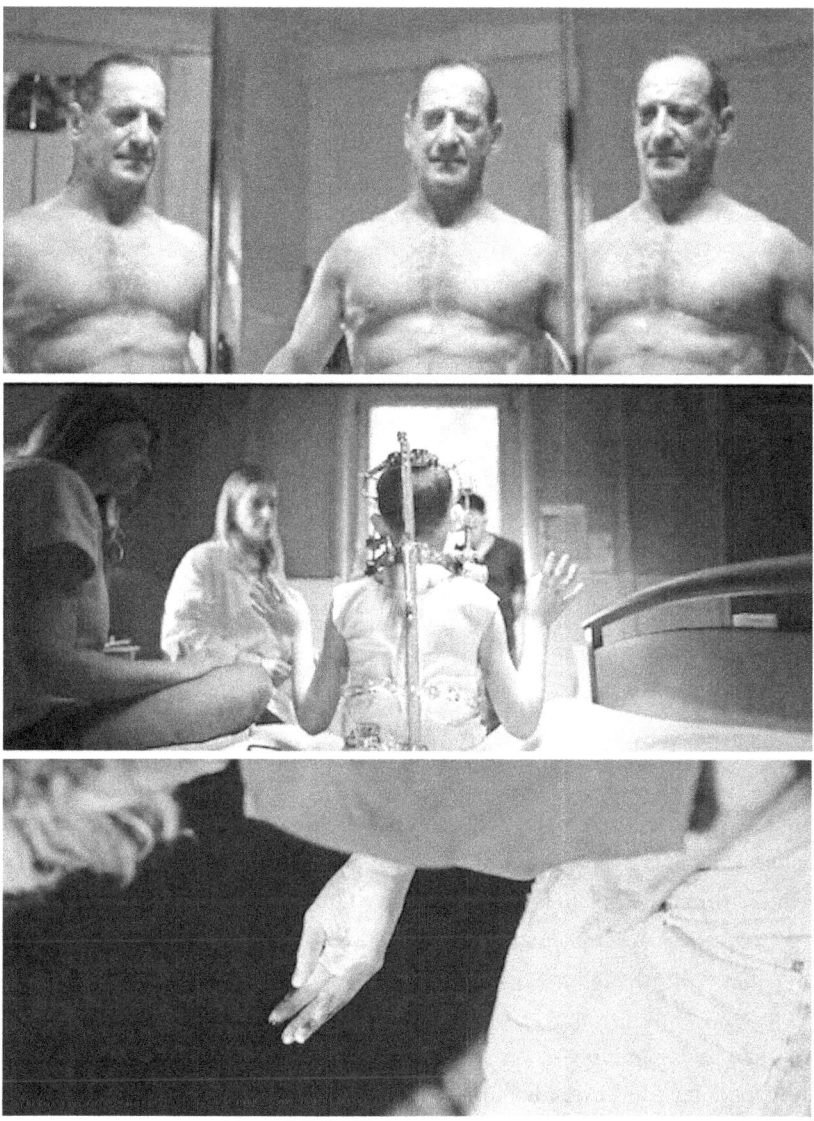

Figure 7.4 Three bodies in *Titane* (2021).

pornography. Filmmakers like Kōta Yoshida (*Woman's Hole/Onno no anna*, 2014), Kazuhiro Yokoyama (*Sundome New*), Yûki Aoyama and Iggy Coen (*What's Going on With My Sister?/Saikin, imôto no yôsu ga chotto okashii n da ga?*, 2014) and even the prolific Sono Sion (*Guilty of Romance* and *Antiporno/Anchiporuno*, 2016) are mostly unafraid of the censor, keen to exploit a large market that sits within a field of highly sexualized and violent manga and anime imagery.

8

Life, death and states of being

While the joy of life is often celebrated by filmmakers, the concept of the 'human condition' is one that is inevitably punctuated by the theme of death, a theme that often makes for a more challenging film experience. Death as a cinematic theme can be handled in a poignant manner, such as in Yōjirō Takita's *Departures*, where the preparation of bodies for the funeral process in a Japanese village is handled in a (mostly) caring way, or in Michael Haneke's *Amour* (2012), where an elderly couple faces their mortality in their Paris apartment. Such films offer discourses on the fundamental, or even existential, states of being – discourses that oscillate between universal and culturally specific beliefs and practices. They force us, the audience, to question our own mortality and how we will deal with the death of loved ones, or the impending finality of our own lives. While French films may be underpinned by beliefs developed through Western religions, Japanese films can reflect attitudes honed through an amalgam of Eastern concepts such as Buddhism and Shintoism, with some reference to Catholicism and other forms of Western religion that have found their way to Japan over the years. The cinematic landscape, as it were, can therefore be strewn with images influenced not just by the art and techniques of film but by the sacred underpinnings that birthed modernity's secular societies. Sono Sion has shown an understanding of this in *Love Exposure/Ai no Mukadashi* (2008) when he offers 'Japanese perceptions of Western religion and iconography' through the portrayal of images of the cross and allusions to Christianity, sacrifice and martyrdom (Pugsley 2013: 118).

The power of film to tap into our emotions is strong, and as Kuhn notes, '[t]hrough its organization within the frame of space, time, stillness and motion, film is capable ... of replaying or re-evoking certain states of being which are commonly experienced as inner' (2005: 407). Filmmakers seek to exploit these 'states of being' by triggering emotional responses, and through narratives based on key themes such as death, joy, pain or love, they are able to negotiate the emotional terrain that can be culturally specific or universal in nature. The very act of storytelling follows what seems to be a natural arc from birth to life to death. While this may seem an obvious path to follow in the construction of a story or film, it presupposes a linearity that is not necessarily present in all cultures. Juzo Itami, best known in the West for his films with female protagonists, the noodle-shop-based *Tampopo* and the 'eroticised tales of coercion and bureaucracy' (Pugsley 2013: 53) in *A Taxing Woman* and its sequel, sums up this different approach: 'In Japanese films, instead of a straight line you have a circle. The time frame in Christian societies and Japanese society is totally different . . . In the Christian worldview, time is moving toward a conclusion – the Last Judgement – and cannot be reversed' (Schilling 1999: 78). Itami muses on how this reflects on the narrative structure of Japanese films, reflecting, 'I don't know whether it's right to try and make Japanese films in the Western straight-line time frame' (Schilling 1999: 78).

Death has been a key theme in Japanese cinema, often utilizing 'straight-line time frames', despite Itami's musings. The linear form of the temporal, inevitable march towards death is central to the narrative of films such as Ōshima Nagisa's 1968 *Death by Hanging/Kôshikei*, and *In the Realm of the Senses/Ai no Korîda*, Yasuzô Masumura's *Blind Beast/Môjû* (1969), Yoshishige Yoshida's 1969 *Eros + Massacre/Erosu Purasu Gyakusatsu*, and any number of Kurosawa's films, especially *Ran* where valour, honour and sacrifice are key themes. The final act of Ozu's *Tokyo Story*, for instance, centres on the death of Grandmother Tomi. During the funeral service, the youngest son Keizō gets up and walks out of the service, to sit on the verandah of the temple. His eldest sister follows, and he tells her that he hates the sound of the monks chanting – 'As I hear it, I feel as if Mother were becoming smaller, bit by bit' – but then reasons with himself, in reference to an earlier joking comment from his colleague – 'I can't lose her now. No one can serve his parents beyond the grave' – and he returns to the service. Keizō's acceptance signals his acknowledgement of the cycle of life and its ultimate endpoint, death.

Tokyo Story also allows for discussions of a more existential nature. Following the death of Grandmother Tomi, the rest of the family can barely hide their eagerness to divide up their mother's belongings so they can return quickly to Tokyo. Kyoko, the youngest child, is a schoolteacher left at home to care for her widower father, who speaks her mind to her sister-in-law, Noriko, telling her that the other siblings are all selfish:

> **Kyoko**: Wanting her clothes right after her death. I felt so sorry for poor mother. Even strangers would have been more considerate!

Noriko, ever the optimist, tries to reason:

> **Noriko**: But look, Kyoko. At your age I thought so too. But children do drift away from their parents. A woman has her own life away from her parents, when she becomes Shige's [eldest sister's] age. So she meant no harm, I'm sure. They have to look after their own lives.
> **Kyoko**: I wonder. I won't ever be like that. Then what's the point of being family?
> **Noriko**: It is. But children become like that gradually.
> **Kyoko**: Then you too?
> **Noriko**. Yes. I may become like that, in spite of myself.

After a short pause, Kyoko responds:

> **Kyoko**: Isn't life disappointing?
> **Noriko**: (smiling) Yes, it is.

Kyoko turns away. Ozu's reflection on the pathos of things (*mono no aware*) is at its strongest in this scene, concisely summarized in these final lines and Noriko's quiet acceptance.

The 'straight-line' narrative also features in many French films. *Amour* stars veteran actors Jean-Louis Trintignant (. . . *And God Created Woman/Et Dieu . . . créa la femme*, 1956; *Three Colors: Red/Trois Couleurs: Rouge*, 1994), as Georges, and Emmanuelle Riva (*Hiroshima, Mon Amour*), as Anne. As a mostly set-piece drama that takes place in their apartment in Paris, *Amour* presents the dilemma of a loving couple forced to adapt to a new life when Anne becomes disabled through a stroke. The freedom of movement beyond their apartment takes on a greater importance, as family and friends question whether they should consider moving to an aged-care facility. Haneke's film is, like many of his others, intensely claustrophobic, with the confines of the (relatively large) apartment accentuated through close-ups and amplified sounds of breathing, a boiling kettle or doors closing, that all add to the cloying atmosphere of impending death that frequents the film (Figure 8.1).

The threat of dying also plays a major thematic role in an earlier film, Julian Schnabel's *Le Scaphandre et le Papillon/The Diving Bell and The Butterfly* (2007). It is based on the true story of the life of top magazine editor Jean-Dominique Bauby (Mathieu Amalric), whose paralysis after a stroke sees him trapped inside his own body. The spectre of death looms large, as either a sorry end to a dynamic life or as a sweet relief from the torture and humiliation of

Figure 8.1 Jean-Louis Trintignant watches and listens in *Amour* (2012).

being totally dependent on others for daily survival. Schnabel explores the psychological trauma of Bauby's entrapment, made all the more frightening because

> one of the distinctive features of film's organization of space within the frame and its play of stasis and movement is its capacity to express and evoke – at the levels of feeling and memory – highly invested objects, spaces and passages, in particular those which have to do with the task of negotiating inner and outer worlds. (Kuhn 2010: 96)

For Bauby, this includes not just the inanimate objects that he can no longer reach (books, food) but the personal touch of his wife, children or lover. As with the portrayal of deafness noted earlier in *The Family Belier* and *My Summer in Provence,* or blindness in *Radiance*, the representation of what is seen as disability creates tensions around authenticity and realism. Although writing on Japanese cinema, Wren's thoughts prove universal when he writes:

> the disabled subject must be repeatedly inscribed; and the (d)enunciatory act of inscription erases in order to maintain that subject, in precisely the same manner in which collective, national – able-bodied and participating – subjects must trace and retrace their spatial and temporal boundaries and the identity of part and whole and past and present in order to remain in circulation. The disabled occupy not the border but a place beyond and without, an entirely alien location where they are outcasts. (2016: 236)

While this paints a seemingly dire picture (and perhaps rightly so in relation to Wren's central focus on Akira Kurosawa's 1970 *Dodes'ka-den/Dodesukaden*), we can imagine that it also conjures up the internal struggles faced by the disabled characters – whether Bauby in *The Diving Bell* or the stroke-afflicted Anne in *Amour* – who find themselves in 'a place beyond and without'.

In *Rust and Bone*, Marion Cotillard's Stéphanie is a water park entertainer who performs with killer whales. During a show, one of the whales misjudges the distance to the stage and lands almost on top of Stéphanie, tearing away the platform she is standing on. In the turmoil, Stéphanie is severely injured and after coming out of a coma finds that both her legs have been amputated below the knee. The psychological impact weighs heavily on her, and she soon tries to take her own life. When her attempt fails, she continues her rehabilitation in the hospital, only to return home still plagued by suicidal thoughts and despair. Stéphanie's developing relationship with the emotionally distant Ali, nevertheless, helps her to slowly emerge from her ongoing trauma, with *Rust and Bone* ending on a note of positivity and Stéphanie's recovery and acceptance of her new life with prosthetic legs.

Another filmmaker to reflect his thoughts on the concept of death as an integral part of life's *mono no aware* is Jun Ichikawa (who has paid homage to Ozu in a number of his films, perhaps no more overtly than in 1995's *Tokyo Siblings/Tōkyō Kyodai*). In an interview discussing his *Dying at a Hospital/Byoin de Shimu to iu Koto*, Ichikawa states that 'Death is an equaliser' (Schilling 1999: 105). Ichikawa's cinematic approach to death affects his visual style, to the point that, as he admits, 'I didn't want to do the closeups of doctor's faces or suffering patients that you usually find in hospital films', preferring to portray a more detached sentiment, 'images that would be similar to a picture painted from a middle distance' (Schilling 1999: 105). In one of his final films, Ichikawa's *Tony Takitani/Tonî Takitani* (2004), the director draws on historical photographs from Japan's tragic involvement in its invasion of China and the immediate post-Second World War period to set up the story of the eponymous Tony, the son of a Jazz musician, Shozaburo (Issei Ogata), who was captured in China (then released), who returns to Japan and marries a short time later. Shozaburo's wife dies just after giving birth, and the musician decides upon an American name for his son, Tony, both in honour of a foreign friend but also because he feels that the American presence in Japan will be around for a long time into the future. Tony's father continues to tour with his music, so the boy has a lonely upbringing, which Ichikawa presents through the film's opening of a young man's sparse voiceover narration (by Hidetoshi Nishijima). These scenes are accompanied by an unembellished piano score and a vignette of still and moving images, with the young Tony occasionally speaking in synchronicity with the voiceover, thereby narrating his own story, but in the third person. The effect is slightly unnerving, adding a melancholy air to the film, and a sense of impending doom. An almost identical voiceover narrative style is used throughout the generational family drama, *Eternity/Éternité* (2016), by French/Vietnamese director Tran Anh Hung. Given that this was Tran's first film after his Japanese-made adaptation of Haruki Murakami's bestselling novel *Norwegian Wood/Noruwei no Mori* (2010), perhaps this later film was influenced by Ichikawa.

When the opening titles to *Tony Takitani/Tonî Takitani* arrive, some twelve minutes into the film, they act as a temporal divide. Suddenly, Tony (Issei Ogata plays both the father and the son) is a grown man, an artist making his living from illustrating, perhaps in his forties, but an insular, solitary man. The film tracks quickly, with Tony now possibly in his fifties and successful in his work, but still living alone, when he meets the younger Eiko (Rie Miyazawa), who works for one of his clients. Again, Ishikawa employs the 'voiced' voiceover technique, as Tony muses aloud, watching Eiko walk off into the distance, 'She reminded me of a bird flying off to a faraway land . . .', before cutting to the vision of Eiko walking in slow-motion, and the original voiceover speaker finishing the thought, '. . . Like a bird wrapped in its own special wind . . .'. After some setbacks, Tony is finally able to marry Eiko, but even this is not enough to provide him with the security the relationship could have brought to him, and Ichikawa again invokes the shift of dialogue from the narrator to Tony.

> **Narrator**: When he woke in the morning, she was the first thing he looked for. Finding her sleeping next to him was a relief. Not seeing her there made him uneasy. To Tony, not being lonely was somewhat strange. Having become not lonely, he fell captive to the fear of becoming lonely again. Every now and then . . .
> **Tony**: . . . the thought sent me into a cold sweat.

So, while Tony's marriage has brought him happiness, he is unable to remove himself from the possibility that this is a temporally constrained feeling. While Tony continues to work, Eiko develops an addiction to buying new clothes. Ultimately, tragedy strikes, bringing Tony's prophesied concern for loneliness back to him. To assist with his grief, he hires a young assistant, Hisako (also played by Rie Miyazawa) on the provision that she wears the clothes that Eiko had accumulated. In a series of hauntingly slow close-ups, Ishikawa takes the audience through the many jackets Eiko has left behind, a poignant reminder of loss, as the narrator speaks:

> **Narrator**: The clothes looked like shadows his wife had left behind.

A cut away reveals a stunned, grief-stricken Tony peering into the closet. The scene returns to the closet.

> **Narrator** (*cont.*): Filled with the warm breath of life, the shadows had once moved as his wife moved. But those in front of him now, had been cut from the root of life. They were just rows of shadows withering further and further. As Tony . . .

Cut back to the forlorn Tony, who finishes the thought:

> **Tony**: . . . stared at them, he felt he was suffocating.

Tony dismisses Hisako, and then rids himself of the clothes, part of the process that he later describes as 'forgetting' Eiko. He also seems to have no memory of Hisako, but in the film's final moments, it becomes apparent that he has not forgotten her. *Tony Takitani* is embedded with a sense of grief. Ichikawa's selection of wide horizontal shots, even from interior scenes, is intercut by naturally forming swipe edits, where the camera tracks to one side with a wall or doorway providing the dark image that ends one scene and opens on to another. The use of limited movement throughout the film adds to the foreboding atmosphere, generally the entire film is made up of slow tracking shots where there is limited movement on screen, or completely static shots, where the only movement is from the actors or nature, such as leaves blowing in the wind. This could be seen as Ichikawa adopting a formalist approach, leaning towards Eisenstein and Meyerhold's 'primacy of movement' which 'seeks to liberate acting from the task of psychological and narrative representation, turning it toward "play-acting" and improvisation' (Arsenjuk 2018: 71). In other words, the movements, limited as they are in *Tony Takitani*, become equally important in the overall 'message' of the film, and the delivery of dialogue (usually seen as the prime method of pushing the narrative forward) by Ogata and Miyazawa becomes secondary, or supplementary, to the holistic performance (Figure 8.2).

A sense of impending death is also found in *Tokyo Fiancée*, where Amélie's curiosity in Rinri's (her boyfriend's) house leads her to a room with a collection of samurai artefacts. She finds a book of *yokai* (traditional Japanese monsters), and is looking through it when Rinri appears behind her shoulder, and he

Figure 8.2 Static shot as Eiko emerges in *Tony Takitani* (2004).

gestures towards one of the yokai. 'Yamanba', he tells her. Amélie replies, 'She scares me'. Rinri explains, 'That's Yamanba, the witch. When you die, she'll come for you.' In the later scene, where Amélie survives her night on the mountain, she reasons, 'Yamanba was left empty-handed. She didn't catch me'. As she returns to Tokyo, Amélie reconsiders her life:

> **Amélie** (v/o): I'd been lost in Japan. Mt Fuji had found me again. It taught me a lesson. Taught me that you can escape death. That is, a rigid image you have of yourself. I was 20 years old. I had yet to find what I was searching for. And that's why I loved life. That day, I learned that to love, I had to be free. That day I learned that birth means both pain and joy. That day I learned that I had to become all the people I was, all the people I hadn't met yet. I learned that day I was as large as life.

Amélie's existential epiphany could be read in a number of ways, the first as a distinctly French philosophical view of the self, a realization of Sartre's *Being and Nothingness* where he states:

> Man can will nothing unless he has first understood that he must count on no one but himself; that he is alone, abandoned on earth in the midst of his infinite responsibilities, without help, with no other aim than the one he sets himself, with no other destiny than the one he forges for himself on this earth.

Amélie can also be seen here to be taking on a Japanese philosophical aesthetic. A poetical view that searches for meaning within oneself, borne partly from

Buddhist notions of dualism and 'a worldview in which oppositional forces coexist and hold each other in balance and order' (Wee 2011: 49). Thus, rather than running from Japan, Amélie can be seen as taking on the values of her new society, or as Amélie later states, she is now part of 'this world of impermanence'.

The state of being for Japan's salaryman (or woman), as noted earlier in Kiyoshi Kurosawa's *Tokyo Sonata*, presents a conflict between financial security and a feeling of entrapment. The gendered codes of Japanese society, however, dictate that 'masculine mobility is escapist fantasy; immobility, or involuntary mobility, is a dull immovable reality' (Gill 2003: 3). The sense of self-worth attached to Japanese masculinity is an important factor, and one often tied to high rates of male suicide, where '[d]espite gradual shifts in social and legal norms, custom and state institutions still tend to valorize the nuclear family centred on the male breadwinner' (2003: 23). In the post–Second World War environment, the concept of family was shaken up by the immense loss of life, especially among young males, and by the return to civilian life, for many young, discharged soldiers. Akira Kurosawa's *Stray Dog* touches on this theme in a scene where detectives Murakami and Sato are tracking down a suspected criminal, Yusa. They question his sister and her husband, poor rural people who took him in after the war.

> **Yusa's Sister**: He changed completely after he was repatriated. His bag, with everything he owned, was stolen. It changed him.
> **Brother-in-law**: You spoiled him.
> **Yusa's Sister**: You were too strict.
> **Brother-in-law**: Blaming the world, the war, playing the martyr. He didn't work.
> **Yusa's Sister**: His friend is to blame. A bum who comes to see him sometimes. He has a quiff; that disgusting haircut. He's a bad one.
> **Murakami**: What's his name?
> **Yusa's Sister**: Sei. They were buddies at the front.

Kurosawa reflects the inability to fit back into society and to retain links forged during the war, no matter how unsavoury. Later, Murakami himself admits that he saw 'men turn bad very easily', during the war, and Sato refers to these damaged men as part of the post-war, or as he recalls the French term the *après-guerre* generation. Murakami confesses that on his return from war, all his belongings had been stolen too, but that he had chosen to become a policeman rather than lapse into a life of seeking revenge. For Sato, there are only two types of *après-guerre* citizens: those who turn to criminality, and those, like Murakami, who take an honest approach to life. When Murakami confronts Yusa's girlfriend, Harumi (Keiko Awaji) he again relates the story of his misfortune, adding:

> **Murakami**: Times are very bad. But that's no excuse for doing wrong.
> **Harumi**: Bad people eat good food and dress well. They're the winners!
> **Murakami**: You really think so? Why not do the same?

The ultimate reflection on life, though, comes from Detective Sato late in the film, when, laid up in a hospital, he instructs Murakami to look out of the window at the city below and surmises:

> **Sato**: Many bad things will happen under those roofs. Many good people will be hurt.

He tells Murakami to put the past behind him and move on. His message is fatalistic, an attempt to snap Murakami out of his abstraction of searching for *why* things happen and look to the future.

The shift in the film between fiction and fact-based narratives, between diegetic and non-diegetic sounds and images can impact upon notions of whether the lives presented on screen are perceived as 'real' or not. The work of Takeshi Kitano, as noted, often features savage and sudden bursts of violence. In his 1993 *Sonatine*, released four years before his landmark *Hana-Bi*, Kitano had established his 'new version of gangster cool' (Schilling 1999: 341), in an international climate still reeling from the success of Quentin Tarantino's 1992, *Reservoir Dogs*. The impact of *Sonatine* led Mark Schilling to exclaim, 'I have seldom seen a film in which death is so drained of drama and emotion: Kitano seems to be saying that because his characters' lives have no meaning, their deaths can have no charge' (1999: 341-2). The link between Kitano the film star and his many other guises including director, producer, author, screenwriter, TV comic and visual artist (painter and sculptor) often sees a blurring of his personas, and as Dyer muses, this may be '[b]ecause stars have an existence in the world independent of their screen/"fiction" appearances, it is possible to believe . . . that as people they are more real than characters in stories' (Dyer 1998: 20). A motorcycle accident in 1994 damaged Kitano's face, with a partial paralysis down one side giving even more credence to his realist film roles as a gangster or rogue cop, extending 'the specific repertoire of gestures, intonations, etc. that a star establishes' that enables them (in this case, Kitano) to project an image 'just as much as the "inert" element of appearance, the particular sound of his/her voice or dress style' (Dyer 1998: 142).

Hirokazu Kore-eda: Contemplations on life

Focusing on several key films of Hirokazu Kore-eda's twenty-four directorial credits (including his Japan/France co-production that had the working title *The Truth About Catherine*, filmed in France with a strong French cast including Juliette Binoche and Catherine Deneuve – since released in 2019 as *The Truth/La Vérité*) provides some insights into the way he presents Japanese culture through his often-gentle reflections on families, individual characters and the personal traits they embody. These sensitivities are central to Kore-eda's films where it seems apparent that 'a Buddhist worldview pervades his cinematic narratives' (Yamada 2016: 1). Winner of the 2018 *Palme d'Or* at Cannes, with another family-centred film, *Shoplifters/Manbiki Kazoku*, Kore-eda's work serves as a vital link between Japan and cinema audiences around the globe.

In Kore-eda's *Our Little Sister*, the nuclear family ideal is destroyed when the siblings' estranged father dies and the teenage stepsister, Suzu Asano (Suzu Hirose), comes to stay with her older sisters. Suzu watches with keen interest as the adult women deal with loneliness and attempts at romance. In one scene, Suzu watches as impulsive twenty-two-year-old Yoshino (or Yochan) (Masami Nagasawa) paints her toenails.

> **Suzu**: Are you going on a date, Yochan?
> **Yoshino**: I wish I was. But I'm not in the mood for that right now.
> **Suzu**: I see.
> **Yoshino**: So, I'm not doing this for a man, I'm doing it for me. (pause) A good pedicure lifts your spirits. Want one?
> **Suzu**: No thanks. I'd ruin it playing soccer.

This brief scene helps to establish not just Suzu's approach to life and the functionality of sport but allows her to see into her elder sister's perception of herself as an independent woman. Suzu's lonely existence up until this time, growing up as the only child in a household where she was neglected by both parents, allows Kore-eda to explore how she might feel as she observes the actions of those around her: the squabbles, the banter and the raw emotions of her 'respectable' elders. Such imagery recalls the observances of *Tokyo Story*'s Kyoko (see earlier) or even the young Antoine (Jean-Pierre Léaud) in the early scenes of *The 400 Blows*, each film utilizing the innocence of youth to highlight the absurdity or cruelty that permeates the world of the adult.

Kore-eda broaches the topic of death in many of his films, *Air Doll/Kuki Ningyo* (2009), for example, couples the theme of death with a deeper existentialist discourse of what it means to be alive, when Nozomi (played by Korean actor, Bae Doona), an inflatable, life-size sex doll, suddenly comes to life and becomes part of society, but begins to question her place within the world. At one point, she wanders the streets, looking at her environment, and encounters an old man (Masaya Takahashi) with a walking frame and an oxygen tank, in obvious ill-health, sitting on a bench. They sit and chat, and when Nozomi tells him that she is empty inside, he responds 'A marvelous coincidence. I'm the same. I'm all empty', and taps his chest, indicating that his life is now, or soon to be, exhausted (Pugsley 2013: 99). The consistent referral to matters of life, death and existence in Kore-eda's films 'thematize the process of finding release from the illusionary and self-centered thoughts that can entangle individuals in the experiences of the material world and their own egocentric desires' (Yamada 2016: 3). For Nozomi, her sudden 'birth' as a fully formed adult means that she has little experience of the material (or spiritual) world to draw from. The final scenes of *Air Doll* offer an even more poignant insight into the differences between the physical realities of the human form compared to the empty, deflatable nature of Nozomi's body, as she makes an innocent, but bloodied attempt to 'inflate' her lover.

In 2008's *Still Walking/Aruitemo Aruitemo*, death is also a key theme, with Kore-eda presenting a familiar trope of a family coming together to commemorate a death in the family, that of the eldest son, Junpei, who drowned fifteen years ago saving a child. In an early scene, as the only surviving son travels to be with his family, he is accompanied by his new wife (a widow) and her son. They stop for a meal, and when the mother momentarily leaves the new stepfather, Ryota (*Thermae Romae*'s Hiroshi Abe, a regular in Kore-eda's films) with his pre-teen stepson, Atsushi (Shohei Tanaka), the father asks, with deep concern about an earlier incident involving a pet rabbit:

> **Ryota**: Your mother told me yesterday about the rabbit. Why did you laugh when it died?
> **Atsushi**: It was funny.
> **Ryota**: What was?
> **Atsushi** (*staring into his drink*): Rena started saying we should write letters to the rabbit.
> **Ryota** (*attempting to brighten the mood*): What's wrong with writing letters?
> **Atshushi** (*finally making eye contact with his stepfather*): Letters no one will read?

Ryota is taken aback and is unable to answer the boy's logic. The scene establishes a common theme throughout the film around the formalities of dealing with death. Atsushi ignores the conventions and traditions of Japanese culture and beliefs in rebirth or an afterlife, but Kore-eda leaves open the possibility whether this is through naivete or the boy's hidden pain where he wishes to put any thoughts of the rabbit and its death behind him. Later, some of the family go to visit Junpei's grave, high on a hillside. As the grandmother, Toshiko (Kirin Kiki), spoons water over the headstone, she explains:

> **Toshiko**: It was so hot all day. The water must feel good.

Kore-eda cuts to Atsushi, who stands at the side of the headstone, watching silently. His eyes dart from the headstone to his grandmother, a look that suggests she might well be crazy. As they walk home from the cemetery, Atsushi's mother suggests that he should come with her to visit their father's grave. Atsushi, who cannot remember playing with his father, responds with a deadpan, 'whatever', indicating his non-committal attitude towards taking part in the emotional expectations of the adult world.

The concept of death as a waste of a productive life is repeated throughout *Still Walking*. Not only is Ryota an art restorer struggling to find work, and therefore a disappointment to his father, he wears the stigma of not being as good as his late brother – who was slated to become a doctor following in his father's footsteps. In a poignant, but mostly comic series of scenes, the boy that Junpei saved, comes to pay his respect. He is now an overweight, clumsy slob of a man named Yoshio, twenty-five years old and unemployed and with a nihilistic outlook. As Ryota bundles him out the door at the end of the visit, he tries to be optimistic.

> **Ryota**: You're just 25. You can be anything you want.
> **Yoshio**: No, I can see my life won't go anywhere.

Grandmother Toshiko, seemingly indifferent to this comment, simply says, 'Come again next year. Promise, okay? We'll be waiting.' Yoshio smiles and agrees that he will be back. He leaves, but once out the door Toshiko launches into a series of unkind comments about how fat he is. The family returns to the living room, a tatami-style room that opens to the garden. Kore-eda frames this scene (and a number of others) as a direct homage to Ozu, the camera low inside the room and fixing the family within the physical parameters of the room, but with action also taking place in the distant garden, beyond the central characters, creating a multilayered depth to the scene. The grandfather, Kyohei

(Yoshio Harada) has been sitting on the step facing away from the others during the visit, and when they re-enter the room including his three grandchildren, he bitterly voices the sentiment that runs deep through the previous scenes.

> **Kyohei:** That ... that useless piece of trash. Why did my son have to save him? There were plenty of others.

As Ryota tries to defend the young man, his father persists.

> **Kyohei:** There's no point in him being alive.

The family all add their thoughts, but this does nothing to appease the old man.

> **Ryota:** Stop comparing his life to others' ... he's doing the best he can. Things don't always work out the way you want. How can you sit in judgement, Dad? Calling him 'useless' and 'trash'?

Ryota begins to get angry, and his father responds.

> **Kyohei:** What are you so defensive about? This has nothing to do with you.
> **Ryoto:** Is being a doctor so important? Advertising is a fine profession. Who knows how Junpei would have turned out if he were still alive? (pause) We're only human.

The family falls into a contemplative silence, waiting for Kyohei to raise his voice in anger, fortunately Ryota's goofy brother-in-law bursts in with a funny self-deprecating joke, and the mood seems to lift. Kyohei stands and it seems the matter is finished with, but as he walks through the busy household, he angrily mutters, 'Nobody asked him to live Junpei's life!' (Figure 8.3).

Still Walking is an exploration of how individuals cope with death. While it seems that Kyohei is the one most affected by Junpei's death, years ago, a later conversation reveals that Grandmother Toshiko harbours ill-feeling towards Yoshio. Ryota suggests that they stop inviting him because he can see it is painful for her, but she refuses.

> **Toshiko:** Can't have him forgetting after just a dozen years. It was his fault Junpei died. ... Not having someone to hate makes it all the worse for me. So once a year, I make him feel awful too. (she begins to cry) Will the gods punish me for that too? So, I'll invite him next year and the year after.

Ryota tells her that he thinks that she is cruel.

> **Toshiko:** I'm not cruel. I think it's normal.

Figure 8.3 Framing the grandfather in *Still Walking* (2008).

She ends the conversation by turning it back on Ryota, acerbically suggesting that he would not understand because he is not a 'real' parent.

Superstition is also part of *Still Walking*, when a butterfly finds its way into Grandmother Toshiko's house in the evening she chases it around, addressing it, 'You followed us home from the grave, right?' Ryota slides open a door to let it out, but Toshiko tells him to close it, because, 'It might be Junpei'. She follows it around the room as if in a trance, repeating her son's name. Her husband enters, and rather than showing empathy, remarks, 'Cut it out, you're pathetic.' Finally, it lands, and she cries 'See, it is Junpei!'. Ryoto captures the butterfly and then releases it out the door. Toshiko watches, then explains, 'On my grandma's 17th memorial, a butterfly flew in at night'. She is shaken and suddenly appears to be very frail.

Kore-eda's multi-award-winning *Like Father, Like Son/Soshite Chichi ni Naru* (2013) presents an intimate study of family life, in a traditional one-child Japanese family. The film investigates the value of parenthood and whether biological bloodlines impact the raising of a child. While Kore-eda's films generally fit into the category of art-house films that receive great critical acclaim, but a less successful response at the box office, *Like Father, Like Son* was Japan's tenth highest-ranked box-office hit in 2013, taking over US$31 million. Kore-eda explores the role of parenting across two families, divided by location (urban/rural), wealth, education and opportunity. Kore-eda's background in TV documentaries has been noted as a reason for the observational realism that permeates each of his films. In making *Like Father, Like Son*, Kore-eda's documentary grounding resulted in a production where he has stated that he 'did not provide a script at all, preferring to talk over the scenario with the actors before shooting and then construct the scene based on their real responses to his questions' (Yamada 2016: 24).

Centred on a plot of a baby mix-up in the hospital, the action takes place several years after the mix-up as upper-middle-class couple Ryota and Midori Nonomiya (Masaharu Fukuyama and Machiko Ono) are preparing their son Keita Nonomiya (his real name) to enter an expensive, exclusive primary school. Once informed of the mix-up, they are put into contact with the couple who have raised their biological son, Ryusei (Shôgen Hwang), a slovenly, unrefined rural shopkeeper, Yudai Saiki (Lily Franky) and his meek wife, Yukari (Yōko Maki). The differences between the two couples are made clear both visually through expected motifs such as the clothes they wear and the cars they drive, but also in their behaviours, with Yudai's unrefined eating and drinking habits a constant focus. Yudai's use of Osakan dialect, common with comedians often in exaggerated form (similar to the use of, say, an over-emphasized Yorkshire accent, or an overly drawled American 'Deep South' accent), is used to signify a stereotyped version of a poorly educated person. On the other hand, Ryota uses a more formal standard Japanese dialect where 'his language shows him to be a classic salaryman in that he tends to favor less informal forms of pronouns and prefers linguistically polite forms over plain ones' (SturtzSreetharan 2017: 47). Ryota has worked hard to earn his privileged background (his father gambled away any money that he had earned) which means he is well connected in the business world, and calls upon an old classmate, now a successful lawyer to assist him in their case against the rural hospital where the mix-up occurred, and in any potential custody issues over the boys. *Like Father, Like Son* therefore explores themes of the responsibilities of parenthood and the ethical dimensions that can arise in challenges to these roles.

The issue of how to resolve the custody of each boy tests Ryota's approach where he is suddenly in a situation where he cannot control what will happen. The hospital administrators work towards the families by simply 'swapping' the boys back, and urge the couples to begin with simple sleepovers, where the boys stay with their 'new' family for a night. As Ryota pulls up to Yudai's shop to drop off Keita and pick up Ryusei, he cannot control his prejudice, and at the sight of the shop mutters, 'It's pathetic'. Ryota's sense of his own superiority clouds his view of the world, and yet it is apparent that Yudai's playful, but immature ways render him closer to his own children (they have two younger siblings to

Ryusei) than the detachment that the workaholic Ryota has with Keita. While it would be all too easy for Kore-eda to paint Ryota as the uncaring father, the film works on a number of emotional levels, and Ryota's concern for Keita quickly rises, replacing to a large degree his blind ambition for career success. Yudai approaches life from a different mindset, and when exchanging the boys at the end of the first visit he openly states in front of Midori, and his own wife, that his motto is 'Put off till tomorrow whatever you can', resulting in Yukari, who has obviously heard this many times, joylessly stating 'Right. Your life will be over before you know it.' Yudai retorts, 'Trying to scare me. I've still got some life left to live.'

Yudai's down-to-earth philosophies help to lift his character from what could have easily been a comic foil, the country yokel. Speaking with Ryota, who refuses to join the children in an inflatable ball pit in a childrens' play centre, Yudai admonishes Ryota for not spending more time with Keita. Ryota replies that he is busy, and there are some things (in the company) that only he can do. Yudai looks at him and challenges, 'But no one can take your place as your son's father.' Ryota falls silent. Kore-eda plays with the audience by offering a switch in compassion, while Ryota at first seems the ideal parent because he can provide economically for his son, Yudai, with his manic enthusiasm and seemingly careless use of his regional dialect, 'becomes the voice of warmth and familial interdependence, which regulates and becomes indexical of the kind of fatherhood he practices' (SturtzSreetharan 2017: 49). Ryota's strict adherence to his own socio-economic codes disallows him the opportunity to relax into his relationships, whether with his wife, child or others.

Like Father, Like Son serves to highlight Japan's cultural differences around the showing of affection between members of a family and the unofficial codes of politeness in various social groups. The relationship between Ryota and all members of his family is one of detachment; there is little to no physical interaction, even when Keita is heading for bed, Ryota merely smiles at his son and says goodnight, making no attempt to hug or kiss the boy. Keita is played for all his cuteness, his wide eyes dominating his features, giving a manga-style effect to his face (as used to great effect to create Audrey Tautou's waif-like look in *Amélie*). Midori is also a little restrained with her touch, something that almost goes unnoticed until later when Keita is with Yukari and she hugs him, Keita either does not know what to do or is apprehensive about whether he should respond by folding his arms around her. Ryota's detachment develops into a bitter coldness, emboldening Midori, who confronts him several times about the disjuncture between his words and actions. At one point she calls him 'Liar', but the word provokes no immediate reaction. Ryota's behaviour replicates the forms of etiquette required of him in his salaryman role where clear logic must rule over emotion.

Kore-eda is ultimately a storyteller, a filmmaker who began his craft (as noted) in the field of documentary-making, leaving a legacy of 'sustained interest in actuality' (Wada-Marciano 2012: 58) in all his dramas. Such devotion to realism emerges in the storytelling of *Like Father, Like Son*, which offers Ryota a transformative experience when Ryusei, his biological son, comes to live with them. Ryota sees an opportunity to reset his life, at first seemingly with no regrets at having returned Keita to his biological family, but then a visual reminder of his 'lost' son brings the pain of his conflicting emotions to the fore. In a touching postscript to the film, just as the final credits roll, Kore-eda overlays the simple piano score with the sound of the children playing, a simple reminder of the joys of family.

Kore-eda's films embrace some of the more traditional elements of Japanese family life, mirroring the idea, as in the immediate post-war films of Ozu and Mizoguchi, that 'the figure of the father, while perhaps on the edge of cataclysmic change, remains the source of stability and emotional security for the members of his family' (Iles 2008: 193). While his films contain many strong female characters, they are often positioned as a foil to the male protagonist, or to help spur him on to a decision. Thus, it would be a struggle to read Kore-eda's films as feminist texts; rather they capture a slice of contemporary Japan through which he explores life, death and the simple act of 'being'.

The connectivity and disconnectivity of family in French cinema

Familial bonds in contemporary French cinema run deep and yet these bonds often oscillate wildly. The family dynamic is often deployed as a means to interrogate wider issues to do with intergenerational tension, freedom and liberation, or an attempt to move away from the strictures of the domestic setting. As Geoffrey Nowell-Smith reminds us, melodrama's concern is typically the family:

> [In film melodrama] the locus of power is the family and individual private property, the two being connected through inheritance ... Patriarchal right is of central importance. The son has to become like his father in order to take over

his property and his place within the community (or . . . the father is evil and the son must grow up different from him in order to be able to redistribute the property at the moment of inheritance). (1977: 115)

Whether Oedipal, patriarchal or concerned with *transmission* and inheritance, the conflict between father and son is seeded through much of contemporary French cinema. Themes of filiation and its persistent presence can be noted in examples ranging from dominant representations of the indelible haunting of a family by an absent father in Orso Miret's *De l'histoire ancienne* (2001) and Mia Hansen-Løve's *Father of My Children/Le Père de mes enfants* (2009) to the challenge presented by both medical progress and post-colonial discourses to structures of paternalistic identity in Claire Denis's *The Intruder/L'Intrus* (2005).

Other recent films confirm the ongoing sustainability in French cinema of a father–son grand narrative that constantly replays patriarchal conflicts and filial angst. Films like Ismaël Ferroukhi's *The Great Journey/Le Grand voyage* (2004) and Michael Haneke's *Hidden/Caché* (2005) express themselves in mediated forms of alienation and resentment: freighted silences, passive-aggressive behaviour and determination on the son's part to carve out a life remote from the father's. Most notable is Xavier Legrand's *Custody/Jusqu'à la garde* (2017), a searing portrait of a hostile custody battle between a divorcing couple and the young son at the centre.

The role of the family takes centre stage in *The Belier Family/La Famille Bélier* (2014, dir. Eric Lartigau), featuring a young girl, Paula (Louane Emera), an integral member of her small farming family in rural France. Paula's parents, mother Gigi (Karin Viard) and father Rodolphe (François Damiens), and brother Quentin (Luca Gelberg), are deaf, so Paula is tasked with accompanying them in their daily life, visits to the doctor or serving at their market stall. Lartigau's popular film (France's second-highest-grossing film for 2014, it took over US$55 million at the box office) highlights the difficulty facing those in rural communities with the constant loss of young people leaving for better education and employment prospects in the big cities. Paula is selected to go to Paris to try out for a music scholarship. Gigi and Rodolphe are played, somewhat controversially, by non-deaf actors, feeding into what Fraser refers to as the 'problematic on-screen portrayal of disability by ablebodied actors' (2016: 6). The parents have volatile personalities, so the added stress of losing Paula to the bright lights of Paris emphasizes their predicament. *The Belier Family* explores what Fraser (2016: 5) refers to as 'film's unique representational significance as it relates to ableism, disability and the interdependence of all human lives'. The film is ultimately centred on Paula though, and it is her life, and especially her independence, that is framed by her relationship with her family.

Hearing impairment also features in an earlier French comedy/drama, although less popular at the box office (taking just US$3.1 million), the 2013 *My Summer in Provence/Avis de Mistral* (the French title has a more literal meaning approximating 'The Impending Winds', referring to the seasonal mistral breezes that flow around that area of Europe), directed by Rose Bosch and starring Jean Reno (*Wasabi*; *La Femme Nikita*, 1990, dir. Luc Besson; *Godzilla*, 1998, dir. Roland Emmerich), also features a deaf character, this time the youngest brother of three children, Theo (Lukas Pelissier). The film opens with a high-definition close-up of a young boy about seven or eight years old (Theo) sleepily gazing out of a train window as it travels through the countryside. Simon and Garfunkel's 'Sounds of Silence' plays, and as the boy rouses from his sleepiness, he looks around to see others soundlessly speaking to him, Bosch's way of quickly establishing the boy's deafness. He is travelling with his grandmother, Irene (Anna Galiena), his surly teenage sister, Léa (Chloé Jouannet), and their angry brother Adrien (Hugo Dessioux), neither of whom is happy about having to spend their summer in the French countryside, with a grandfather they have never met, Paul (Reno). Paul is estranged from his daughter – the children's mother – since she left their farm after becoming pregnant at the age of seventeen. As with Keita in *Like Father, Like Son*, Theo's eyes (although a rich blue compared to Keita's dark brown) are a factor in drawing out his innocence and are used in early scenes to show how cold Paul can be, as he resists giving any comfort to the young boy.

My Summer in Provence presents a dysfunctional family where the grandparents have to look after the children for several months in their old farmhouse, the home where their mother was raised. The children's mother is in Canada working, and following her recent divorce, their father has deserted them. The older children, hurt by the divorce, have a negative attitude to the concept of marriage, with Léa claiming 'Count me out of that. Marriage is for retards!', reasoning that her parents 'married and lived miserably ever after!'. The city-bred children search desperately for phone reception, anxious that their friendship networks and social media links will be severed. Their efforts to leave are thwarted, with their mother insisting, from afar, that they stay. On a trip to the local village, Léa and Adrien both run across some potential romantic interests, and they get to see how welcomed their grandparents are in the local community. For much of the first part of the film, Theo's role is merely as a silent onlooker, rather than an active character, but Paul begins to soften towards him, noticing the young boy's curiosity with the animals around the farm and drawing him into more activities as a more significant part of the family.

In an effort to annoy the ever-grumpy Paul, Adrien creates a Facebook account in his name and then begins replying to Paul's long-estranged acquaintances as they respond. When a group of Paul's old motorbike-riding hippy friends arrive en masse (at Adrien's invitation), Paul is initially angry, but this soon subsides and the closeness he shares with his friends replicates the affinity that he should be sharing with his family. Adrien begins to worry about Paul who appears to be hiding a deep hurt and trying to cover it with excessive drinking. Paul finally reaches a turning point, admitting that his drinking is out of hand, and confesses to the family that he can only give up if the children can help him. Ultimately Paul proves to be strong, realizing the fragility of the family, and when the summer ends and the children must leave, promises them, 'I'll be here'. While *My Summer in Provence* draws on a limited range of stereotyped characters (and celebrity cameos such as musician Hugues Aufray), Reno's Paul represents a type of old-fashioned patriarch, stubborn in their righteousness, even if it means distancing those they love dearest. It is unclear whether Theo's character is an instance of what Fraser sees as harnessing disability for narrative exploitation (2016: 6), or whether he exists to provide a normative aside to the family dramas that unfold.

Olivier Assayas deals with a different family predicament in the form of the spirit world in *Personal Shopper* (2016), a critically acclaimed co-production between France, Germany, Belgium and the Czech Republic, that won him the Best Director award at Cannes. Starring US actor Kristen Stewart (of the *Twilight* series) as Maureen, an American biding her time in Paris as a personal shopper for a wealthy, but a very demanding celebrity, the film centres around her quest to re-establish contact with her dead twin brother, Lewis. Both saw themselves as mediums, in touch with the afterlife, so Maureen is sure that Lewis will keep his pact with her to make contact. She spends nights in the almost empty mansion where he died, experiencing strange shifts and seeing ghostly apparitions, but is not convinced that these are Lewis. When Maureen begins to get text messages from an unknown source, she becomes anxious. The mysterious person (or being?) sending the texts asks her what she finds unsettling, and she responds (in Assayas perhaps toying with the idea of the Fourth wall) 'Horror movies'. When the texter asks why, she responds, 'A woman runs from a killer and hides'. The response is 'What you find unsettling is fear. Are you often scared?', to which Maureen replies, 'No', which seems to contradict her behaviour up until this point, and again, in a self-referential way, is probably the response a heroine in a horror film might give. As they continue the conversation, the tone shifts to more daring, sexually charged responses, as Maureen confesses to a minor discretion that occurred with her employer, and posts 'No desire if it's not forbidden.'

The use of media as a conduit for spirits is explored further in *Personal Shopper* when Maureen watches a 1970s film on her smartphone (continued later on her laptop) about Victor Hugo and his belief in the power of the seance. Instead of Assayas just showing Maureen watching the film, the scenes are edited into this film to indicate how absorbed Maureen is in the subject. Following a major development in the story, the text messages take on a sinister tone, as Assayas increases the tension for Maureen and the audience. Maureen seeks some form of closure from Lewis before her life can continue, so while Assayas's film explores the afterlife, it is just as much focused on bereavement and the living.

The role of the family also frames *Back to Burgundy*, with Jean returning to France after ten years of travelling and eventually setting up a vineyard in Australia with his girlfriend. Seemingly estranged from his father and his two siblings, his return is unexpected after nearly five years of not making contact with them. Their mother has died in the interim, and now Jean's father is gravely ill. He returns in time to see his father briefly, before the elder man dies. Jean still has a strong emotional attachment to his younger sister, Juliette (Ana Girardot) and brother Jérémie (Francçois Civil), and to the family vineyard. The father's death creates problems for the younger siblings who must work to keep the vineyard productive, so Jean stays on to help them, even though his girlfriend and young son remain behind in Australia. When the father's will dictates that the property must be shared equally between all three, and unearths a large tax bill, Jean is torn between the financial constraints of trying to sell his share (although his siblings have no money) and allowing them all to sell off portions of the estate. His circumstances are further complicated with him having to decide between his family in France and his 'new' family back in Australia.

Compounding Jean's problems are his own feelings of guilt around his actions towards his father over the years, and in several flashbacks, their tumultuous, but ultimately loving, relationship is explored. Caught up in the financial problems and his commitments to helping Juliette and Jérémie continue to produce wine, Jean stays on for several seasons, passionately involved in the running of the vineyard. When his girlfriend, Alicia (María Valverde), and son Ben (Sean O'Gara-Micol) unexpectedly arrive, the connection of the two families seems complete; however, financial commitments back in Australia mean that Jean and Alicia (and Ben) must soon return home.

Back to Burgundy features one more complex family relationship through Jérémie's relationship with his wife's, Océane (Yamée Couture), wealthy family who own a neighbouring vineyard estate. Océane's overbearing father, Anselme (Jean-Marie Winling), looks down upon Jérémie, his new son-in-law, but is willing to support him for his daughter's sake. Anselme repeatedly offers Jérémie managerial positions in his vineyard, away from the act of winemaking, but Jérémie refuses. During a celebration at Anselme's estate, the older man offers to buy out the siblings' vineyard, but their attachment to the land their parents nurtured is too great. An obviously drunk Jean refuses to acquiesce. Unaccustomed to not getting his way, Anselme pulls Jérémie aside and tries to reason with him. The relatively gormless Jérémie attempts to explain:

> **Jérémie**: That's my brother. That's how Jean is.
> **Anselme**: Didn't anybody teach him to spit at a tasting? He's acting like a child. It's unbelievable!

Anselme's insinuation is that Jean cannot control himself around alcohol. After an awkward pause, Jérémie becomes emboldened, also a little drunk.

> **Jérémie**: I don't spit either. We don't spit in our family. Our grandfather taught us that. He said only wimps spit.

Anselme begins to step towards the younger man, a physical movement meant to intimidate. Jérémie retreats but continues his defence.

> **Jérémie** (cont:). We like to drink!
> **Ansleme**: Do you have something to say?
> **Jérémie** (*nervously*): No. No. Yes! Even . . . yes! Absolutely. This isn't working, Anselme. You can see how you are with me. Yes! You know. (*angrily*) And what's with that spitting business? What is that? If we don't want to spit! (*calm*) That's all.

In the preceding argument, Jérémie's reference point is always his family, the 'we' of his outburst going back generations, from Jean back to his grandfather. So, although Anselme is now Jérémie's father-in-law, it is the blood relations that connect Jérémie to his family and to their land.

Aside from *Back to Burgundy*, two other contemporaneous French films take as their starting point stories about wine that eventually morph into intense family psycho-dramas. In *First Growth/Premiers crus* (2015, Jérôme Le Maire), a wine critic in Paris returns home to take over his father's vineyard on the verge of bankruptcy, and at the same time falls in love with the daughter of his father's rival. In *You Will Be My Son/Tu seras mon fils* (2011, Gilles Legrand), a demanding winemaker is dissatisfied at the prospect of his son taking over his vineyard and seeks to literally and symbolically disown him. An extraordinary dream sequence takes place in this latter film: Martin (Loràmt Deutsch), passed out after a night of heavy drinking, finds himself trapped inside a wine barrel, submerged and struggling to escape. He tries to scramble out but looks up to see his father repeatedly pushing him back under the fermenting wine and then sealing him in. A garish red filter and the father's demonic smile add to this horrific setting, all the more dreadful because up to this point, Legrand's film has been a restrained tale of familial tension within the rarefied world of a Saint-Emilion *domaine*. Here, the father is slowly, painstakingly, emasculating the son (Figure 8.4).

These films are not just about wine, then – equally compelling is the way each film diagrams a variation of Oedipal anxiety through the ongoing narrative complexities within the child–parent/son–father bond. Fraught issues of transmission, legacy, loyalty and patriarchal ownership of the land all play out in these works; at the same time, each charts the mythic, eco-poetical connection that exists between wine and the land in France. Subtextually, *You Will Be My Son*, *First Growth* and *Back to Burgundy* are films apprehensive about fatherhood, depicting crises in paternity and masculinity. By exploring the obsession with absent or ineffectual father figures, these films offer up contested readings of strong-willed patriarchs, the passing of knowledge from father to son, and the preservation of a certain way of life as embodied by wine, landscape and *terroir*.

Figure 8.4 A father and son divided in *You Will Be My Son* (2011).

As Klapisch acknowledged, 'if I wanted to make a film about wine it was because I wanted to talk about family. What we inherit from our parents, what we pass on to our children' (2017).

The visceral hatred on the father's part to the son in *You Will Be My Son* prevents any possibility of transmission or knowledge transfer. In *First Growth* and *Back to Burgundy*, however, the practical problem of transferring knowledge from one part of the organization to another – that is, from father to son in the former; from Australian perspective to French in the latter – creates a revival of the fortunes not just of the failing vineyards and company finances, but also of the family itself.

Conclusion

The humanist values and emotive traits of filial relationships found in the earlier films illustrate how cinema reflects the verisimilitude of our lives. Storytelling techniques expose the frailties of existence and the inextricable webs of family relationships. The metaphysical elements so tactfully hinted at in Kore-eda's films are dragged to the surface in many French films. The gregariousness of French culture is shown through cinematic characters unable to conceal their passions, including bursts of anger, with and against members of their own families. These contrast heavily with the restrained manner of Japanese society, the quiet contemplative characters that populate the films of Kore-eda, or Kawase or dozens of other filmmakers.

9

Adapting literary and visual texts

The esoteric nature of filmmaking as a creative practice offers filmmakers an almost limitless palette on which to tell a story. Influences can come from a variety of origins found in local texts or sourced from the inexhaustible exchange of cultural texts across borders, languages and ethnicities. One way this has been done across almost the entirety of cinema's existence has been to draw on existing texts (often novels or short stories, but equally through manga/comics or anime/animations) and adapt them for the sensory experience of the audio and visual world of the cinema. Both French and Japanese cinema are filled with examples of such films and have been extensively explored elsewhere. In France, for example, *Variety* (2015) reminded readers that one in five French films is based on a literary source, and that around 40 per cent of the films that sell over 500,000 tickets in France each year are based on books. What we are particularly interested in demonstrating in this final chapter is how the creative use of adaptation in both national contexts can be deployed to maintain or rework particular genre styles. In the case of France and Japan in recent years, there has been a parallel strand of adapted film work competing alongside the more culturally respectable adaptations of classic literary texts. Popular genres, such as fantasy and adventure, have become increasingly visible, and have much to say about the film tastes and trends of contemporary France and Japan.

Adaptations

The transformation of an existing text into a film is a complex process that creates 'an ongoing whirl of intertextual reference and transformation, of texts generating other texts in an endless process of recycling, transformation, and transmutation, with no clear point of origin' (Stam 2000: 66). This is especially the case for filmmakers in Japan who are highly reliant on manga and anime as the basis for screenplays, but may just as easily call upon local, national or global literary novels, folklore, theatre, religious texts or traditional oral stories. Many live-action films are adaptations, or loosely based interpretations of these existing texts, including recent films such as *Assassination Classroom*, *Ace Attorney/Gyakuten Saiban* (2012, Takashi Miike), or *Bakuman* (2015, Hitoshi Ohne) that have their most direct origins in manga. Such inspiration has also been found in French filmmaking, with film series such as *Astérix* (or *Astérix le Gaulois*) based on the original comics by René Goscinny and Albert Uderzo, and successful feature-length versions produced in both animated and live-action films. At the more prestigious end of the spectrum, the French film *Blue Is the Warmest Colour/La Vie d'Adèle – Chapitres 1 & 2*, which won the Palme d'Or at Cannes in 2013, was based on the graphic novel *Le bleu est une couleur chaude* by Jul Maroh. Luc Besson's *The Extraordinary Adventures of Adele Blanc-Sec/Les Aventures Extraordinaires d'Adèle Blanc-Sec* (2010) and his later *Valerian and the City of a Thousand Planets* (2017) were also based on comics. These adaptations reflect Stam's observation that such films 'are hypertexts derived from preexisting hypotexts that have been transformed by operations of selection, amplification, concretization and actualization' (2000: 66).

The successful *Adele Blanc-Sec* series of texts is a steampunk fantasy/adventure that began in comic form in 1976, and while the film version retains many of the features of the original comic, it borrows heavily from Hollywood films ranging from *Night at the Museum* (2006, dir. Shawn Levy), *Lara Croft: Tomb Raider* (2001, dir. Simon West), *Jurassic Park*, *The Mummy* (1999, dir. Stephen Sommers), *Pirates of the Caribbean* (2003, dir. Gore Verbinski) and *Raiders of*

Figure 9.1 Comic-book aesthetic in *Valerian & the City of a Thousand Planets* (2017).

the Lost Ark (1981, dir. Steven Spielberg). Besson's all-star cast includes former TV presenter and model, Louise Bourgoin as Adele, and César Award-winning actor/director, Mathieu Amalric (*The Diving Bell and the Butterfly*). While these films may have been the result of multiple transitions from an original source, Stam suggests a cautious approach to reading a filmed adaptation, stating that 'our statements about films based on novels or other sources need to be less moralistic, less panicked, less implicated in unacknowledged hierarchies, more rooted in contextual and intertextual history' (2000: 75). In other words, a film such as *Adele Blanc-Sec* need not be judged by its 'accuracy' to the source text, but in relation to all the texts it draws from, including the world of film, to be judged (if need be) on its own merits rather than for its authenticity to the source comic.

Whether a cinematic adaptation of a manga or anime is authentic or not, does not equate to a guaranteed strong box office, due to the 'seemingly yin-yang nature of the relationship between comic art to motion pictures' (McAllister et al. 2006: 109), where decisions have to be made not only regarding the type of work to be adapted but how it will be adapted. Will the adapted film aim for a popular audience by keeping a bright comic-book appearance and theme, or will it follow the often-darker path of the graphic novel, and risk only attracting a niche audience? This latter path has been well-documented in terms of Hollywood cinema, where films such as *Hulk* (2003, dir. Ang Lee), and Robert Rodriguez's *Sin City* (2005) adhered to the darkness of their original comic book or graphic novel forms, and although they achieved reasonably strong box- office returns, they ranked fourteenth and thirty-second in box-office takings for their respective year (Box Office Mojo figures). These films nevertheless paved the way for greater economic success for the studios and their associations with the Marvel and DC Comics companies who then tailored subsequent films to create, respectively, the Avengers and X-Men, and DC Universe franchises, that utilize '[b]ig casts, big costs, big distribution, big spectacle, and big revenue' (McAllister et al. 2006: 110). For French and Japanese cinema, this type of franchising of live action, comic-inspired films has yet to reach the levels of the Hollywood model despite the production of numerous successful sequels. In Japan this includes the 2015 and 2016 *Assassination Classroom* series, or *Gantz* and *Gantz 2: Perfect Answer*, both released in 2011, and the occasional merging of two characters, perhaps most notably beginning with Ishirō Honda's *King Kong versus Godzilla/Kingu Kongu Tai Gojira* in 1962 (although not a comic adaptation), with another US remake, this time with the title reversed as *Godzilla vs. King Kong* (dir. Adam Wingard) released in 2021.

In France, again, we can point to the phenomenally popular *Astérix et Obélix* series, or more recently in the drama based on a 2011 graphic novel by French comic artist, Bastien Vivès, *Polina/Polina danser sa vie* (2016, dirs. Valérie Müller and Angelin Preljocaj). *Polina* features the eponymous Polina (Anastasia Shevtsova) as a young Russian dancer aspiring to perform with the Bolshoi Ballet. While the graphic novel sees Polina (who does reach the Bolshoi, only to see her ambitions move beyond the restrictive classical style) move from Russia to Germany (and back to Russia), the French film includes a foray into France to dance with her French boyfriend, Adrien (Niels Schneider) under the tutelage of Liria Elsaj (Juliette Binoche). When Polina is injured, and the lead role opposite Adrien falls through, she heads to Belgium, seemingly an end to her dancing career. Polina's creativity shines through though, and she is soon drawn back into dance by her new lover, Karl, (Jérémie Bélingard), and they create a new contemporary dance performance that suggests that Polina will go on to greater success. While the foray into France is relatively brief in the context of the almost two-hour film, it briefly shows the Aix-en-Provence, allowing Polina to remark, as she gazes out of a bus window, 'It's beautiful here', to which Adrien simply replies, 'You like it?', as Polina smiles. By including the 'French' section in *Polina*, husband and wife co-directors, Müller and Preljocaj (the latter, a contemporary dancer and choreographer of some renown), are able to physically locate the film in the homeland of the original author. The final act of the film, where Polina and Karl create their choreographed work for entry into the Festival Montpellier Danse, a festival now in its forty-first year, locates the drama within a real setting.

Unlike the minimalist brushed-ink style of the original, using just black, white and beige imagery, *Polina* is shot in a high-contrast way, emphasizing shadows and darkness shot through with bursts of colour, or more often, the light tone of the dancer's skin. Nowhere is this more evident than in the final dance piece: Polina and Karl's intensely dramatic and punishingly physical performance that cuts directly from their practice dance to impress a visiting dance director from the Montpellier Festival to their ultimately commissioned theatrical performance in a dark forest setting, the floor dusted with 'snow'.

Another form of adaptation can be found in the attraction of the gothic style (especially in young people's clothing) in Japanese culture that has been found in a vast number of text formats. One extremely popular manga series, set in nineteenth-century London, that became a long-running TV anime series was

Black Butler. In 2014, a live-action feature was released under the same title, *Black Butler/Kuroshitsuji*, directed by Kentarō Ōtani (whose debut film in 1999 had a French title, *Avec mon mari/Abekku mon mari*, lit. *With My Husband*) and Kei'ichi Satō. The cinematic *Black Butler* is set in an unnamed city in the future of 2020. With a strong emphasis on costuming, including top hats, canes and capes, the film was a stylistic success, but only a moderate box-office success, reaching sixty-seven in the top 100 films for the year with a gross of just over US$5 million (Box Office Mojo 2018). Critics of the film were again quick to measure its success in contrast to the manga and anime, pointing to the unfaithfulness of the text and the 'disappointment we feel when a film adaptation fails to capture what we see as the fundamental narrative, thematic, and aesthetic features of its literary [or comic] source' (Stam 2000: 54). Even slight changes to the look of a character, their costume or even their gender, can create a storm of controversy among fans, while critics pick up on shifts in narrative or the watering down of extreme elements that ultimately change the tone or mood found in the originating source.

A Bride for Rip Van Winkle/Rippu Van Winkuru no hanayome (2016) is another adaptation, this time based on a novel by Shunji Iwai, who adapted the screenplay and directed the film. It features softly spoken and painfully shy school teacher Nanami (Haru Kuroki), who soon loses her job because of her inability to command respect from her students. She takes up online tutoring, but even then, is so timid that she fails to help students. When one student asks what use 'cubic functions' are in the real world, she responds, 'Well . . . I'm not sure'. The student challenges 'You don't know?', and Nanami replies 'I'm sorry', before adding, meekly, 'I'll look it up for you.' Nanami meets a fellow schoolteacher, the similarly reserved Tetsuya (Gô Jibiki) through an online dating site, and they soon become engaged, much to her mother's disappointment that due to Nanami's lack of ambition she failed to hook a doctor or a millionaire. Iwai uses the narrative to explore the strict politeness and honour codes that guide Japanese society. When arranging their wedding, Tetsuya teases Nanami that she will only have two guests (her parents, who have delayed their divorce in order to not shame Nanami on her wedding day). Nanami has a mysterious friend on social media, who puts her in contact with a businessman, Amuro (Gô Ayano) who arranges for hired wedding guests for the day.

On the day of the wedding, Tetsuya discovers Nanami's online avatar, Clammbon (the name of a Japanese musical group, but she later changes the name to Campanella, in reference to a fantasy novel from the 1920s), who is also getting married on the same day, but he is too naïve to realize it is his own bride. The expensive Western-style wedding and reception goes ahead as planned. As the couple settles into domestic life, Nanami finds a woman's earring on the floor of their apartment and takes it to Amuro to see if he can discover whether her new husband is being faithful. Amuro sets a fee of US$3,000, allowing Nanami to pay by instalments, and she agrees.

As noted, *A Bride for Rip Van Winkle* was written by Iwai, furthering his ability to work across mediums as he did with 'Hana and Alice', which he originally made as a teen romance film in 2004 as *Hana and Alice/Hana to Arisu*, and extended with an anime prequel, *The Murder Case of Hana and Alice/Hana to Arisu Satsujin Jiken* in 2015, that Iwai also directed. This film was then serialized as a manga. Iwai also works with other filmmakers, and in 2012 produced writer/director Eriko Kitagawa's Paris-set romance *I Have to Buy New Shoes*.

Before Amuro returns to Nanami, a man appears at her apartment claiming that he has evidence that Tetsuya is having an affair with his girlfriend. Later, Nanami visits him at his apartment. Until now, Iwai's directional style has been unremarkable, but as Nanami enters his apartment, the camera turns to a Dutch tilt, with a fisheye lens, giving the appearance of a series of surveillance cameras. Over a glass of wine, Nanami discovers that the man has now dumped his girlfriend, and he asks her if she thinks Tetsuya should be killed for his infidelity. The camera shifts to a floor level, still canted angle, as the entire mood of the film shifts to hint at something sinister. He tries to get her to have sex with him, and they struggle, only their legs in shot. His offer is a deal that if she gives herself to him, he will 'take care' of her husband. She seems to acquiesce, as he reasons:

> **Man**: Betraying your husband, that only makes things even. Think of it as a fresh start.

He begins to undress, undoing his pants as she crouches against a door.

> **Man**: Remember, we're both victims.

Nanami asks to use the bathroom, interrupting his predatory behaviour. Inside the bathroom, in distress, she texts Amuro for help. He replies that he is coming to help, and then posts an inappropriate, jovial photo of him saluting. These shifts in mood are not unusual in novel, manga or anime forms; however, they are less common in what appear to be rom-com films, that generally stick to their genre, rather than turn into something more sinister. These darker tones, both visually and thematically, can be clearly detected in a genre that has, in recent years, become increasingly prevalent in French and Japanese cinema – fantasy.

Fantasy

The 2016 sci-fi *Cutie Honey: Tears/Kyūtī Hanī Tiāzu* (dir. Takeshi Asai) is a high-budget, high-tech manga remake that shares a visual style with Luc Besson's *The Fifth Element*. A more serious adaptation than the pop-styled, playful *Cutie Honey: Live Action/Kyûtî Hanî* (2004) directed by Hideaki Anno of *Shin Godzilla/Shin Gojira* fame (2016, co-directed with Shinji Higuchi), and a 'supervising director' on three of the Evangelion feature-length anime series, *Tears* explores a class-based future, where the world's elite live in a pristine environment at skyscraper level, while the poor live at street-level among the refuse and polluted air piped down from above, introduced as a 'vertical, multi-layered and self-sufficient city', the entire 'world' was initially designed as the 'special zone of Tatehama, the utopia of a metropolis'. When the evil android Jiru (Nicole Ishida) gains control of the city, she creates a division between the two levels, where 'the ground floor is hell'. An early model android, fitted with human emotions by her adopted father, Professor Kisaragi, Hitomi Kisaragi (Mariya Nishiuchi), known as Honey Kisaragi in earlier versions more closely aligned with the manga, transforms into the eponymous leather-clad Cutie Honey when her fighting skills are needed. Asai's influences, aside from Besson are also found in the *Blade Runner*-esque landscapes of the underworld. Both the hero and villain of the film are female, as are some of the key sidekicks, challenging some of the gender stereotypes often found in sci-fi films until recent years. Hooded characters, curiously named 'Sodoms', prowl the streets, reflective of the *Star Wars* Stormtroopers in their ruthlessness and anonymity. The threat to unleash an immediately toxic fog on the unsuspecting lower class is an environmental message that is highly pertinent to Japanese audiences in the wake of the Fukushima radioactive leaks of 2011. The poisonous gas breaches the division between the two worlds, so Kisagari must transform into Cutie Honey to prevent the alienation of all citizens. In true superhero fashion, she defeats the hero, and then in an act of self-sacrifice, dies while saving the planet, albeit with the possibility of her regeneration.

One of Japan's most recognized manga and anime series is Death Note, a thrilling murder/fantasy series about a magical notebook that, when someone's name is written in it, will cause them to die (although, to make things more intriguing, there are a number of caveats, such as the person writing the name, must know the face of the person they are killing). The Death Note series has spawned two live-action adaptations and a sequel since 2006, each with a bigger budget than the previous film. The series' incredible success across all mediums is attributed to its mix of 'attractive characters, sexual tensions, emotional conflicts, physical battles, supernatural powers and open-ended subplots' (Freedman 2017: 40). To avoid too much controversy over the age of the lead character, the film series made the major character, who holds the death notebook, a university student (rather than a high-school student). In 2016, Shinsuke Sato directed *Death Note: Light Up the New World*/*Desu Nōto Light up the NEW* (*sic*) *World*, using an original story that develops characters and storylines from the 2006 *Death Note 2: The Last Name*/*Desu Nōto the Last Name*, directed by former *kaijū eiga* (monster film) filmmaker, Shūsuke Kaneko. The film works the ten-year time difference into its narrative, the earlier holder of the book, Yagami Raito (played by Tatsuya Fujiwara in all three live-action films), also known as Light Yagami, or Kira (a phonetic transposition of 'Killer'), used the book to dispense justice by killing off known criminals. The book, or as it appears, books, have fallen into other hands, following Kira's death in the previous film, and indiscriminate killings are occurring across Tokyo. At the summoning of Beppo, a large, golden 'extra-dimensional' Shinigami (lit. 'Death God', in this instance, a speaking beast in the mould of the H.R. Giger-designed skeletal monster in the *Alien* films), the authorities are able to determine the number of books currently in circulation.

The Death Note series has also been effective in adaptation form because of its melding of different mediums as part of its overall plot. The magical powers of the ancient notebooks 'dramatizes the coexistence of old and new media; screens (of computers, televisions, cell phones, videogames and more) are a plot device and visual motif' (Freedman 2017: 36), something that allows the filmmakers to utilize special effects and explore the possibilities of not-too-futuristic technologies such as holographic projections.

Technology also plays a significant role in *Fullmetal Alchemist*/*Hagane no Renkinjutsushi* [*Alchemist of Steel*] (2017, dir. Fumihiko Sori), an adaptation of a highly successful manga series and an equally successful, fifty-one-episode anime series. While the Fullmetal Alchemist series has long been compared to the Harry Potter texts (from the search for a 'Philosopher's Stone', to the alchemy motif), the live-action *Fullmetal Alchemist* (*FMA*) opens with sweeping views of what looks like French countryside, with grassy, rolling hills and a brick chateau.

Two young golden-haired brothers, Ed and Al Elric, run to their dark-haired mother, who is hanging out washing, but rather than being European, they are Japanese in appearance and language, and it is established that the year is 1904. The Harry Potter influences abound, from the musical score, the visual sign of steam trains to the timber-clad library where the boys practice their sorcery; however, *FMA* has a sci-fi element in the mechanical armour features of several lead characters, in line with *Robocop* or the more recent *Avengers* series of film. As the film cuts to a later scene, an aerial view of a European village (mostly shot in the Tuscany region in Italy) is supported by a title card that indicates the (fictitious) town of Reole, and a pony-tailed Ed, now in his late teens, appears running along rooftops in a long red coat that flares like a superhero's (or manga hero's) cape. A sustained battle using magical powers eventuates as Ed corners a bad guy in a busy *piazza*, and alluding to the Potter series, a bystander with a Potter haircut and round-rimmed glasses adds a brief comment to the action. Interestingly, all characters appear to be Japanese, including bystanders in the village scenes (some in blonde wigs), despite the use of foreign locations, reflecting the predominantly monocultural, or monoracial features of Japanese society, and in keeping with the original manga series. The Romanized names such as Edward (Ed, sometimes referred to as Edo) or Al (Alphonse) are taken directly from the original manga series, providing the characters with a sense of the foreign exotic.

The manga style is replicated throughout *FMA*, with Ed (Ryôsuke Yamada from *Assassination Classroom*) striking the necessary melodramatic poses, such as in a sombre scene with Dr Marcoh (veteran actor Jun Kunimura from *Kill Bill 1 & 2*, *Ichi the Killer*), when the doctor advises him to stop searching for the magical Philosopher's Stone:

Marcoh: Play with the devil and you'll end up in Hell.
Ed: (pause) I've already been to hell!

During this scene Ed stands, leaning on a table looking up through his blonde fringe at the doctor, a common pose in manga and anime that forces the character (actor) to raise their eyebrows giving the appearance of larger eyes. Following a failed alchemy experiment to bring back their dead mother, Ed's brother Al is destroyed. Ed's only hope is to rescue Al's spirit, which he does by sacrificing his right arm (later replaced by a mechanical prosthetic), but as he is unable to resurrect his brother's physical body, he embeds the spirit into a large suit of armour that was in their house. In his new form, Al lives his life

Figure 9.2 Al and Ed in *Fullmetal Alchemist* (2017).

trapped as the large, armoured figure, reminiscent of popular 1950s manga and anime icon, Tetsujin 28 (lit. Iron Man 28, known more commonly in the West as Gigantor), and its more muscular version from the 1980s, New Tetsujin-28. Ed's quest, that he believes will be solved if he can find the Stone, is to return Al's body to him. Due to the number of episodes in both the manga and the anime, the story is based on an amalgamation of episodes, emphasizing (or omitting) some characters at the expense of others, something aggrieved fans are eager to point out in online fora (Figure 9.2).

The transition of *FMA* to live action presents some difficulties in the presentation of different creatures, such as the Skeletor-like beings created by Colonel Hakuro (Fumiyo Kohinata, the father in 2016's *Survival Family*) in a bid to create his own army. The creatures are deformed, one-eyed zombies, but their undeveloped brains render them unsuitable for following orders, and they must be destroyed. While in manga or comic form, they may be relatively benign to the reader or viewer, in their cinematic realist form, they could be seen as overly frightening for a younger audience, especially when coupled with the number of characters and evil 'Homunculi' that are burnt to death throughout the film.

Drama

Films adapted from novels have existed since the beginning of feature films, often aiming to create a new text that is faithful to the original. Drawing examples from *Madame Bovary* and *The Grapes of Wrath*, Stam notes that the 'words of a novel... have a virtual, symbolic meaning; we as readers, or as directors, have to fill in their paradigmatic indeterminances' (2000: 55). Stam explains how the reader's imagination creates an image of Emma Bovary and her beauty, or of Ma Joad and the newspaper clippings she holds, and that any filmed version will seldom match the viewer's imagination. This recalls Roland Barthes and his notion of anchorage, where an image can take any form in the imagination but may become fixed through, for example, the addition of written text to a visual image, or in the hands of a director, marrying a visual image with dialogue, sounds, movement or even written text. This shift in imagination is perhaps most keenly felt when one sees a film before reading its literary source and projecting the image of the film star into the book (Colin Firth as Mr Darcy in *Pride and Prejudice*, for instance, or Henry Fonda's Tom Joad in *The Grapes of Wrath*), or feeling a disjuncture between the two, where the casting of the star seems at odds with the literary description.

The privileging of the source text comes from a long history that Stam says 'quietly reinscribes the axiomatic superiority of literary art to film' (2000: 58). One example can be found in Shun Nakahara's 1990 *The Cherry Orchard/Sakura no Sono*, another manga adaptation, and nominated in the Best Film category of the Japan Academy Prize. The film features members of a theatre group in a girl's school who are preparing to stage a performance of the Chekhov play. In 2008, Nakahara directed a remake under the title *The Cherry Orchard: Blossoming*, with changes to character names and the use of more diverse locations throughout the film. Nakahara's use of this as the title of both films could be seen as a direct way to attract an audience of those with the literary capital that may not otherwise be interested in a teen comedy-drama. The original 1990 film begins with a schoolgirl, Kaori Shiromaru (Miho Miyazawa, now an established TV actor), giving a quick retelling of the plot of the play to her disinterested boyfriend, who is more interested in making out with her. They are in the theatre, with the set in place for the play. She explains to him that the school stages the same play each year. When one of the lead girls, Sugiyama (Miho Tsumiki), is caught smoking, it looks like the play will be cancelled for this year rather than allow the miscreant to represent the school. The imagery of the cherry blossom is invoked, as one tearful student exclaims:

> **Student**: The cherry blossoms bloom the same way every year. I don't like it [the cancellation] at all. The students come and go. But the blossoms stay here. It's not fair.

The passing of time is therefore invoked, a reference to the girls not being at school for much longer. During the long (fifty minutes) set up to the premise of the cancellation, Nakahara begins to hint at the original manga's 'lesbian narrative' (Welker 2005: 130, n.28), when he includes three or four cutaway close-ups – a girl's lips as she drinks from a straw, another student's hair blowing in the breeze, or legs swinging under a table (Figure 9.3). When Sugiyama comments on another girl's, Shimizu (Hiroko Nakajima) haircut, she suggests that it was done to impress another girl, Kurata (Yasuyo Shirashima). Sugiyama asks her, 'Because you wanted her to see it, right? You like her, don't you?'. Shimizu plays coy, and Sugiyama awkwardly responds, 'Uh . . . just what I said. I don't know why, but I always thought you . . .'. Rather than end the conversation, Shimizu blushes, but then prompts, 'Thought you . . . what?'. Sugiyama continues, 'I can't explain, but I've watched you', then quickly adds, 'I don't mean you're a lesbian', and the conversation falls silent. At the mention of Kurata, it seems that Sugiyama is also romantically interested in her. They then settle in to discussing why a girls' school suits them, and the teasing they were subjected to by boys in their junior schools. Later, Shimizu admits that she does like Kurata, a feeling that is soon reciprocated.

The reason for staging *The Cherry Orchard* each year is revealed late in the film when the school principal admits that he worked backstage on a production of the play when he was young, soon after the war, admitting, 'it was odd to do a play about rich Russians. Our friends criticised us, "Why not face reality? Describe the real Japan!" But we could get money more easily for a classic like this. It helped us financially and we could survive. And we hoped that someday we'd

Figure 9.3 Eroticized close-up in *The Cherry Orchard* (1990).

do a play relating to real life.' Both the 1990 and 2008 films touch on the possible same-sex relationships between the girls, following the 'girls' love' (*gūruzu rabu*, or the often homoeroticized *yuri*) trope found in the original manga, but one handled with subtlety rather than overt scenes of physical love. In a sense, this provides a cover for the filmmakers and manga writers to obfuscate the issue so that the reading could be explained as a girl-crush between friends, rather than an unambiguous turn into homosexuality. The appearance of the original film in the 1990s, targeted at a mainstream audience, played an important role in highlighting the possibility of same-sex relations for Japanese girls or women, and as Welker writes (2005: 137):

> While the Japanese lesbian community has not emerged as rapidly or on the scale of its male counterpart, Japanese lesbians have, through translation and borrowing, but most importantly through telling their own stories created a viable and vibrant lesbian community.

The ability to transpose this part of the storyline from the manga to the film, therefore, had a significant role in broader discourses circulating in Japanese society.

In creating an adaptation, what is important is, as Stam (2000: 58) argues, not a strict fidelity to the source text, 'but rather to the essence of the medium of expression', an equally subjective proposition. It is here that an adaptation can be 'less an attempted resuscitation of an originary word than a turn in an ongoing dialogical process' (Stam 2000: 64); in other words, the filmed adaptation is advancing a discourse rather than offering a reductive, limiting remaking of the source text. In our discussion of *Departures/Okuribito* in Chapter 5, the theme of death was seen as central to the story of Daigo and his new position preparing the dead for their funeral ceremony. An adaptation of the novel *Nōkanfu Nikki/Diary of an Undertaker* (1993, then revised 1996) by Aoki Shinmon, *Departures* differed from the novel by excising many of the religious themes found in the earlier text, causing friction between the author and the filmmaker, and seen as 'one of the reasons the author did not allow the title of his book to be used for the film' (Mullins 2010: 102, n. 2). Aoki's personal experience as a 'coffinman' fed directly into his novel, and he was initially critical that the film ignored the theme of the ultimate fate of the dead (in a spiritual sense). Following the success of the film (winning a slew of Japanese film awards along with the 2009 Academy Award for Best Foreign Language Film), sales of Aoki's book rose sharply, with the author hoping that this would extend the themes that were not fully developed in the film, and this would lead readers 'to reflect more deeply about the meaning of death and the final destination of the dead (*okurareta saki*)' (Mullins 2010: 103, n.4). In this way, the film is part of the 'ongoing dialogical process', perhaps limited in the themes it can develop due to the constraints of the feature film, in this case already over 130 minutes long.

The impact of *Departures* both in Japan and abroad indicates the ability to strike a chord with audiences. While its focus may not have been true to the wishes of the original author, it focuses heavily on the roles of those having to deal with death from a pragmatic approach. When Daigo visits his boss's (Sasaki) personal living area above the shop, he notices a picture of Sasaki's wife. Without prompting, Sasaki speaks:

> **Sasaki**: My wife: She died on me nine years ago. (pause) One of you always goes first, but it's hard being left behind. (he wistfully stares into the distance) I made her beautiful and sent her off.

The practicalities of dealing with the dying are again highlighted when the bathhouse keeper, Mrs Yamashita dies, and her son expresses a wish to watch the cremation process, out of a sense of honour, rather than a macabre wish. As the crematorium operator prepares to light the furnace, he pauses, and contemplates aloud to the son:

> **Man**: Working here all these years, I've often thought that maybe death is like a gateway. Dying doesn't mean the end. You go through it and onto the next thing. It's a gate. And as the gatekeeper, I've sent so many on their way, telling them, 'Off you go. We'll meet again'.

He ignites the furnace. In this way *Departures* offers a closer link to the novel in a way that is not necessarily tied to one specific theological set of beliefs. When Daigo is faced with a personal tragedy, the death of an elderly family member, he questions:

> **Daigo**: So, what was his life for, anyway? Living seventy-some years and leaving one box of stuff?

With these questions, Daigo is able to present an alternative view to the 'gateway', suggesting that there are no ongoing repercussions from one's life. As he prepares the body, he discovers a small icon that triggers a memory, and, turning to the now pregnant Mika, the film closes on a scene that seems to answer his questions, again keeping the film aligned with the novel's quest to encourage thought about death and 'final' destinations.

Keeping the title of a source text for a filmed adaptation is a way of capitalizing on a pre-existing market for a known text (some recent Japanese examples include *Bakuman* and *Thermae Romae*), but often filmmakers will choose to change the title to indicate 'the transformations operative in the adaptation' (Stam 2000: 65). The example of Akira Kurosawa's *Throne of Blood/Kumonosu-jō* (lit. *Spider Web Castle*), clearly based on Shakespeare's Macbeth, indicates a shift to focus on the object of pursuit (the castle and all it symbolizes) rather than the ambitious individual at the centre of the action. Hutchinson, however, sees problems in Western scholarship failing to move beyond measuring the worth of the film against its original text, arguing that Kurosawa's films are too often read 'not only in terms of hierarchy and fidelity, but also in terms of cultural essentialism' (2006: 181). The critics, she argues, 'revert to using a hierarchical structure of the (superior) original Western format versus the Japanese adaptation which is to be judged by Western standards' (original parentheses) (Hutchinson 2006: 181).

Stam suggests that a filmmaker can deliberately choose to ignore fidelity to the source text in the name of temporal social or political comment or for comic effect, where he notes that 'the cinema offers possibilities of disunity and disjunction'. Stam uses the soundtrack to Stanley Kubrick's Dr *Strangelove* (1964), loosely based on the dramatic 1958 novel Red Alert, where an instrumental version of 'Try a Little Tenderness' plays against a background of nuclear-armed planes on a bombing run as an example, where the 'possible contradictions between tracks become an aesthetic resource, opening the way to a multitemporal, polyrhythmic cinema' (2000: 60). Could it be, as Hutchinson suggests, that an 'adaptation may in fact be seen as privileged, in that it has claimed power over the original through the act of appropriating it' (2006: 181)? In other words, in a particular cultural environment, can it be 'better' than the original because it adds to the existing text, it becomes an interpretation, rather than a translation, and therefore becomes its own, perhaps incomparable, text.

Miwa Nishikawa's touching 2009 rural drama *Dear Doctor* is an adaptation of her own screenplay that won a slew of awards in Japan, including four Kinema junpo awards, four Yokohama Film Festival awards (including Best Film at both) and three Blue Ribbon awards (judged by film journalists from across Japan). Nishikawa has also written two novels, bringing one of them, *The Long Excuse/Nagai iiwake*, published in 2015, to the screen in 2016, and in 2020 her adaptation of the 1990 novel, Mibuncho [lit. Inmate Files], about a reformed yakuza gangster, was released as *Under the Deep Sky/Subarashiki Sekai* [lit. Wonderful World], premiering at the Toronto International Film Festival.

Released in 2012, *Signal: Luca on Mondays/Shigunaru – Getsuyôbi no Ruka* (dir. Masaaki Tanaguchi) is a poignant love story, sparked in a cinema projection booth, and based on a 2008 novel by Hisashi Sekiguchi. The film is not only about the blossoming romance between its two lead characters, Keisuke (played by *Love Exposure*'s Takahiro Nishijima) and Ruka (Azusa Mine in her acting debut), but also about the love of cinema, reminiscent of films such as *Cinema Paradiso/Nuovo Cinema Paradiso*, (1988, dir. Giuseppe Tornatore) or even the 2005 Indonesian film *Joni's Promise/Janji Joni* (dir. Joko Anwar). Keisuke takes on a summer job as a projectionist assisting the 'Chief Engineer', the beautiful, soft-spoken Ruka, in an old theatre that specializes in screening 'classic' films. With an air of mystery, Ruka has an internal sadness and lives in the cinema in a small room beside the projection booth. She has a small garden on the roof of the cinema but has not left the building for three years. The owner of the cinema has employed Keisuke on the proviso that he does not ask Ruka about her past, nor is he to fall in love with her.

Ruka eventually begins to open up to Keisuke, and hands him a cherished document, the cinema's handwritten 'bible' (*Tora No Maki*), which begins with the words:

> Movies only exist as what we project on the screen. Protect this theatre and be proud as an engineer.

The sense of cinematic tradition runs throughout the film, and Keisuke reminisces about how the cinema was a refuge for him and his brother from a home filled with domestic violence, claiming, 'When the movie started, I could forget everything that was happening in real life'. And while all those that work in the cinema profess a love for the building and its old technologies, Ruka laments, 'In reality, they don't need movie projectionists anymore. Everything is digital. If you press a button you can project movies perfectly'. The drama in *Signal* is heightened by Ruka's mysterious past, and her former emotionally charged lover, the wealthy Reiji (Kengo Kora), who has a powerful hold over Ruka, with a symbolic link to Mondays (as per the film's title). There is a melancholy awareness throughout the film that the cinema has a very limited future.

Mumon: The Land of Stealth/Shinobi no Kuni (2017, directed by the prolific Yoshihiro Nakamura, with fifteen feature films and six TV episodes since 2008), is a comic *jidaigeki* (period action film), loosely based on sixteenth-century historical events, and adapted from a novel and a manga series. Well over half of Nakamura's films have been adaptations of novels by a variety of authors, with most of the remainder made up of manga adaptations. Nakamura's comic adaptation of Ryō Wada's hit two-part 2013 novel 'The Pirate's Daughter/Murakami Kaizoku no Musume' into *Mumon*, shifts the focus away from the pirate-led sea battles that dominate the early parts of the novel to the on-land battles that ultimately determine power in the region. It also lightens the mood from the 'Shinobi no Kuni' manga, published from 2009 until 2011 which Wada wrote, with artwork handled by an established manga artist. Mumon (boy-band idol, Satoshi Ohno) is the region's most stealthy ninja, but also relatively lazy. The film was a reasonable hit at the box office, taking almost US$18 million (ranking twenty-first for the year according to boxofficemojo). The only impetus for Mumon to carry out his work is his lustful desire for his gorgeous, but chaste, wife Okuni (Satomi Ishihara from *Shin Godzilla*). When the warring samurai group, led by the fresh-faced, petulant Oda Nobukatsu (another boy-band star, Yuri Chinen), attacks Mumon's province, he has to decide whether to stay and fight or make a hasty escape. Among the constant barrage of action, the film addresses themes of greed, honesty, trust and generational change. Given the use of boy-band actors, the soundtrack uses pop songs and a contemporary rock and pop score, rather than traditional instrumentation that might be expected in a historically set film.

The Many Faces of Ito: The Movie/Itô kun A to E (2018), directed by Ryuichi Hiroki, who had a minor hit with the grungy apartment-based comedy-drama *Tokyo Trash Baby/Tôkyô Gomi Onna* in 2000, is adapted from a successful Netflix-commissioned TV series, *Itô kun A to E*, that was adapted from a 2013 novel by Asako Yuzuki, who also worked as a screenwriter on both the series and the film. This romantic-comedy stars Fumino Kimura (from the TV series) as Rio Yazaki, a cynical young, but successful, screenwriter and teacher trying to find a new angle for her next drama. Yazaki is a strong, independent woman, resentful of the way her female fans yearn for romance, and following one public lecture and focus group with her readers, confides to her publisher, Shinya Tamura (Kei Tanaka):

> **Yazaki**: It is pointless to lecture women who have no sense of self-actualization. Don't they have anything better to do than come here?

The women have filled out surveys about their lives, loves and ambitions, and as Tamura reads through some of them, she states:

> **Yazaki**: They are all pathetic.

Tamura suggests that she uses their responses as a base for her next TV drama, Yazaki gives this some thought and then begins a process of meeting the respondents individually to gather information. Her focus is on their darker moments and failed relationships, a reflection of her own troubled personal life.

The film draws on the structure of the novel and its story where the brash, often rude Seijiro Ito (Masaki Okada) develops relationships with five different women (respondents 'A' to 'D' from Yazaki's study), as well as through his interactions with Yazaki, whom he knows from their screenwriting cram school, and later becomes the 'E' of the story. Yazaki dispenses sage advice to the women, and they begin to use the sessions with her as a form of therapy. The common link between the women, unbeknownst to Yazaki, is Ito and his ruthless regard for their feelings. Despite appearing to show concern for the women, Yazaki maintains her detachment. She realizes that two of the women ('C' and 'D') are interested in the same man (although she does not realize it is Ito), so suggests to Tamura that in order to make for a more exciting drama:

> **Yazaki**: We need these women to get dirtier in order to achieve that feat.

Yazaki is not troubled by her ethical actions, informing 'D' that it would be wise to surrender her virginity if she wants to keep her man, but telling 'C' that she needs to act quickly if she wants to attract him. Ito writes a screenplay about the events and submits it to Tamura, who, as an objective TV producer, feels that Ito's script is better than Yazaki's because he is writing from his personal experiences, whereas Yazaki is writing 'from the side'. This theme resonates with the idea of an adaptation, where the perspective of whose story is being told is important. The title alone of *The Many Faces of Ito* suggests it is a story about him, yet most of the narrative is driven by Yazaki, and she is the character who experiences the arc of the story.

One French film to have travelled the route from novel to screen, *Rémi: Nobody's Boy/Rémi sans famille* (2018, dir. Antoine Blossier), also has the heritage of being a Japanese anime. Originally published in 1878 as an episodic novel by Hector Malot, *Sans Famille* (its original title) has had a number of film and TV remakes across territories including the Soviet Union, Italy and Hong Kong. This tale of a young orphan who joins a travelling entertainer who mentors him and teaches him about humanity deals with a number of universal themes that no doubt added to its international success. Appearing in Japan first as a feature-length anime in 1970 as *Little Remi and Famous Dog Capi/ Chibikko Remi to Meiken Kapi* (dir. Yugo Serikawa), the anime was distributed across the global market in versions including French, Spanish, Italian and Russian. By 1977 a fifty-one-episode animated TV series had been put into production under the title *Nobody's Boy: Remi/le Naki Ko* [lit. *Child without a Family*], and another feature-length anime was produced in 1980 by the same production team and studio. A gender-switched TV series was also produced by Fuji TV in 1996–7 under the name *Rémi: Nobody's Girl*.

This latest French production of *Rémi*, closely follows the visual characteristics of the earlier versions, including the 1970 anime, and features the internationally recognized Daniel Auteuil as the Italian minstrel, Vitalis, who saves Rémi (Maleaume Paquin) from being taken to an orphanage and takes him on the road with his 'troupe' that consists of himself alongside a dog (the original novel has three dogs) and monkey that perform tricks for the audience. The film achieved moderate success at the box office (taking around US$7.5 million). *Rémi* opens with a night-time, gothic-style view of a large chateau or manor house during a violent thunderstorm. Inside, a young boy is lying in bed, frightened by the storm. He soon runs downstairs, only to collide with a shadowy figure who turns out to be an old man named Rémi (Jacques Perrin), who comforts the boy by retelling his story. The rest of the film takes place as an extended flashback, with occasional voiceovers by the older Rémi, until it returns to the present day and the revelation that Rémi had found his birth mother back in England, before going on to become a famous opera singer. With many of the location shots taken in the Occitanie region of Southern France, and the rolling grasslands of Aubrac, *Rémi* captures the episodic and visually adventurous tone of the original novel (in essence a 'road-trip' film).

A more contemporary film, *In Harmony/En équilibre* [aka *In Balance*] (2015, dir. Denis Dercourt), is based on the literary memoir *Sur mes quatre jambes* [on my Four Legs] by equestrian stunt rider, Bernard Sachsé, co-written with Véronique Pellerin. *In Harmony* is the story of the fictitious stuntman, Marc Guermont (based on Sachsé, but played by Albert Dupontel, one of the stars of Gaspar Noé's *Irréversible*). Following a similar trajectory to *The Diving Bell and The Butterfly* (but ultimately less tragic), *In Harmony* tracks the aftermath of an incident where a man becomes physically impaired and must deal with adapting to their altered circumstances. Guermont's spine is crushed following a fall while shooting a stunt for a German film. Assigned to his insurance claim is the loss adjuster, Florence (Cécile de France), who finds him confrontational, but spirited. A mutual attraction develops between the two, and soon Florence realizes that there is the possibility of a life beyond her husband and two children.

Figure 9.4 Albert Dupontel as a stuntman in *In Harmony* (2015).

Guermont makes Florence realize that her life lacks passion, and their bond over classical music sees Florence return to her first love, the piano. The obstinate Guermont similarly embraces his passion for horses and is soon back on his horse competing in equestrian events as a 'paraplegic rider', as one television commentator calls him (Figure 9.4).

While *In Harmony* may over-romanticize Sachsé's life (unlike Guermont, he was married and his wife helped him through his recovery), Dercourt firmly establishes the *équilibre* between the characters, most clearly shown in some of the film's later moments. Dercourt presents parallel images of Guermont in full dressage mode on his horse, intercut with an emotionally moved Florence finally finding the inspiration she needs to play a rousing étude on her piano, and deciding to pursue her playing at a higher level.

Conclusion

The practicalities of taking an existing text and transforming it in another medium may give rise to a range of practices and praxis. To end this chapter on adaptation, it is perhaps necessary to return to François Truffaut's famous essay 'A Certain Tendency in French Cinema' (first published in *Cahiers du cinéma* in 1954), in which he excoriated the so-called 'tradition of quality' which turned French literary classics into predictably well-furnished, well-spoken and stylistically formulaic films (Stam 2013: 178). Truffaut's words have been used ever since to denounce and push to the margins a whole range of films by directors whose reputations and careers were severely diminished by the article. But in one sense, Truffaut was right: film – as an art form distinct from literature – deserved themes and narrative structures that would be emboldened by visual storytelling practices. The range of films, genres and approaches outlined earlier serves once again to reiterate the ongoing vitality of French and Japanese cinema in the realm of adaptation and demonstrates how the complex conceptual relationship between images and words affects the viewing experience. These films are not the bland reproduction of an 'original' text; rather, they expand upon and inject new ways of seeing into both text and film.

Conclusion

Where to next for the cinematic influence?

At first glance, the films produced by France and Japan are about as widely different as any two national cinemas can be. While both enjoy the support of developed economies and a well-educated society with high regard (and funding) for the status of film, their cultural and linguistic differences signal a vast range of areas where commonalities may be hard to trace. We hope to have shown in this book how each film industry has been influenced by the other, and where deliberate or even serendipitous parallels can be found.

The concept of the *nouvelle vague* in France was not only effective for the marketing of French film, and for distinguishing it as cinema beyond the West's already-exotic reputation of French films, but the concept was also utilized in Japan, with Shōchiku Studios using the French phrase to promote the films of Ōshima and Yoshida. As Standish notes though, neither of these artists was pleased with 'this labelling as their films [as they saw them] grew from a spontaneous reaction to the events of the post-war period and in no way were they an emulation of the French' (2011: 157, n. 3). Tracing the links, as we have attempted in this book, nevertheless leads to inevitable similarities between the two cinemas.

For Japanese filmmakers in the 1960s and 1970s, 'there was a desire to overcome the narratives of history being institutionalized through mainstream cinema' (Standish 2011: 148) resulting in the *nuberu bagu* and the subsequent incorporation of 'pink' elements in films that confronted mature audiences in their telling of contemporary Japan. Standish points to the efforts to deny entry of select Japanese films to European festivals as evidence of 'the efficacy of these counter-discourses to unsettle certain elements within both the film industry and the government who intervened on behalf of Eiren' (2011: 148) to prevent particular cinematic images of Japan being unleashed on the world. This, then, takes us back to the power of the cinematic form and its ability to act as a messenger across cultures.

The importance of film has perhaps been no better explored than in Bazin's work, where we can:

> interpret his criticism as grounded in a view of the distinctiveness of cinema's being as resting on how the world inside the edges of the film frame reveals itself to us, and how we may enter into that world in the act of watching a film. (Kuhn 2005: 405)

The privileging of film as a multi-faceted text that delivers a visual and audio sensory experience has long been seen by filmmakers in France and Japan as an entry point for the construction of representations of the self. Projecting the culturally determined meanings encoded in films can be manipulated through styles ranging from realism to formalism, each making a different impact on the audience. The filmgoers of France and Japan are perhaps more willing to take risks than audiences in other nations, allowing avant-garde productions to live within the scope of commercially viable films, in an industry increasingly global, and increasingly dependent on economic return at the box office.

There are, of course, a number of paths that we have been unable to trace in this book. For instance, there remains fruitful work to be done in the world of animation, where Japan is well represented in France at events such as the prestigious Annecy International Animated Film Festival. Many top prizes have been awarded to Japanese films across its sixty-year history, with the 2017 Cristal for a Feature Film awarded to Masaaki Yuasa for *Lu Over the Wall*, and the festival's Jury Award to Sunao Katabuchi for *In This Corner of the World*. In 2019, the festival featured a showcase of Japanese animation with feature screenings of films by past and present animators, while at the 2021 festival, the first episode of *Japan Sinks: 2020, The Beginning of the End* (again directed by Yuasa) won a Jury Award for a TV Series.

Any further investigation of these two national cinemas would warrant a closer exploration of how gender impacts French and Japanese films, in terms of subject matter, narrative style, directors and even the issue of 'gaze'. Within both French and Japanese culture, gender plays an important role even in the base form of communication in linguistic forms and grammar. Politeness codes and gendered forms of address are important in France, and in Japanese society, with 'the masculine/feminine division of social roles . . . encoded in the topographical terms *soto* and *uchi*', with *soto* referring to the 'outside public world, the domain of men and the masculine', and *uchi* referring to 'the inside, private world symbolized by the home, the family unit, and by extension the feminine' (Standish 2006: 310). The role of female characters in films such as *Tokyo Story* and *Tokyo Sonata*, even though each was made decades apart, sees a familiar placement of the married woman. In the latter film, there is an opportunity for release, as Megumi runs from her husband and family in crisis, but she soon returns, providing stability and a sense of closure to the family unit.

The rise of the strong female character as the leading protagonist in films began in earnest in the 1970s. Japanese studios were keen to release prolific series that not only featured tough, sassy and sexy lead women but these women also became stars in their own right such as Sugimoto Kiki in the *Girl Boss* films, and then Kaji Meiko, first in the *Stray Cat Rock* films and then with the *Lady Snowblood* and *Female Convict Scorpion* films (Desser 2016: 115–19). The *Lady Snowblood* concept was later 'reimagined' as the futuristic *The Princess Blade* (2001, dir. Shinsuke Sato), starring Yumiko Shaku.

Despite the importance of the two 'Tokyo' films, the role of the female protagonist is not one that is necessarily tied to the domestic sphere in Japanese films, with many contemporary films presenting women in active, and at times, actively violent roles. Sono Sion's *Guilty of Romance* and *Tag* are both films where female leads take control, upsetting, outsmarting and at times defeating their male adversaries. Even Seijun Suzuki's films from the 1960s toyed with ideas of female empowerment, although not always with positive results, often ending in the death or rejection of the active female. From France, the success of *Amélie* exploited the cuteness (*kawaii*) of its female protagonist and her anime-like eyes, a character that rendered 'iconic of a certain form of French femininity (slight unreal gamine as opposed to sex kitten)' (Vanderschelden 2007: 45). Regardless of Amélie's romantic allusions, she controls her own destiny.

Japan's male protagonists are often constructed to represent their own form of masculinity measured against their career and their family life. Films such as *Hana-Bi* deliver a complex rift between the violent, physical demands of police work, the criminal environment and the joy and pathos of domestic life. Similarly, *Tokyo Sonata* explores the life of the salaryman and the unemployed, the dichotomy of the masculine provider/non-provider. On the other hand, there is the floating life of the itinerant worker, the Tora-sans of Japan, although Tora-san has the advantage over many itinerant workers in that he 'can wander freely, but he can also come home to a cozy family situation' (Gill 2003: 23). The option of marriage is not so pressing for Tora-san as it is for many Japanese men, and '[t]here is a poignancy in his ability to marry and settle down, but the family is always there for him' (Gill 2003: 23). The death of the eldest, cherished son in Kore-eda's *Still Walking* leads grandfather

Kyohei to defend himself against his wife's charge that as the local doctor, 'He was so busy that he couldn't be here when his own son was dying'. His response reflects what he, or his generation, sees as the duty of the male breadwinner:

> **Kyohei**: I couldn't help it, I had a rash of food-poisoning patients. [then, accusingly at his wife] You don't have a clue how important work is to a man!

In Yaguchi's *Survival Family* (2016), it is through the use of its stereotyped gender roles and the challenges faced by the family, especially by Yoshiyuki, that it investigates the role of individuals within the collective unit. The bumbling patriarch and his son discover the ability to compromise and to work together with Mizue and Yui.

Japan's liberal attitudes to gender also account for responses to on-screen sexual acts where sexual violence is portrayed as a reflection of anxieties faced by those who do not fit the collectivist nature of Japanese society. Sexuality can be found in all manner of texts, from ancient art through to manga and anime. This embeddedness in society leads to the conclusion that 'there is a broad legal acceptance that sexuality and violence are a part of one's normal social experience, and that citizens, even young people, might be exposed to materials portraying sexuality and violence as long as those portrayals are not so explicit that they violate a sense of public decorum' (Alexander 2003: 168). Thus, filmmakers such as Ōshima and, more recently, Sion Sono and Mika Ninagawa have been able to continue to make films that challenge audience perceptions of society. In France, similar attitudes have also remained as legacies of art and literature. French-born American writer Anaïs Nin, most famously romantically linked to another American writer, Henry Miller (as explored in Philip Kaufman's 1990 *Henry and June*, based on Nin's novel of the same name), was openly inspired by French literary and philosophical thought and the works of eminent figures such as Marcel Proust and Jean Cocteau.

An over-representation of male directors is not unique to Japan, but there are indications that female directors 'are beginning to make their voices heard and achieve recognition; not simply as "women directors" but as representatives of the Japanese movie industry' (Taylor-Jones 2013: 164).

Audience and reception

In an interview in 1980, Donald Richie noted that it was a difficult time for Japanese cinema because '[w]hat is different about Japanese cinema is that the minority audience was never particularly catered for' (Burnett 1980: 180), aside from the support of the Art Theatres Guild and other smaller film appreciation societies. Richie's less-than-positive appraisal of Japanese cinema at the time claimed that a shift had occurred, and with the arrival of television, Japan's 'major audience is gone', accompanied by a subsequent movement from what used to be 'a director's cinema' to 'a producer's cinema' (Burnett 1980: 180). In other words, the auteur movement that had so strengthened Japanese cinema from the late 1940s had given way in the 1970s to the austere, characterless filmmaking of economic necessity. Richie also points to the impenetrable gap between film and television in Japan, where television's commercial focus sees a fixation with the continuous production of content but using the same formats from decades earlier. Richie despairs that in Japan, 'I don't think a Kurosawa film has ever been on television' (Burnett 1980: 182), yet the arrival of video, DVD, cable and streaming services in Japan from that point forward no doubt saw a shift in access for Japanese audiences in their own homes. The much-anticipated arrival of the Netflix streaming service in 2015 proved to be enormously successful, and by 2018 Japan had the largest catalogue of streaming titles in all of the Netflix 190 national markets. Netflix Japan (at the time of writing) has over 6,300 titles compared to the United States with 5,600 titles (Champion Traveller 2018).

In working towards a greater appreciation of the connections between French and Japanese cinemas, it is instructive to recall Noël Burch's comment on film theory that 'the critical framework developed in France over the past decade [1960s/1970s] (partly through an investigation of Eastern thought) provides elements towards an understanding of the far-reaching theoretical implications of *le texte japonais*' (1979: 13). In other words, Western perceptions of Japan were already being critically assessed, and Burch refers to the mutual appreciation of each other's culture through the (clichéd) example of a Japanese scholar stating that 'French was the only language precise enough to render with precision the full imprecision of the *nō* play' (Burch 1979: 13). The interplay between these two cinemas could also be seen as part of a larger system that creates 'cultural fragmentation under the impact of imports as the audience for the local cultural product is fractured and seemingly "lost" to other cultures' (O'Regan 2004: 280). The impending domination of Hollywood blockbusters on box office takings around the world is an example, especially in those nations with either small populations or film industries unable to push back against the might of the corporate Hollywood.

The respect for each other's film industry can be found in frequent 'Retrospective' events such as the Kenji Mizoguchi Retrospective held by *La Cinémathèque Française* in March–April 2018, which not only project widely known and obscure films from bygone eras but also open up for debate between participants, film experts and special guests. Other films from Japan, including anime, are commonly featured in screenings, festivals and conferences across France, for example, the anime, *Hana and Alice Lead the Investigation/Hana to Arisu Satsujin Jiken* (directed by Shunji Iwai and released in 2015) featured among the screenings at the *Musée de la Cinémathèque* in May 2018.

The importance of festivals in promoting French and Japanese films to foreign audiences is undeniable. In Carroll Harris's study of Australian festivals, she notes how the decline in small independently run cinemas has been offset by a rise in festivals that have become 'increasingly professionalised, moving from community outings to fully fledged commercial events complete with sponsorship from businesses and national-cultural organisations' (2017: 48). The concentration of genre or national films within a festival period means that the 'festival's distributive and commercial power . . . is in its status as a curated, live, film-cultural event' (Carroll Harris 2017: 49). In the case of festivals held in Australia, Carroll Harris cites figures showing that locally produced films are able to 'enjoy a considerable, predictable and ongoing measure of popular success . . . that eludes them at the box office' (2017: 50). Festivals, she surmises, offer 'a pathway to a clear-cut market' (50), something that can also be said for the various annual French and Japanese festivals that traverse the United Kingdom, the United States, Canada and Australia, where the potential audience consists of those with an existing, defined interest in those particular national cinemas.

The importance of film festivals extends beyond just their marketing and economic potentials, with Naomi Kawase, in reference to her own involvement in the Nara International Film Festival, noting that 'The film festival isn't just about viewing movies, but it's also about connecting people and making movies. It's a very creative place for us' (Kawase 2012). The importance of festivals in drawing attention to films from 'other' places is perhaps no better illustrated than in Hamaguchi's nomination for the Palme d'Or and his win in the Best Screenplay category for *Drive My Car* at Cannes in 2021. The exposure given to this ultimately modest film is immense in bringing it to the attention of global audiences and creating a momentum for other festival screenings. In Hamaguchi's case, the accreditation from Cannes judges undoubtedly led to the film's nomination in the Best Picture category at the 2022 Oscars.

Such a creative place is also found in the intersections between French and Japanese cinema. For more than a century, personal interactions and technical and thematic influences have passed between the two national cinemas. Mutual respect for the power and beauty of cinema and the cinematic form can be found. Increasingly, funding opportunities and investments through co-productions appear to be more commonplace, with formal and informal agreements between studios, production houses and various state institutions perpetuating the interchange of filmmakers, crew and acting talent that traverse the European continent and East Asia. In the two parts of this book, we first traced the historical and stylistic links between French and Japanese cinemas. We then presented examples from films across the decades that draw out symmetries in themes, ideas and approaches that maintain ongoing and, at times, highly recognizable motifs and exchanges across the two cinemas. In this way, we can see the crucial role played by the cinematic influences that have shaped French and Japanese films up to the present day.

Films cited

2 Autumns, 3 Winters/2 Automnes, 3 Hivers. 2013. Dir. Sébastien Betbeder. Envie de Tempête Productions: France.

2001: A Space Odyssey. 1968. Dir. Stanley Kubrick. Metro-Goldwyn-Mayer, Stanley Kubrick Productions: USA/Great Britain.

A Better Tomorrow/Ying Hung Boon Sik. 1986. Dir. John Woo. Cinema City: Hong Kong.

A Bride for Rip Van Winkle/Rippu Van Winkuru no hanayome. 2016. Dir. Shunji Iwai. Rockwell Eyes, BS Fuji, Hikari TV, Kinoshita Group, Nihon Eiga Senmon Channel, Papado Music Publishers, Pony Canyon, Toei Company: Japan.

Ace Attorney/Gyakuten Saiban. 2012. Dir. Takashi Miike. Nippon Television, Toho Company, Yomiuri Telecasting Corporation: Japan.

Achilles and the Tortoise/Akiresu to Kame. 2008. Dir. Takeshi Kitano. Bandai Visual, Office Kitano, TV Asahi, Tokyo FM, Tokyo Theatres K.K., WOWOW: Japan.

Adrift in Tokyo/Tenten. 2007. Dir. Satoshi Miki. Style Jam, Geneon Entertainment, Zak Corp., Aoi Promotion: Japan.

A Fistful of Dollars/Per un Pugno di Dollari. 1964. Dir. Sergio Leone. Constantin Film, Jolly Film, Ocean Films: Italy/Spain/Germany.

After the Rain/Ame agaru. 1999. Dir. Takashi Koizumi. Asmik Ace Entertainment, Kurosawa Production Co., 7 Films Cinéma: Japan/France.

Air Doll/Kiku Ningyo. 2009. Dir. Hirokazu Kore-eda. Engine Film: Japan.

Alibi.com. 2017. Dir. Philippe Lacheau. Fechner Films, TF1 Droits Audiovisuels, StudioCanal, TF1 Films, CN5 Productions: France.

All is Forgiven/Tout est pardonné. 2007. Dir. Mia Hansen-Løve. TPS Star, Les Films Pelléas, Centre National de la Cinématographie: France.

Amélie [aka: The Fabulous Destiny of Amélie Poulain/Le Fabuleux Destin d'Amélie Poulain]. 2001. Dir. Jean-Pierre Jeunet. Claudie Ossard Productions, UGC, Victoires Productions Canal +, France 3: France.

Amour/Love. 2012. Dir. Michael Haneke. Les Films du Losange: France.

Anatomy of Hell/Anatomie de l'enfer. 2004. Dir. Catherine Breillat. Flach Films, CB Films, Canal+, CNC, Animatógrafo II [PT]: France, Portugal.

. . . And God Created Woman/Et Dieu . . . créa la femme. 1956. Dir. Roger Vadim. Cocinor: France.

Antiporno/Anchiporuno. 2016. Dir. Sono Sion. Django Film, Nikkatsu: Japan.

Asako I and II/Netemo Sametemo [lit. Even if You Wake Me]. 2018. Dir. Ryûsuke Hamaguchi. Bitters End, C&I Entertainment, Comme des Cinémas, Elephant

House, Nagoya Broadcasting Network, Netemo Sametemo Production Committee: Japan/France.

Assassination Classroom/Ansatsu Kyôshitsu. 2015. Dir. Eiichirô Hasumi. Robot Communications: Japan.

A Summer's Tale/Conte d'été. 1996. Dir. Eric Rohmer. Canal +, La Sept Cinéma, Les Films du Losange, Sofilmka: France.

A Tale of Sorrow and Sadness/Hishū monogatari. 1977. Dir. Seijun Suzuki. Shōchiku: Japan.

A Taxing Woman/Marusa no onna. 1987. Dir. Juzo Itami. New Century Producers, Itami Productions: Japan.

A Trip to the Moon/Le voyage dans la lune. 1902. Dir. Georges Méliès. Star Film Company: France.

Avec mon mari/Abekku mon mari [lit. With my Husband]. 1999. Dir. Kentarō Ōtani. Mutô Kiichi Office: Japan.

Babel. 2006. Dir. Alejandro Gonzalez Iñarritu. Paramount Pictures, Paramount Vantage, Anonymous Content, Zeta Film, Central Films, Media Rights Capital: USA/Mexico/France.

Back to Burgundy/Ce qui nous lie. 2017. Dir. Cédric Klapisch. Ce Qui Me Meut Motion Pictures, StudioCanal, France 2 Cinéma: France.

Bakuman. 2015. Dir. Hitoshi Ohne. Office Crescendo, Toho Pictures, Toho Company: Japan.

Balzac and the Little Chinese Seamstress/Balzac et la petite tailleuse chinoise. 2002. Dir. Dai Sijie. Les Productions Internationales Le Film: France.

Battle Royale/Batoru Rowaiaru. 2000. Dir. Kinji Fukasaku. AM Associates, Gaga, Kobi, MF Pictures, Nippon Shuppan Hanbai, Toei Co., WOWOW: Japan.

Battle Royale 2: Requiem/Batoru rowaiaru II: Chinkonka. 2003. Dir. Kinji Fukasaku and Kenta Fukasaku. Fukasaku-gumi, Gaga, Nippon Shuppan Hanbai, Toei Co., WOWOW, TV Asahi, Sega, Tokyo FM Broadcasting: Japan.

Before We Vanish/Sanpo Suru Shinryakusha. 2017. Dir. Kiyoshi Kurosawa. Shōchiku, Nikkatsu: Japan.

Beloved/Les Bien-aimés. 2011. Dir. Christophe Honoré. Why Not Productions, France 2 Cinéma, Sixteen Films, Negativ: France.

Black Butler/Kuroshitsuji. 2014. Dirs. Kentarō Ōtani and Kei'ichi Satō. Warner Bros., Avex Entertainment, Square Enix Company, A Station, GyaO, Tokyu Recreation, RoC Works, C&I Entertainment: Japan.

Black Rain. 1989. Dir. Ridley Scott. Paramount Pictures, Jaffe-Lansing, Pegasus Film Partners: USA.

Black Snow/Kuroi Yuki. 1965. Dir. Takechi Tetsuji. Daisan Productions: Japan.

Blind Beast/Môjû. 1969. Dir. Yasuzô Masumura. Daiei Motion Picture Co.: Japan.

Blue Velvet. 1986. Dir. David Lynch. De Laurentiis Entertainment: USA.

Branded to Kill/Koroshi no rakuin. 1967. Dir. Seijun Suzuki. Nikkatsu: Japan.

Breathless/À bout de souffle. 1960. Dir. Jean-Luc Godard. Les Films Impéria: France.
Bullet Ballet. 1998. Dir. Shin'ya Tsukamoto. Kaijyu Theatre: Japan.
Cape No. 7/Hǎijiǎo Qī Hào. 2008. Dir. Wei Te-sheng. ARS Film Production: Taiwan.
Château de la Reine/Ohi no Yakata. 2014. Dir. Hajime Hashimoto. D.I.G., Commes des Cinémas: Japan/France.
Chocolat/Chocolate. 1988. Dir. Claire Denis. Caroline Productions: France.
Cinema Paradiso/Nuovo Cinema Paradiso. 1988. Dir. Giuseppe Tornatore. Cristaldifilm, Les Films Ariane, Rai 3, Forum Picture: Italy/France.
Claire's Knee/Le genou de Claire. 1970. Dir. Éric Rohmer. Les Films du Losange: France.
Cleo from 5 to 7/Cléo de 5 à 7. 1962. Dir. Agnès Varda. Ciné Tamaris: France.
Confidentially Yours/Vivement dimanche! 1983. Dir. François Truffaut. Les Films du Carrosse, Films A2, Soprofilms: France.
Cutie Honey: Live Action/Kyûtî Hanî. 2004. Dir. Hideaki Anno. Gainax, WOWOW: Japan.
Cutie Honey: Tears/Kyūtī Hanī Tiāzu. 2016. Dir. Takeshi Asai. Toei Company: Japan.
Daguerreotype/Le Secret de la chambre noire. 2016. Dir. Kiyoshi Kurosawa. Film-In-Evolution [FR], Celluloid Dreams [FR], Frakas Productions [BE], Arte France Cinéma, Bitters End [JP]: Japan, France, Belgium.
Dawn of the Felines/Mesuneko Tachi. 2017. Dir. Kazuya Shiraishi. Nikkatsu, Django Films: Japan.
Dear Doctor/Dia Dokutâ. 2009. Dir. Miwa Nishikawa. Bandai Visual Co., Denner Systems, Dentsu, Eisei Gekijo, Engine Film, Yahoo Japan, TV Man Union: Japan.
Death by Hanging/Kôshikei. 1968. Dir. Nagisa Ōshima. Art Theatre Guild, Sozosha: Japan.
Death Note/Desu Nōto. 2006. Dir. Shūsuke Kaneko. Nippon Television Network (NTV), Shueisha, Warner Bros. (Japan): Japan.
Death Note: Light Up the New World/Desu Nōto Light up the NEW World. 2016. Dir. Shinsuke Sato. Chukyo TV Broadcasting Company, D.N. Dream Partners, Dentsu, Django Film, Fukuoka Broadcasting System, Hiroshima Telecasting, Horipro, Hulu, Miyagi Television Broadcasting, Nikkatsu, Nippon Television Network, Sapporo Television, Shizuoka Daiichi Television, Shōchiku Company, Shueisha, Video Audio Project, Warner Bros., Yomiuri Telecasting Corporation: Japan.
Death Note 2: The Last Name/Desu Nōto the Last Name. 2006. Dir. Shūsuke Kaneko. Horipro, Konami, Nikkatsu Studio, Nikkatsu, Nippon Television Network, Shōchiku Company, Shueisha, Video Audio Project, Warner Bros., Yomiuri Telecasting Corporation: Japan.
Demonlover. 2002. Dir. Olivier Assayas. Citizen Films, Cofimage, Elizabeth Films: France.
Departures/Okuribito. 2008. Dir. Yôjirô Takita. Amuse Soft Entertainment: Japan.
Dien Bien Phu. 1992. Dir. Pierre Schoendoerffer. Flach Film, France 2 Cinéma: France.

Dodes'ka-den/Dodesukaden. 1970. Dir. Akira Kurosawa. Toho Company, Yonki-no-Kai Productions: Japan.

Drive My Car/Doraibu mai kā. 2021. Dir. Ryusuke Hamaguchi. Bitters End, Bungeishunju, C&I Entertainment, Culture Entertainment, Drive My Car Production Committee, L'espace Vision: Japan.

Dr Strangelove or: How I Stopped Worrying and Learned to Love the Bomb. 1964. Dir. Stanley Kubrick. Columbia Pictures, Hawk Films: USA/UK.

Dying at a Hospital/Byôin de Shimu to Iu Koto. Dir. Jun Ichikawa. Kindai Eiga Kyokai, OPT Communications, TV Tokyo: Japan.

Early Spring/Sôshun. 1956. Dir. Yasujirô Ozu. Shōchiku Eiga: Japan.

Electric Dragon 80000 V/Erekuto Rikku Doragon 80000V. 2001. Dir. Gakuryû Ishii (as Sogo Ishii). Suncent CinemaWorks, Taki Corporation: Japan.

Emmanuelle. 1974. Dir. Just Jaeckin. Trinacra Films, Orphée Productions: France.

Enter the Void. 2009. Dir. Gaspar Noé. Fidélité Films, Wild Bunch, BUF Compagnie, Les Cinémas de la Zone, Essential Filmproduktion [Germany], BIM Distribuzione [IT], Canal+, Paranoid Films: France, Germany, Italy.

Eraserhead. 1977. Dir. David Lynch. American Film Institute, Libra Films: USA.

Eros + Massacre/Erosu Purasu Gyakusatsu. 1969. Dir. Yoshishige Yoshida. Gendai Eigasha, Bungakuza: Japan.

Fat Girl/A ma soeur! 2001. Dir. Catherine Breillat. Arte France Cinéma, CB Films, Canal+, Flach Film, CNC, Immagine e Cinema [IT], Urania Pictures S.r.l. [IT]: France, Italy.

Fear and Trembling/Stupeur et Tremblements. 2003. Dir. Alain Corneau. Canal+: France.

Firefly/Hotaru. 2000. Dir. Naomi Kawase. DENTSU Music And Entertainment, Imagica Corp., Les Films de L'Observatoire, Suncent CinemaWorks, Tokyo Theatres K.K.: Japan/France.

Fireworks/Hana-Bi. 1997. Dir. Takeshi Kitano. Bandai Visual Co.: Japan.

Five/Panj, [aka Five Dedicated to Ozu]. 2003. Dir. Abbas Kiarostami. Behnegar/MK2 Diffusion: Iran/France.

Foujita. 2015. Dir. Kōhei Oguri. Eurowide, Office Kōhei Oguri: France/Japan.

Frantz. 2016. Dir. Francois Ozon. Mandarin Films, FOZ, X-Filme Creative Pool [DE], Mars Films, France 2 Cinéma, Playtime: France, Germany.

Fullmetal Alchemist/Hagane no Renkinjutsushi. 2017. Dir. Fumihiko Sori. Oxybot, Square Enix Company, Warner Bros.: Japan.

Gantz. 2011. Dir. Satō Shinsuke. Chubu-nippon Broadcasting Company, Toho, Nikkatsu, Nippon Television, Yomiuri Telecasting Corporation: Japan.

Gantz 2: Perfect Answer. 2011. Dir. Satō Shinsuke. Horipro, J Storm, Nikkatsu, Nippon Television, Shueisha, Toho, Video Audio Project, Yomiuri Telecasting Corporation: Japan.

Ghost. 1990. Dir. Jerry Zucker. Paramount Pictures: USA.

Gladiator. 2000. Dir. Ridley Scott. Dreamworks, Universal Pictures: USA.

Glory to the Filmmaker/Kantoku: Banzai!. 2007. Dir. Takeshi Kitano. Bandai Visual, Tokyo FM, Dentsu, TV Asahi, Office Kitano: Japan.
Godzilla/Gojira. 1954. Dir. Ishirô Honda. Toho Film (Eiga): Japan.
Godzilla/Gojira. 1998. Dir. Roland Emmerich. Contropolis Film Productions, Fried Films, Independent Pictures II, Toho Co., Tristar Pictures: USA/Germany/Japan.
Godzilla vs. King Kong. 2021. Dir. Adam Wingard. Legendary Entertainment, Warner Bros.: USA.
Goodbye to the Summer/ Au Revoir L'Été/ Hotori no Sakuko [lit. Neighbouring Sakuko]. 2013. Dir. Kôji Fukada. Wa Entertainment: Japan.
Guilty of Romance/Koi no Tsumi. 2011. Dir. Sono Sion. Django Film, Nikkatsu: Japan.
Hana and Alice/Hana to Arisu. 2004. Dir. Shunji Iwai. Rockwell Eyes: Japan.
Harmonium/Fuchi ni tatsu. 2016. Dir. Kôji Fukada. Comme des Cinémas: France/Japan.
Helter Skelter/Herutā Sukerutā. 2012. Dir. Mika Ninagawa. WOWOW, Asmik Ace: Japan.
Himizu/Mole. 2011. Dir. Sono Sion. GAGA Corporation, Kodansha, Studio Three: Japan.
Hiroshima, Mon Amour/Hiroshima, My Love. 1959. Dir. Alain Resnais. Argos Films: France/Japan.
H Story. 2001. Dir. Nobuhiro Suwa. DENTSU, Imagica, J-Works, Suncent CinemaWorks: Japan.
Hulk. 2003. Dir. Ang Lee. Universal, Marvel Enterprises, Good Machine, Valhalla Motion Pictures: USA.
Humanity/L'humanité. 1999. Dir. Bruno Damont. 3B Productions, Arte France Cinéma, Canal+, CRRAV: France.
Ichi the Killer/Koroshiya 1. 2001. Dir. Miike Takashi. Omega Project, EMG, Star Max, Alpha Group, Spike Co., Excellent Films: Japan.
I Have to Buy New Shoes/Atarashii Kutsu wo Kawanakucha. 2012. Dir. Eriko Kitagawa. Toei Company, King Records, Kinoshita Komuten, Rockwell Eyes, TV Asahi, Toei Video, Dentsu, Big Apple, Nature Lab, Gento-sha: Japan.
Indochine/Indochina. 1992. Dir. Régis Wargnier. Canal+, Paradis Film: France.
In Harmony/En équilibre. 2015. Dir. Denis Dercourt. Mandarin Cinéma, StudioCanal Cinéfrance 1888, France 3 Cinéma: France.
In the Realm of the Senses/Ai no Korîda. 1976. Dir. Nagisa Ōshima. Argos Films, Ōshima Productions: France/Japan.
Intimate Enemies/L'Ennemi intime. 2007. Dir. Florent Emilio Siri. Les Films du Kiosque: France.
Irma Vep. 1996. Dir. Olivier Assayas. Dacia Films, Canal+: France.
Irreversible. 2002. Dir. Gaspar Noé. 120 Films: France.
It's Tough Being a Man/Otoko wa Tsurai yo. 1969. Dir. Yoji Yamada. Shōchiku Eiga: Japan.
Joni's Promise/Janji Joni. 2005. Dir. Joko Anwar. Kalyana Shira Film: Indonesia.

Journey to the Shore/Kishibe no Tabi. 2015. Dir. Kiyoshi Kurosawa. Comme des Cinémas, Office Shirous, WOWOW Films: France/Japan.

Jurassic Park. 1993. Dir. Steven Spielberg. Universal Pictures: USA.

Kamikaze Girls/Shimotsuma Monogatari. 2004. Dir. Nakashima Tetsuya. Amuse Pictures: Japan.

Kill Bill: 1 & 2. 2003/2004. Dir. Quentin Tarantino. Miramax, A Band Apart, Super Cool ManChu: USA.

King Kong versus Godzilla/Kingu Kongu Tai Gojira. 1962. Dir. Ishirō Honda. Toho: Japan.

Labyrinth of Dreams/Yume no Ginga. 1997. Dir. Gakuryû Ishii (aka Sogo Ishii). KSS: Japan.

Lady Maiko/Maiko wa Redî. 2014. Dir. Masayuki Suo. Fuji Television Network, Toho Company, Kansai Telecasting (KTV), Dentsu, Kyoto Shimbun, KBS Kyoto, Altamira Pictures Inc.: Japan.

La Femme Nikita. 1990. Dir. Luc Besson. Gaumont, Les Films du Loup, Cecchi Gori Group Tiger Cinematografica: France/Italy.

L'avventura/The Adventure. 1960. Dir. Michelangelo Antonioni. Cino del Duca, Produzioni Cinematografiche Europee, Societé Cinématographique Lyre: Italy/France.

Le Jour se lève/The Day Rises [Daybreak]. 1939. Dir. Marcel Carné. Productions Sigma: France.

Let the Sunshine In/Un beau soliel intérieur. 2017. Dir. Claire Denis. Curiosa Films, FD Production, Playtime, Ad Vitam, Versus Production [Belgium], CNC: France.

Like Father, Like Son/Soshite Chichi ni Naru. 2013. Dir. Hirokazu Kore-eda. Amuse, Fuji Television, GAGA: Japan.

Like Someone in Love/Raiku Samuwan In Rabu. 2012. Dir. Abbas Kiarostami. Centre National du Cinéma et de L'image Animée (CNC), MK2 Productions, Euro Space: France/Japan.

Little Astroboy. 2019. Dir. Virgile Trouillot. Something Big, Tezuka Productions: France/Japan.

Little Remi and Famous Dog Capi/Chibikko Remi to Meiken Kapi. 1970. Dir. Yugo Serikawa. Toei Animation: Japan.

Little Soldier Zhang Ga/Xiao Bing Zhang Ga. 1963. Dir. Wei Cui. Beijing Film Studio, Ningxia Film Studio: China.

Love Exposure/Ai no Mukadashi. 2008. Dir. Sono Sion. Omega Project: Japan.

Lucy. 2014. Dir. Luc Besson. Europa Corp., TF1 Films Production, Canal +, Cine+: France.

M. Hulot's Holiday/Les vacances de Monsieur Hulot. 1953. Dir. Jacques Tati. Discina Film: France.

Man's Pain/Ningen Ku. 1923. Dir. Suzuki Kansaku. Japan.

Memoirs of a Geisha. 2005. Dir. Rob Marshall. Columbia Pictures Corporation, DreamWorks, Spyglass Entertainment, Amblin Entertainment, Red Wagon Entertainment: USA.

Microbe and Gasoline/Microbe et Gasoil. 2015. Dir. Michel Gondry. Partizan, StudioCanal: France.
Mon Roi/My King. 2015. Dir. Maïwenn. Les Productions du Trésor, StudioCanal, France 2 Cinéma, Les Films de Batna, Arches Films, 120 Films: France.
Mood Indigo/L'écume des Jours. 2013. Dir. Michel Gondry. Brio Films, StudioCanal, Scope Pictures, France 2 Cinéma, Hérodiade, Radio Télévision Belge Francophone, Belgacom: France, Belgium.
Moulin Rouge. 2001. Dir. Baz Luhrmann. Twentieth Century Fox, Bazmark Films: Australia.
Muddy River/Doro no Kawa. 1981. Dir. Kōhei Oguri. Kimura Productions: Japan.
Mumon: The Land of Stealth/Shinobi no Kuni. 2017. Dir. Yoshihiro Nakamura. Toho Company, Tokyo Broadcasting System: Japan.
My Fair Lady. 1964. Dir. George Cukor. Warner Brothers: USA.
My Neighbor Totoro/Tonari no Totoro. 1988. Dir. Hayao Miyazaki. Tokuma-Shoten, Studio Ghibli, Nibariki: Japan.
My Summer in Provence/Avis de Mistral. 2013. Dir. Rose Bosch. Légende Films, Gaumont, France 2 Cinéma: France.
My Uncle/MonUncle. 1958. Dir. Jacques Tati. Specta Films, Gray-Film, Alter Films, Film del Centauro, Cady Films: France/Italy.
My Way/Maiwei. 2011. Dir. Kang Je-gyu. SK Planet, CJ Entertainment: Korea.
Night and Fog in Japan/Nihon no Yoru to Kiri. 1960. Dir. Nagisa Ōshima. Shōchiku Eiga: Japan.
Nodame Cantabile: The Final Score – Movie I/Nodame Kantâbire: Saishu-gakushou – Zenpen. 2009. Dir. Hideki Takeuchi. Cine Bazar, Fuji TV, Kodansha, Toho Co, Commes des Cinémas: Japan/France.
Norwegian Wood/Noruwei no Mori. 2010. Dir. Tran Anh Hung. Asmik Ace, Dentsu, Fuji Television, Kodansha, Sankei Shimbun, Sumitomo Corporation, WOWOW: Japan.
Old Boy/Oldeuboi. 2003. Dir. Park Chan-wook. CJ Entertainment: South Korea.
Our Little Sister/Umimachi Diary. 2015. Dir. Hirokazu Kore-eda. Toho Company, GAGA Film, Fuji Television Network, Shogakukan, TV Man Union: Japan.
Outrage/Autoreiji. 2010. Dir. Takeshi Kitano. Bandai Visual, Office Kitano, Omnibus Japan, TV Tokyo, Tokyo FM Broadcasting: Japan.
Outrage Beyond/Autoreiji: Biyondo. 2012. Dir. Takeshi Kitano. Bandai Visual, Office Kitano, Omnibus Japan, TV Tokyo, Warner Bros.: Japan.
Outrage Coda/Autoreiji sai shūshō. 2017. Dir. Takeshi Kitano. Office Kitano: Japan.
Pale Flower/Kawaita hana. 1964. Dir. Shinoda Masahiro. Shōchiku Company: Japan.
Parade. 1974. Dir. Jacques Tati. *Gray-Film, Sveriges Radio: France/Sweden*.
Paris, je t'aime. 2006. Multiple Directors. Canal +, Victoires International, Pirol Stiftung: France/Liechtenstein/Switzerland/Germany/USA.
Pauline at the Beach/Pauline à la plage. 1983. Dir. Éric Rohmer. Les Films du Losange, Les Films Ariane: France.

Personal Shopper. 2016. Dir. Olivier Assayas. CG Cinéma, Vortex Sutra, Sirena Film, Detailfilm, Arte France Cinéma, ARTE Deutschland: France, Germany, Belgium, Czech Republic.
Pigs and Battleships/Buta to gunkan. 1961. Dir. Shōhei Imamura. Nikkatsu: Japan.
Pistol Opera/Pisutoru Opera. 2001. Dir. Seijun Suzuki. Ogura Jimusyo Co., Dentsu, Eisei Gekijo, Geneon Entertainment, Nippon Herald Films, Shōchiku Company: Japan.
Play Time/Playtime. 1967. Dir. Jacques Tati. Specta Films, Jolly Film: France/Italy.
Polina/Polina danser sa vie. 2016. Dirs. Valérie Müller and Angelin Preljocaj. Everybody on Deck, TF1 Droits Audiovisuels, UGC Images and France 2 Cinéma: France.
Portrait of a Lady on Fire/Portrait de la jeune fille en feu. 2019. Dir Céline Sciamma. Lilies Films, Arte France Cinéma, Hold Up Films: France.
Postcard/Ichimai no Hagaki. 2011. Dir. Kaneto Shindo. Kindai Eiga Kyokai: Japan.
Princess Raccoon/Operetta: Tanuki Goten. 2005. Dir. Seijun Suzuki. Ogura Jimusyo Co., Dentsu, Eisei Gekijo, Geneon Entertainment, Nippon Herald Films, Shōchiku Company: Japan.
Psycho. 1960. Dir. Alfred Hitchcock. Shamley Productions: USA.
Pure as Snow/Blanche Neige. 2019. Dir. Anne Fontaine. Mandarin Cinéma, Cine @: France.
R100. 2013. Dir. Hitoshi Matsumoto. Phantom Film: Japan.
Radiance/Hikari. 2017. Dir. Naomi Kawase. Comme des Cinémas, Kino Films, Kumie, MK2 Productions: France/Japan.
Raging Bull. 1980. Dir. Martin Scorsese. Chartoff-Winkler Productions: USA.
Raid: Special Unit/Raid Dingue. 2016. Dir. Dany Boon. Pathé, Les Productions du Ch'timi, TF1 Films Production, Artémis Productions [BE]: France, Belgium.
Ran. 1985. Dir. Akira Kurosawa. Greenwich Film Productions, Herald Ace, Nippon Herald Films: France/Japan.
Rashomon. 1950. Dir. Akira Kurosawa. Daiei Motion Picture Company: Japan.
Red Sorghum/Hóng gāoliáng. 1987. Dir. Zhang Yimou. Xi'an Film Studio: China.
Rémi: Nobody's Boy/Rémi sans famille. 2018. Dir. Antoine Blossier. Jerico, TF1 Films Production, Nexus Factory, Umedia: France/Belgium.
Requiem for a Vampire/Vierges et vampires. 1971. Dir. Jean Rollin. Les Films ABC: France.
Reservoir Dogs. 1992. Dir. Quentin Tarantino. Live Entertainment, Dog Eat Dog Productions: USA.
Reunion/Itai: Asu e no Tōkakan. 2012. Dir. Ryoichi Kimizuka. Fuji Television Network: Japan.
Riding the Breeze/Nanpū. 2014. Dir. Kōji Hagiuda. Dream Kid, Glee Entertainment [TW]: Japan and Taiwan.
Romance. 1999. Dir. Catherine Breillat. Flach Film, Arte France Cinéma, CB Films: France.

Run Lola Run/Lola Rennt. 1998. Dir. Tom Tykwer. X-Film Creative Pool, Westdeutscher Rundfunk, Arte: Germany/France.
Rust and Bone/De rouille et d'os. 2012. Dir. Jacques Audiard. Why Not Productions, Page 114, France 2 Cinéma, Les Films du Fleuve [BE], Lumière, Lunanime [BE]: France, Belgium.
Ryuzo and the Seven Henchmen/Ryûzô to 7 nin no Kobun Tachi. 2015. Dir. Takeshi Kitano. Bandai Visual Company, Office Kitano, Tohokushinsha Film Corporation, Warner Bros: Japan.
Samba. 2014. Dir. Olivier Nakache and Éric Toledano. Quad production, Canal+, Gaumont, Korokoro, Ciné+, Ten Films, TF1 Films Production: France.
Sanjuro/Tsubaki Sanjūrō. 1962. Dir. Akira Kurosawa. Toho Company, Kurosawa Production Co.: Japan.
Sansho the Bailiff/Sanshô dayû. 1954. Dir. Kenji Mizoguchi. Daiei Studios: Japan.
Shara/Sharasôju. 2003. Dir. Naomi Kawase. RealProduct: Japan.
Shoplifters/Manbiki Kazoku. 2018. Dir. Hirokazu Kore-eda. AOI Promotion, Fuji Television, GAGA: Japan.
Shin Godzilla/Shin Gojira. 2016. Dir. Hideaki Anno and Shinji Higuchi. Cine Bazar, Toho Co., Toho Pictures: Japan.
Signal: Luca on Mondays/Shigunaru – Getsuyôbi no Ruka. 2012. Dir. Masaaki Tanaguchi. TV Asahi, Sony Music Entertainment, Ten Carat, Hakuhodo Casting & Entertainment, Gentosha, Horipro: Japan.
Silent Running. 1972. Dir. Douglas Trumball. Universal Pictures, Trumbull/Gruskoff Productions: USA.
Sin City. 2005. Dir. Robert Rodriguez. Dimension Films, Troublemaker Studios: USA.
Siworae/Il Mare [The Sea]. 2000. Dir. Lee Hyun-seung. Blue Cinema, CJ Entertainment, Dream Venture Capital, Sidus, UniKorea Pictures: South Korea.
Sonatine. 1993. Dir. Takeshi Kitano. Bandai Visual, Shōchiku Eiga, Yamada Right Vision Corporation: Japan.
Spirited Away/Sen to Chihiro no Kamikakushi. 2001. Dir. Hayao Miyazaki. Studio Ghibli, Tokuma Shoten, Nippon Television, Dentsu, Beuna Vista Home Entertainment, Tohokushinsha Film Corp., Mitsubishi: Japan.
Spirit's Homecoming/Gwihyang. 2016. Dir. Cho Jung-rae. JO Entertainment: Korea.
Splash. 1984. Dir. Ron Howard. Touchstone Pictures: USA.
Stagecoach. 1939. Dir. John Ford. Walter Wanger Productions: USA.
Still Walking/Aruitemo Aruitemo. 2008. Dir. Hirokazu Kore-eda. Bandai Visual Company, Cinequanon, Eisei Gekijo, Engine Film, TV Man Union: Japan.
Stray Dog/Nora Inu. 1949. Dir. Akira Kurosawa. Film Art Association, Shintoho Film Distribution, Toho Company: Japan.
Strip Mahjong: Battle Royale/Datsui-mâjan batoru rowaiaru. 2011. Dir. Mak P. Forever. Chance In, JollyRoger, New Connect: Japan.

Strip Mahjong Idol: Warring States (Naked) Battle Royale/Datsui-mâjan Idol Sengoku jidai batoru rowaiaru. 2015. Dir. Mak P. Forever. Albatros Films: Japan.
Sundome. 2007. *Sundome 2.* 2008, *Sundome 3.* 2008. Dir. Daigo Udagawa. Total Media Corporation: Japan.
Sundome New, Sundome New 2. Dir. Kazuhiro Yokoyama. Aphrodite, Odessa Entertainment: Japan.
Survival Family/Sabaibaru Famirî. 2016. Dir. Shinobu Yaguchi. Altamira Pictures, Dentsu, Fuji Television Network, Toho Company: Japan.
Suzaku/Moe no Suzaku. 1997. Dir. Naomi Kawase. Bandai Visual, WOWOW: Japan.
Tag/Riaru Onigokko [lit. Real Tag]. 2015. Dir. Sono Sion. Asmik Ace Entertainment: Japan.
Tales of Ugetsu/Ugetsu monogatari. 1953. Dir. Kenji Mizoguchi. Daiei Studios: Japan.
Takeshis'. 2005. Dir. Takeshi Kitano. Bandai Visual, Tokyo FM, Dentsu, TV Asahi, Office Kitano: Japan.
Tampopo [lit. Dandelion]. 1985. Dir. Juzo Itami. Itami Productions, New Century Productions: Japan.
Taxi 2. 2000. Dir. Gérard Krawczyk. ARP Sélection, Canal +, Leeloo Productions, TF1: France.
Taxi Driver. 1976. Dir. Martin Scorsese. Columbia Pictures: USA.
Tetsuo, the Iron Man. 1989. Dir. Shin'ya Tsukamoto. Japan Home Video, K2 Spirit, Kaijyu Theater, SEN: Japan.
That Obscure Object of Desire/Cet Obscur Objet du Désir. 1977. Dir. Luis Buñuel. Greenwich Film Productions, Les Films Galaxie, In-Cine Compañía Industrial Cinematográfica: France/Spain.
The Ballad of Nureyama/Narayama Bushikô. 1983. Dir. Shôhei Imamura. Toei Company: Japan.
The Battleship Island/Gunhamdo. 2017. Dir. Ryoo Seung-wan. Filmmaker R&K: Korea.
The Belier Family/La Famille Bélier. 2014. Dir. Eric Lartigau. Jerico, Mars Films, France 2 Cinéma, Quarante 12 Films, Vendôme Production, Nexus Factory, Umedia: France.
The Cherry Orchard: Blossoming/Sakura no Sono. 2008. Dir. Shun Nakahara. Arcimboldo Y.K., Dentsu, G.T. Entertainment, Hakusensha, Kinoshita Komuten, Oscar Promotion, Shōchiku Company, Shueisha, TV Asahi: Japan.
The Cherry Orchard/Sakura no Sono. 1990. Dir. Shun Nakahara. New Century Producers, Suntory: Japan.
The Diabolical Dr. Z/Miss Muerte. 1966. Dir. J.(Jesús) Franco. Spéva Films, Ciné-Alliance, Hesperia Films S.A.: France/Spain.
The Discreet Charm of the Bourgeoisie/Le Charme Discret de la Bourgeoisie. 1972. Dir. Luis Buñuel. Greenwich Film Productions: France.
The Diving Bell and The Butterfly/Le Scaphandre et le Papillon. 2007. Dir. Julian Schnabel. Pathé Renn Productions: France/USA.

The Eel/Unagi. 1997. Dir. Shôhei Imamura. Eisei Gekijo, Groove Corporation, Imamura Productions, KSS, NHK Enterprises, Satellite Cinema, Shōchiku Eiga: Japan.

The Eight Hundred/Bābǎi. 2020. dir. Guan Hu. Beijing Diqi Yinxiang Entertainment, Huayi Brothers Media: China.

The Extraordinary Adventures of Adèle Blanc-Sec/Les Aventures Extraordinaires d'Adele Blanc-Sec. 2010. Dir. Luc Besson. EuropaCorp, Apipoulaï, TF1 Films: France.

The Flowers of War/Jīnlíng shísān chāi. 2011. Dir. Zhang Yimou. Beijing New Picture Film, Edko Film [HK], New Picture Company: China.

The 400 Blows/Les Quatre Cents Coups. 1959. Dir. François Truffaut. Les Films du Carrosse, Sédif Productions: France.

The Girl on the Bridge/La Fille sur le Pont. 1999. Dir. Patrice Leconte. Canal+, France 2 Cinéma, Les Films Christian Fechner, Sofica Sofinergie 5, UGCF: France.

The Lake House. 2006. Dir. Alejandro Agresti. Warner Brothers, Village Roadshow, Vertigo Entertainment: USA.

The Land of Hope/Kibō no Kuni. 2012. Dir. Sono Sion. Marble Films: Japan.

The Little Soldier/Le petit soldat. 1963. Dir. Jean-luc Godard. Les Productions Georges de Beauregard: France.

The Long Excuse/Nagai iiwake. 2016. Dir. Miwa Nishikawa. Aoi Promotion, Asmik Ace Entertainment, Bandai Visual Company, Bunbuku, Bungeishunju, TV Tokyo, Television Osaka: Japan.

The Many Faces of Ito: The Movie/Itô kun A to E. 2018. Dir. Ryuichi Hiroki. Netflix, Showgate: Japan.

The Murder Case of Hana and Alice/Hana to Arisu Satsujin Jiken. 2015. Dir. Shunji Iwai. Nippon Television, Pony Canyon, Rockwell Eyes, Shogakukan, Steve N' Steven, Toei Company: Japan.

The Nude Vampire/La Vampire nue. 1970. Dir. Jean Rollin. Les Films ABC, Tigon British Film Productions: France, UK.

The Only Son/Hitori Musoko. 1936. Dir. Ozu Yasujirô. Shōchiku Eiga: Japan.

The Perfect Couple/Un couple parfait. 2005. Dir. Nobuhiro Suwa. Comme des Cinémas [FR], Arte France Cinéma [FR], Bitters End [JP]: France and Japan.

The Pornographers/"Erogotoshi-tachi": yori Jinruigaku nyûmon. 1966. Dir. Shôhei Imamura. Imamura Productions, Nikkatsu: Japan.

The Princess Blade/Shurayukihime. 2001. Dir. Shinsuke Sato. GAGA, Oz Productions: Japan.

The Rape of the Vampire/Le Viol du vampire. 1967. Dir. Jean Rollin. Les Films ABC: France.

Thermae Romae/Terumae Romae. 2012. Dir. Hideki Takeuchi. Dentsu, Enterbrain, Filmmakers, Fuji Television, Toho Co.: Japan.

Thermae Romae II /Terumae Romae II. 2014. Dir. Hideki Takeuchi. Fuji Television, Toei Co., Dentsu, Kadokawa: Japan.

The Road. 2009. Dir. John Hillcoat. Dimension Films, 2929 Productions, Nick Weschler, Chockstone Pictures: USA.

The Seashell and the Clergyman/La Coquille et le Clergyman. 1928. Dir. Germaine Dulac. Délia Film: France.
The Shiver of the Vampires/Le Frisson des vampires. 1971. Dir. Jean Rollin. Les Films ABC, Les Films Modernes: France.
The Story of O/Histoire d'O. 1975. Dir. Just Jaeckin. A.D. Creation, Somerville House, Terra-Filmkunst, Yang Films: France/Germany/Canada.
The Tokyo Trial/Dōngjīng Shěnpàn. 2006. Dir. Gao Qunshu. Beijing Xianming Yinghua Culture & Media, Jiujiang Changjiang Film, Shanghai Film Group: China.
The Transporter Refuelled/Le Transporteur: Héritage. 2015. Dir. Camille Delamarre. EuropaCorp, TF1 Films Production, Fundamental Films, Belga Films Fund: France/China/Belgium.
The Twenty-Six Japanese Martyrs/Les Vingt-Six Martyrs Japonais. 1930. Dir. T. Ikeda. Nikkatsu Studios: Japan.
The Village Fair/Jour de fête. 1949. Dir. Jacques Tati. Cady Films: France.
The Whispering Star/Hiso Hiso Boshi. 2015. Dir. Sono Sion. Sion Production: Japan.
The Wolverine. 2013. Dir. James Mangold. Twentieth Century Fox, Marvel Entertainment, Ingenious Media, TSG Entertainment, Donners' Company: USA/Great Britain.
Three Colors: Red/Trois Couleurs: Rouge. 1994. Dir. Krzysztof Kieślowski. MK2 Productions: France.
Three Men and a Cradle/Trois Hommes et un Couffin. 1985. Dir. Coline Serreau. Flach Film: France.
Throne of Blood/Kumonosu-jō. 1957. Dir. Akira Kurosawa. Toho, Kurosawa Production Co.: Japan.
Tokyo!. 2008. Dirs. Leos Carax, Michel Gondry and Bong Joon Ho. Comme des Cinémas [FR], Kansai Telecasting [JP], Arte France Cinéma [FR], Sponge [KR], Bitters End [JP], Coin Film [DE], WDR/Arte [DE]: France, Japan, South Korea, Germany.
Tokyo Drifter/ Tōkyō Nagaremono. 1966. Dir. Seijun Suzuki. Nikkatsu: Japan.
Tokyo Fiancée. 2014. Dir. Stefan Liberski. Versus Production: France.
Tokyo Fist. 1995. Dir. Shin'ya Tsukamoto. Kaijyu Theatre: Japan.
Tokyo Lullaby/Tôkyô Yakyoku. 1997. Dir. Jun Ichikawa. Kindai Eiga, Shōchiku Eiga: Japan.
Tokyo Siblings/Tōkyō Kyōdai. 1995. Dir. Jun Ichikawa. Yamada Right Vision Corporation: Japan.
Tokyo Sonata/Tōkyō Sonata. 2008. Dir. Kiyoshi Kurosawa. Django Film: Japan.
Tokyo Story/Tôkyô Monogatari. 1953. Dir. Yasujirô Ozu. Shōchiku Eiga: Japan.
Tokyo Trash Baby/Tôkyô Gomi Onna. 2000. Dir. Ryuichi Hiroki. Arcimboldo Y.K., Bonobo Co., CineRocket: Japan.
Tokyo Tribe/Tōkyō Toraibu. 2014. Dir. Sono Sion. Django Film, From First Production Co., Nikkatsu: Japan.

Tomboy. 2011. Dir. Céline Sciamma. Hold Up Films, Canal+, Arte France Cinéma: France.
Tony Takitani/Tonî Takitani. 2004. Dir. Jun Ichikawa. Breath, Wilco Co.: Japan.
Tora-san Meets the Songstress Again/Otoko wa Tsurai yo: Torajiro aiaigasa. 1975. Dir. Yoji Yamada. Shōchiku Eiga: Japan.
Tora-san: Our Lovable Tramp/It's Tough Being a Man/Otoko wa Tsurai yo. 1969. Dir. Yoji Yamada. Shōchiku Eiga: Japan.
Traffic/Trafic. 1971. Dir. Jacques Tati. Les Films Corona, Les Films Gibé, Selenia Cinematografica: France.
Trainspotting. 1996. Dir. Danny Boyle. Channel Four Films, Figment Films, The Noel Gay Motion Picture Company: UK.
Twentynine Palms. 2003. Dir. Bruno Dumont. 3B Productions: France.
Two Days, One Night/Deux jours, une nuit. 2014. Dirs. Jean-Pierre Dardanne and Luc Dardanne. Les Films du Fleuve [BE], Archipel 35, BIM Distibuzione [IT], Eyeworks [BE], France 2 Cinéma, Belgacom [BE], Radio Télévision Belge Francophone [BE]: France, Belgium, Italy.
Typhoon Over Nagasaki/Typhon sur Nagasaki/Wasureenu Bojo. 1957. Dir. Yves Ciampi. Cila Films, Compagnie Industrielle et Commerciale Cinématographique (CICC), Doxa Films, Pathé Overseas, Shōchiku Eiga, Société Nouvelle Pathé Cinéma, Terra Film Produktion: France/Japan.
Until We Meet Again/Mata au hi made. 1950. Dir. Imai Tadashi. Toho: Japan.
Vagabond/Sans toit ni loi. 1985. Dir. Agnes Varda. Ciné-Tamaris, Films A2: France.
Valerian and the City of a Thousand Planets/Valérian et la Cité des Mille Planètes. 2017. Dir. Luc Besson. EuropaCorp, Fundamental Films, Gulf Films, River Road Entertainment: France/China/UAE/USA.
Warm Water Under a Red Bridge/Akai Hashi no Shita no Nurui Mizu. 2001. Dir. Shōhei Imamura. BAP Inc., Comme des Cinémas, Catherine Dussart Productions (CDP), Eisi Gekijo: France/Japan.
Warrior's Gate [aka Enter the Warrior's Gate]. 2016. Dir. Matthias Hoene. Fundamental Films, EuropaCorp, Transfilm, Screen Siren Pictures: China/France/Canada.
Wasabi. 2001. Dir. Gérard Krawczyk. EuropaCorp, Samitose Productions, TF1 Films, Canal+, Victor Company, Destiny: France/Japan.
We Are Little Zombies/Watashitachi wa Ritoru Zonbī. 2019. Dir. Makoto Nagahisa. Dentsu: Japan.
What's Going on With My Sister?/Saikin, imôto no yôsu ga chotto okashii n da ga? 2014. Dirs. Yûki Aoyama and Iggy Coen. Dub, Kadokawa Pictures, Pony Canyon: Japan.
White Material. 2009. Dir. Claire Denis. Why Not Productions, Wild Bunch, France 3 Cinéma: France/Cameroon.
Why Don't You Play in Hell?/Jigoku de Naze Warui. 2013. Dir. Sono Sion. King Record Co., KH Capital, BizAsset, T-Joy, Gansis: Japan.

Wife of a Spy/Supai no tsuma. 2020. Dir. Kiyoshi Kurosawa. C&I Entertainment, ENBU Seminar, Incline, Kirinzi, NHK Enterprises, Weroll: Japan.

Woman's Hole/Onno no anna. 2014. Dir. Kōta Yoshida. Dub, IS Field, Tokuma Shoten, VAP: Japan.

Yojimbo/Yōjinbō. 1961. Dir. Akira Kurosawa. Kurosawa Production Co., Toho Company: Japan.

You Only Live Twice. 1967. Dir. Lewis Gilbert. Eon Productions, Danjaq: UK/USA.

Yuki and Nina/Yuki to Nina. 2009. Dirs. Nobuhiro Suwa and Hippolyte Girardot. Comme des Cinémas [FR], Les Films du Lendemain [FR], Arte France Cinéma [FR], Bitters End [JP]: France and Japan.

Bibliography

Aftab, Kaleem. 2020. 'Mathieu Kassovitz on *La Haine*: "I made the movie because kids die"'. *British Film Institute*. 2 September. Available at https://www.bfi.org.uk/sight-and-sound/interviews/mathieu-kassovitz-la-haine-legacy.

Alexander, James R. 2003. 'Obscenity, Pornography, and the Law in Japan: Reconsidering Ōshima's *In the Realm of the Senses*'. *Asian-Pacific Law and Policy Journal*, 4 (1): 148–68.

Allison, Anne. 2015. 'Precarity and Hope: Social Connectedness in Postcapitalist Japan'. In *Japan: The Precarious Future*, edited by Anne Allison and Frank Baldwin. New York: New York University Press, 36–57.

Anderson, Joseph L. and Donald Richie. 1956. 'The Films of Heinosuke Gosho'. *Sight and Sound*, 26 (2): 77–81.

Anderson, Joseph L. and Donald Richie. 1982. *The Japanese Film: Art and Industry*, Expanded Edition. Princeton: Princeton University Press.

Arsenjuk, Luka. 2018. *Movement, Action, Image, Montage: Sergei Eisenstein and the Cinema in Crisis*. Minnesota: University of Minnesota Press.

Bałaga, Marta. 2019. 'Interview with Robert Guédiguian'. *Cineuropa*, 8 September. Available at https://cineuropa.org/en/interview/377898/.

Barthes, Roland. 1972, c.1957. 'The Romans in Films'. In *Mythologies*, translated by Annette Lavers. New York: Hill and Wang.

Baskett, Michael. 2008. *The Attractive Empire: Transnational Film Culture in Imperial Japan*. Hawaii: University of Hawaii Press.

Bazin, André. 1967. *What Is Cinema?* Vol. I. Berkeley: University of California Press.

Bazin, André. 1982, c.1975. *The Cinema of Cruelty: From Bunuel to Hitchcock*. Translated by Sabine d'Estree. New York: Seaver Books.

Beeton, Sue. 2005. *Film-Induced Tourism*. Bristol: Channel View.

Blum-Reid, Sylvie. 2003. *East-West Encounters: Franco-Asian Cinema and Literature*. London and New York: Wallflower.

Bordwell, David. 1995. 'Visual Style in Japanese Cinema, 1925–1945'. *Film History*, 7 (1), Spring.

Bourdieu, Pierre. 1991. 'First Lecture: Social Space and Symbolic Space: Introduction to a Japanese Reading of Distinction'. *Poetics Today*, 12 (4), National Literatures/Social Spaces: 627–38.

Burch, Noël. 1979. *To the Distant Observer: Form and Meaning in the Japanese Cinema*. Berkeley and Los Angeles: University of California Press.

Burnett, C. Ewan. 1980. 'Donald Richie: Interview'. *Cinema Papers #27*, 180.

Buruma, Ian. 2012, c.1984. *A Japanese Mirror: Heroes and Villains of Japanese Culture*. London: Atlantic Books.

Cardullo, Robert. 2013. 'The Sound of Silence, The Space of Time: Monsieur Hulot, Comedy, and the Aural-visual Cinema of Jacques Tati (An Essay and an Interview)'. *Contemporary French and Francophone Studies*, 17 (3): 357–69.

Carroll Harris, Lauren. 2017. 'Theorising Film Festivals as Distributors and Investigating the Post-festival Distribution of Australian Films'. *Studies in Australasian Cinema*, 11 (2): 46–58.

Cather, Kirsten. 2009. '"I Know It When I Hear It": The Case of the Blind Film Censor'. *The Velvet Light Trap*, 63: 60–2.

Cauliez, Armand J. 1968. *Jacques Tati*. Paris: Seghers.

Champion Traveller. 2018. 'Japan Officially Has the Largest Netflix Catalog in the World, US Falls to Second'. Champion Traveller, 1 February. Available at: www.championtraveller.com/news.

Christley, Jaime N. 2018. 'Kiyoshi Kurosawa's Underseen "Daguerrotype" Is a Cinematic Ghost Tale Par Excellence'. *The Village Voice*, 19 March.

CNC (Centre National du Cinéma et de l'Image animée/French National Centre for Cinema and the Moving Image). 2015. *Producing Films in France*. Paris: CNC.

Comolli, Jean-Luc and (Jean) Paul Narboni. 1971. 'Cinema/Ideology/Criticism'. *Screen*, 12 (1): 27–38. Reprint of 'Editorial' *Cahiers du Cinéma* 216, 217. October–November, 1969.

Criterion Collection. 2014. 'Abbas Kiarostami on *Like Someone in Love*'. Available at: https://www.criterion.com/current/posts/3245-abbas-kiarostami-on-like-someone-in-love [video].

Czach, Liz. 2010. 'Cinephilia, Stars and Film Festivals'. *Cinema Journal*, 49 (2): 139–45.

Danan, Martine. 2000. 'French Cinema in the Era of Media Capitalism'. *Media, Culture & Society*, 22: 355–64.

Davis, Darrell William. 2001. 'Reigniting Japanese Tradition with *Hana-Bi*'. *Cinema Journal*, 40 (4): 55–80.

Desser, David.1988. *Eros Plus Massacre: An Introduction to The Japanese New Wave Cinema*. Bloomington: Indiana University Press.

Desser, David. 2016. 'The Gunman and the Gun: Japanese Film Noir SInce the Late 1950s'. In *International Noir*, edited by Homer H. Pettey and R. Barton Palmer. Edinburgh: Edinburgh University Press, 112–35.

Dixon, Wheeler Winston. 2015. *Black & White Cinema: A Short History*. New Brunswick: Rutgers University Press.

Dyer, Richard. 1998, c.1979). *Stars*, New Edition. London: BFI Publishing.

Ebert, Roger. 2000. Reviews: 'L'Humanité'. *RogerEbert.com*, 23 June. Available at: https://www.rogerebert.com/reviews/lhumanite-2000.

Ehrlich, Linda C. 1996. 'Wandering Fool: Tora-san and the Comic Traveler Tradition'. *Asian Cinema*, 8 (1): 3–27.

EIRAN (Motion Picture Producers Association of Japan). 2021. 'Statistics of Film Industry in Japan'. Available at: http://www.eiren.org/statistics_e/index.html.

Evans, Owen. 2007. 'Border Exchanges: The Role of the European Film Festival'. *Journal of Contemporary European Studies*, 15 (1): 23–33.

Foreman, Liza. 2010. 'UniJapan: Talking about European Cinema in the Japanese Marketplace'. *Cineuropa*, 12 November. Available at: https://cineuropa.org/en/newsdetail/153464/.

Foster, Gwendolyn Audrey. 2016. 'Anatomy of Hell: A Feminist Fairy Tale', *Senses of Cinema*, 80. Available at: https://www.sensesofcinema.com/2016/cteq/anatomy-hell/.

Franco, Judith. 2017. 'The Difficult Job of Being a Girl: Key Themes and Narratives in Contemporary Western European Art Cinema by Women'. *Quarterly Review of Film and Video*, 35 (1): 16–30.

Fraser, Benjamin. 2016. 'Introduction: Disability Studies, World Cinema and the Cognitive Code of Reality'. In *Cultures of Representation: Disability in World Cinema Contexts*, edited by Benjamin Fraser. London and New York: Wallflower Press, 1–17.

Freedman, Alisa. 2017. 'Death Note, Student Crimes, and the Power of Universities in the Global Spread of Manga'. In *The End of Cool Japan: Ethical, Legal, and Cultural Challenges to Japanese Popular Culture*, edited by Mark McLelland. Oxon and New York: Routledge, 31–50.

Gardner, William O. 2004. 'New Perceptions: Kinugasa Teinosuke's Films and Japanese Modernism'. *Cinema Journal*, 43 (3): 59–78.

Gerow, Aaron. 2016. 'Kurosawa Kiyoshi, dis/continuity, and the Ghostly Ethics of Meaning and Auteurship'. In *The Global Auteur: The Politics of Auteurship in 21st Century Cinema*, edited by Seun-hoon Jeong and Jeremi Szaniawski. New York and London: Bloomsbury, 343–59.

Gill, Tom. 2003. 'When Pillars Evaporate: Structuring Masculinity on the Japanese Margins'. In *Men and Masculinities in Contemporary Japan: Dislocating the Salaryman Doxa*, edited by J.E. Roberson and N. Suzuki. London: RoutledgeCurzon, 1–34.

Grandena, Florian. 2008. *Showing the World to the World: Political Fictions in French Cinema of the 1990s and Early 2000s*. Newcastle: Cambridge Scholars Publishing.

Harper, Graeme and Jonathan Rayner (eds). 2010. *Cinema and Landscape: Film, Nation and Cultural Geography*. Bristol and Chicago: Intellect.

Harrod, Mary and Phil Powrie. 2018. 'New Directions in Contemporary French Comedies: From Nation, Sex and Class to Ethnicity, Community and the Vagaries of the Postmodern'. *Studies in French Cinema*, 18 (1): 1–17.

Hilliker, Lee. 1998. 'Hulot vs. the 1950s: Tati, Technology and Mediation'. *The Journal of Popular Culture*, 32 (2): 59–78.

Hilliker, Lee. 2002. 'In The Modernist Mirror: Jacques Tati and the Parisian Landscape'. *French Review*, 76 (2): 318–29.

Hunt, Leon. 2008. 'Asiaphilia, Asianisation and the Gatekeeper Auteur'. In *East Asian Cinemas: Exploring Transnational Connections on Film*, edited by Leon Hunt and Leung Wing-Fai. London and New York: I. B. Tauris, 220–36.

Hutchinson, Rachael. 2006. 'Orientalism or Occidentalism?: Dynamics of Appropriation in Akira Kurosawa'. In *Remapping World Cinema: Identity, Culture and Politics in Film*, edited by Stephanie Dennison and Song Hwee Lim. London and New York: Wallflower Press, 173–87.

Higbee, Will. 2006. 'Diva'. In *The Cinema of France*, edited by Phil Powrie. London and New York: Wallflower, 153–62.

Iles, Timothy. 2008. 'Families, Fathers, Film: Changing Images from Japanese Cinema'. *Japanstudien*, 19 (1): 189–206.

Jacobs, Alexander. 2008. *A Critical Handbook of Japanese Film Directors*. California: Stone Bridge Press.

Japan Times (author not cited). 2016. 'Kiyoshi Kurosawa's Cinematic Apparitions'. *Japan Times*, 15 December.

JFCPC (Japan Film Commission Promotion Council). 2009. 'FAQ'. Available at: http://www.japanfc.org/film-com090329/en/faq.html.

JW Web Magazine. 2017. 'Filming Locations of 8 Famous Movies in Japan! *Memoirs of a Geisha, Kill Bill, Resident Evil* and More! *Japan Travel Guide: Japan-Wireless (JW) Web Magazine*'. Tokyo. Available at: https://jw-webmagazine.com/filming-locations-of-8-famous-movies-f804a8b2393d.

Kawase, Naomi. 2012. 'The Value of Movies: Naomi Kawase at TEDxTokyo'. *TEDx Talks*. Available at: https://www.youtube.com/watch?v=XhOtrGDDRRo.

Keslassy, Elsa. 2015. 'Literary Adaptation Biz Heat Up in France'. *Variety*, 19 January. Available at: https://variety.com/2015/film/news/literary-adaptation-biz-heat-up-in-france-1201409523/.

Keslassy, Elsa. 2016. 'Naomi Kawase to Preside Over Cannes Cinefondation, Short Film Jury'. *Variety*, March 16. Available at: https://variety.com/2016/film/news/naomi-kawase-cannes-cinefondation-short-film-jury-1201730382/.

Keslassy, Elsa. 2018. 'France's 2017 Box Office Scores Third-Largest Haul in 50 Years'. *Variety*, 2 January. Available at: https://variety.com/2018/film/global/frances-2017-box-office-scores-third-biggest-in-50-years-1202650717/.

Komatsu, Hiroshi and Ben Brewster. 1996. 'The Lumière Cinématographe and the Production of the Cinema in Japan in the Earliest Period'. *Film History*, 8 (4): 431–8.

Kriegel-Nicholas, Isadora. 2016. 'The Historical Reception of Japanese Cinema at Cahiers du Cinema: 1951–1961'. Unpublished thesis. Boston University.

Kuhn, Annette. 2005. 'Thresholds: Film as Film and the Aesthetic Experience'. *Screen*, 46 (4): 401–14.

Kuhn, Annette. 2010. 'Cinematic Experience, Film Space, and the Child's World'. *Revue Canadienne d'Études cinématographiques/Canadian Journal of Film Studies*, 19 (2): 82–98.

Lehman, Peter and Luhr William. 2018. *Thinking About Movies: Watching, Questioning, Enjoying*, 4th edition. Hoboken, NJ & Chichester: Wiley Blackwell.

McAllister, Matthew P., Ian Gordon and Mark Jancovich. 2006. 'Blockbuster Meets Superhero Comic, or Meets Graphic Novel?: The Contradictory Relationship Between Film and Comic Art'. *Journal of Popular Film and Television*, 34 (3): 108–15.

McCann, Ben. 2008a. 'Du verre, rien que du verre': Negotiating Utopia in Playtime'. In *Nowhere is Perfect: French and Francophone Utopias/Dystopias*, edited by John West-Sooby. Newark: University of Delaware Press, 195–210.

McCann, Ben. 2008b. 'Pierced Borders, Punctured Bodies: the Contemporary French Horror Film'. *Australian Journal of French Studies*, 45 (3): 225–37.

McKnight, Anne. 2010. 'Frenchness and Transformation in Japanese Subculture, 1972–2004'. *Mechademia Second Arc*, 5 (1): 118–37.

McLelland, Mark. 2017. 'Introduction Negotiating "Cool Japan" in Research and Teaching'. In *The End of Cool Japan: Ethical, Legal, and Cultural Challenges to Japanese Popular Culture*, edited by Mark McLelland. Oxon and New York: Routledge, 1–30.

Mes, Tom. 2001. 'Seijun Suzuki'. *Midnight Eye: Visions of Japanese Cinema*. Available at: www.midnighteye.com/interviews/seijun-suzuki/#sthash.adpHvqsP.dpuf.

Michael, Charlie. 2019. *French Blockbusters: Cultural Politics of a Transnational Cinema*. Edinburgh: Edinburgh University Press.

Moine, Raphaëlle. 2014. 'Contemporary French Comedy as Social Laboratory'. In *A Companion to Contemporary French Film*, edited by Alistair Fox, Michel Marie, Raphaëlle Moine, and Hilary Radner, Chichester: Wiley-Blackwell, 233–55.

Mullins, Mark R. 2010. 'From "*Departures*" to "Yasukuni Shrine": Caring for the Dead and the Bereaved in Contemporary Japanese Society'. *Japanese Religions*, 35 (1&2): 101–12.

Neupert, Richard. 2007. *A History of the French New Wave Cinema*. Madison: University of Wisconsin Press.

NHK (*Nippon Hoso Kyokai*/Japan Broadcasting Corporation). 2018. 'What is Sundance Institute/NHK Award?'. Available at: http://www.nhk.or.jp/sun-asia/sundance/about/index_e.html.

Nochimson, Martha P. 2010. *World on Film: An Introduction*. Malden: Wiley-Blackwell.

Nornes, Abé Mark. 2014. 'Yamagate-Asia-Europe: The International Film Festival Short Circuit'. In *The Oxford Handbook of Japanese Cinema*, edited by Daisuke Miyao. Oxford: Oxford University Press, 245–62.

Nowell-Smith, Geoffrey. 1977. 'Minelli and Melodrama'. *Screen*, 18 (2): 113–18.

Nygren, Scott. 2007. *Time Frames: Japanese Cinema and the Unfolding of History*. Minneapolis: University of Minnesota Press.

O'Brien, Adam. 2018. *Film and the Natural Environment: Elements and Atmospheres*. New York: Columbia University Press/Wallflower Press.

O'Donoghue, Darragh. 2015. 'Monsieur Hulot's History: Jacques Tati Pictures Modern France'. *Cineaste*, 40 (2): 12–17.

O'Regan, Tom. 2004. 'Cultural Exchange'. In *A Companion to Film Theory*, edited by Toby Miller and Robert Stam. Malden: Blackwell Publishing, 262–94.

Ortiz-Moya, Fernando and Nieves Moreno. 2016. 'The Incredible Shrinking Japan'. *City*, 20 (6): 880–903.

Palmer, Tim. 2006. 'Style and Sensation in the Contemporary French Cinema of the Body'. *Journal of Film and Video*, 58 (3): 22–32.

Petterson, David. 2014. 'American Genre Film in the French Banlieue: Luc Besson and Parkour'. *Cinema Journal*, 53 (3): 26–51.

Pettey, Homer B. 2016. 'Early Japanese Noir'. In *International Noir*, edited by Homer B. Pettey and R. Barton Palmer. Edinburgh: Edinburgh University Press.

Phillips, Alistair and Julian Stringer. 2007. *Japanese Cinema: Texts and Contexts*. London: Routledge.

Phillips, Alistair and Ginette Vincendeau. 2017. *Paris in the Cinema: Beyond the Flâneur*. London: Bloomsbury.

Pugsley, Peter C. 2013. *Tradition, Culture and Aesthetics in Contemporary Asian Cinema*. Surrey: Ashgate/Routledge.

Pugsley, Peter C. 2015. *Exploring Morality and Sexuality in Asian Cinema: Cinematic Boundaries*. Surrey: Routledge.

Regelman, Karen. 1995. 'For Japan Fans, Tora-san's the Man (Shōchiku Co. Ltd.'s Comic Film Series Still Popular After 26 Years)'. *Variety*, 359 (4): 66.

Rosenbaum, Jonathan. 2014. 'Jacques Tati: Composing in Sound and Image'. *Criterion.com*, 28. October. Available at: https://www.criterion.com/current/posts/3337-jacques-tati-composing-in-sound-and-image.

Rosenbaum, Jonathan. 2022. 'Trafic'. *jonathanrosenbaum.net*, 19 January. Available at: https://jonathanrosenbaum.net/2022/01/trafic/.

Rosenbaum, Roman. 2010. 'From the Traditions of J-Horror to the Representation of Kakusa Shakai in Kurosawa's *Tokyo Sonata*'. *Contemporary Japan*, 22: 115–36.

Ross, Kristin. 1995. *Fast Cars, Clean Bodies: Decolonization and the Reordering of French Culture*. London and Cambridge, MA: MIT Press.

Ruffo, Elio. 1955. 'Italian and Japanese Cinema'. *East and West*, 6 (3): 269–73.

SAS. 2018. 'Shoot in Japan'. Available at: https://shootinjapan.net.

Sato, Tadao. 2008. *Kenji Mizoguchi and the Art of Japanese Cinema*. Translated by Brij Tankha. Oxford and New York: Berg.

Schilling, Mark. 1999. *Contemporary Japanese Film*. New York and Tokyo: Weatherhill.

Schilling, Mark. 2018. 'Japan Box Office Slides in 2017, as Hollywood Gains'. *Variety*, 25 January. Available at: https://variety.com/2018/film/asia/japan-box-office-slides-in-2017-hollywood-gains-1202676519/.

Schilling, Mark. 2022. 'Japan Box Office Makes Small 2021 Recovery, Puts 'Evangelion' and Toho on Top'. *Variety*, 25 January. Available at: https://variety.com/2022/film/box-office/japan-box-office-2021-evangelion-1235163655/.

Seaton, Philip and Takayoshi Yamamura. 2015. 'Japanese Popular Culture and Contents Tourism – Introduction'. *Japan Forum*, 27 (1): 1–11.

Smith, Murray. 2000. 'Modernism and the Avant-Gardes'. In *World Cinema: Critical Approaches*, edited by John Hill and Pamela Church Gibson. Oxford: Oxford University Press, 11–28.

Stam, Robert. 2000. 'Beyond Fidelity: The Dialogics of Adaptation'. In *Film Adaptation*, edited by James Naremore. New Jersey: Rutgers University Press, 54–78.

Stam, Robert. 2013. 'Adaptation and the French New Wave: A Study in Ambivalence'. *Interfaces*, 34: 177–97.

Standish, Isolde. 2006. *A New History of Japanese Cinema: A Century of Narrative Film*. New York and London: Continuum.

Standish, Isolde. 2011. *Politics, Porn and Protest: Japanese Avant-Garde Cinema in the 1960s and 1970s*. New York and London: Continuum.

Standish, Isolde. 2012. 'The Ephemeral as Transcultural Aesthetic: A Contextualization of the Early Films of Ozu Yasujiro'. *Journal of Japanese and Korean Cinema*, 4 (1): 3–14.

SturtzSreetharan, Cindi. 2017. 'Resignifying the Japanese Father: Mediatization, Commodification, and Dialect'. *Language and Communication*, 53: 45–58.

Taylor-Jones, Kate E. 2013. *Rising Sun, Divided Land: Japanese and South Korean Filmmakers*. New York and London: Wallflower Press.

Tezuka, Yoshiharu. 2012. *Japanese Cinema Goes Global: Filmworkers' Journeys*. Hong Kong: Hong Kong University Press.

Tezuka, Yoshiharu. 2020. 'Japanese Cinema and Europe. A Constellation of Gazes: Europe and the Japanese Film Industry'. In *The Japanese Cinema Book*, edited by Hideaki Fujuki and Alastair Phillips. London and New York: BFI, 541–55.

Tsunagu Japan. 2016. '21 Filming Locations to Expand Your Trip in Japan'. *Tsunagu Japan*. Tokyo. Available at: https://www.tsunagujapan.com/21-filming-locations-to-expand-your-trip-in-japan/.

Turim, Maureen. 2016. 'French Neo-Noir: An Aesthetic for the *Policier*'. In *International Noir*, edited by Homer B. Pettey and R. Barton Palmer. Edinburgh: Edinburgh University Press, 61–84.

Tweedie, James. 2013. *The Age of New Waves: Art Cinema and the Staging of Globalization*. Oxford: Oxford University Press.

UNIJAPAN. 2017a. *UNIJAPAN Certificate*. Tokyo: UNIJAPAN. Available at: http://unijapan.org/english/2017/10/05/CoproSubsidy170924.pdf.

UNIJAPAN. 2017b. *Co-production: Partnering with Japan*. Tokyo: UNIJAPAN. Available at: http://unijapan.org/english/production/partnering.html.

UNIJAPAN. 2017c. *The Statutes of UNIJAPAN*. Tokyo: UNIJAPAN. Available at: http://unijapan.org/english/about/statutes.html.

UNIJAPAN. 2020. *Statistics*. Tokyo: UNIJAPAN. Available at: https://www.unijapan.org/english/overview/statistics.html.

Vanderschelden, Isabelle. 2007. *Amelie: French Film Guide*. London and New York: I.B. Tauris.

Wada-Marciano, Mitsuyo. 2008. *Nippon Modern: Japanese Cinema of the 1920s and 1930s*. Hawaii: University of Hawaii Press.

Wada-Marciano, Mitsuyo. 2012. *Japanese Cinema in the Digital Age*. Hawaii: University of Hawaii Press.

Wee, Valerie. 2011. 'Visual Aesthetics and Ways of Seeing: Comparing *Ringu* and *The Ring*'. *Cinema Journal*, 50 (2): 41–60.

Welker, James. 2005. 'Telling Her Story: Narrating a Japanese Lesbian Community'. *Japanstudien*, 16 (1): 119–44.

Wren, James A. 2016. 'Homes Wretched and Wrecked: Disability as Social Dis-ease in Kurosawa's *Dodes'ka-den* (1970)'. In *Cultures of Representation: Disability in World Cinema Contexts*, edited by Benjamin Fraser. London and New York: Wallflower Press, 230–46.

Yamada, Marc. 2016. 'Between Documentary and Fiction: The Films of Kore-Eda Hirokazu'. *Journal of Religion and Film*, 20 (3): Art. 13.

Yoshimi, Mitsuhiro. 2000. *Kurosawa: Film Studies and Japanese Cinema*. Durham: Duke University Press.

Zahlten, Alexander. 2017. *The End of Japanese Cinema: Industrial Genres, National Times and Media Ecologies*. Durham: Duke University Press.

Index

2 Autumns, 3 Winters/2 Automnes, 3 Hivers (2013)   60–1
2001: A Space Odyssey (1968)   69

Achilles and the Tortoise/Akiresu to Kame (2008)   155
adaptations   189–95
Adrift in Tokyo/Tenten (2007)   129, 132
Agresti, Alejandro   127
Air Doll/Kuki Ningyo (2009)   175
Akiko   119
Akira Kurosawa   3, 36–8, 56–9, 165, 168, 172, 203
Alexander, James R.   128, 154, 159, 160
Alibi.com (2017)   7
All Is Forgiven/Tout est Pardonneé (2007)   99–105
Amalric, Mathieu   191
ambivalence   82–8
Amélie/Le Fabuleux Destin d'Amélie Poulain (2001)   52, 121, 123, 126
Amour (2012)   164, 166–8
Anatomy of Hell/Anatomie de l'enfer (2004)   148
Antonioni, Michelangelo   2
Anwar, Joko   204
Aoki Shinmon   201
art house   158
The Artist (2011)   68
Asako Yuzuki   205
Assassination Classroom, Ace Attorney/Gyakuten Saiban (2012)   190
Assassination Classroom/Ansatsu Kyôshitsu (2015)   123
Assayas, Olivier   160, 184, 185
Astérix et Obélix franchise   190, 192
atomization, working class   99–105
audience   213–16
Auteuil, Daniel   207

Babel (2006)   144
Back to Burgundy/Ce qui nous lie (2017)   134, 135, 185–8

Bakuman (2015)   190
The Ballad of Narayama/Narayama Bushikô (1983)   3
Ballard, J.G.   83
Bandes de filles/Girlhood (2014)   26
banlieue   73
Barthes, Roland   199
Bashō Matsuo   116
Baskett, Michael   140
Battle Royale/Batoru Rowaiaru (2000)   151, 152, 155, 156
Battle Royale 2: Requiem/Batoru rowaiaru II: Chinkonka (2003)   151
The Battleship Island/Gunhamdo (2017)   139
Bauby, Jean-Dominique   166–8
Baudelaire, Charles   24
Bazin, André   19, 36–7, 211
Beaumont, Jeffrey   162
Beeton, Sue   116
Before We Vanish/Sanpo Suru Shinryakusha (2017)   141
Beineix, Jean-Jacques   20
Being and Nothingness   171
The Belier Family/La Famille Bélier (2014)   167, 182
Belleville Rendez-vous/Les Triplettes de Belleville (2003)   56
Beloved/Les Bien-aimés (2011)   120
Belvaux, Lucas   135
Benguigui, Yamina   135
benshi style   48
Bercot, Emmanuelle   109
Berusaiyu no bara/Rose of Versailles (1972-3)   7
Besson, Luc   3, 7, 10, 20–2, 124, 183, 190, 191, 195
The Big Blue/Le Grand Bleu (1988)   21
Big Man Japan/Dai Nipponjin   66
'Bilateral Co-productions'   40–1
Binoche, Juliette   122, 141, 174
Black Butler/Kuroshitsuji (2014)   193
Black Rain (1989)   144

Black Snow/Kuroi Yuki (1965)   127, 128, 146, 153
Blind Beast/Môjû (1969)   165
Blossier, Antoine   206
Blue Is the Warmest Colour/La Vie d'Adèle-Chapitres 1 & 2 (2013)   190
Blue Velvet (1986)   162
Blum-Reid, Sylvie   7
Bong Joon Ho   144
Bonnaire, Sandrine   131–2, 134, 137
Boon, Dany   7
Bordwell, David   9, 47–8
Bosch, Rose   183
Bourdieu, Pierre   4
Bourgoin, Louise   191
Boyle, Danny   149
Branded to Kill/Koroshi (1967)   51, 63
Breathless/À bout de souffle (1960)   2, 20, 24, 63
Breillat, Catherine   25, 148, 162
bricolage approach   52–3
Bride for Rip Van Winkle/Rippu Van Winkuru no hanayome (2016)   193, 194
brutal intimacy   145
Bunka-cho subsidy   43
Buñuel, Luis   38, 65
Burch, Noël   116, 214

The Cabinet of Dr. Caligari/Das Kabinett des Dr. Caligari (1919)   33
Cahiers du cinéma   2, 3, 9, 22, 32
Cannes Film Festival (2005)   36, 39
Cape No. 7/Hǎijiǎo Qī Hào (2008)   140
Carax, Leos   144
Cardullo, Robert   80
Carné, Marcel   19
casual inspection   4
Centre National du Cinéma et de l'image animée (CNC)   40–1
'A Certain Tendency in French Cinema' (Truffaut)   208
Certified Copy/Copie conforme (2010)   39
CGI technologies   60–1
Chaplin, Charlie   79, 82
Chateau de la Reine/Ohi no Yakata (2014)   41
The Cherry Orchard: Blossoming (2008)   199

The Cherry Orchard/Sakura no Sono (1990)   199, 200
Chieko Higashiyama   117
China   9–10
Cho Jung-rae   139
Cinéfondation (2016)   11
cinema. See also individual entries
    art-house   158
    of attractions   147
    concept of   146
    landscape   164
cinéma du look   21
Cinema Paradiso/Nuovo Cinema Paradiso (1988)   204
Claire's Knee/Le genou de Claire (1970)   22
Cocteau, Jean   213
Code inconnu: récit incomplet de divers voyages/Code Unknown: Incomplete Tales of Several Journeys (2000)   141
The Commission du Film Rhône-Alpes   41
Confidentially Yours/Vivement dimanche! (1983)   72
confrontational cinema   145–63
    eroticism   146–51
    sexploitation   146–51
    violence   151–62
constant camera movements   150
contemplative contemporary cinema (CCC)   49
contents tourism (*kontentsu tsūrizumu*)   116
contrasting palettes   67
co-productions   38–9
Corneau, Alain   124
Cotillard, Marion   103, 168
Coulin, Delphine   138
Covid-19 pandemic   6
Craven, Wes   124
Creative Contribution points system   43–4
Criminal Code   146
Crossroads (1928)   33
Cukor, George   120
culture   5
    communication   3
    fragmentation   214

Custody/Jusqu'à la garde (2017)   182
Cutie Honey: Live Action/Kyûtî Hanî (2004)   195
Cutie Honey: Tears/Kyūtī Hanī Tiāzu (2016)   195
Czach, Liz   11–12

Dafoe, Willem   122
Daguerreotype/Le Secret de la chambre noire (2016)   39
Dalle, Beatrice   144
Darboe, Ibrahim Burama   136
Dardenne, Jean-Pierre   103
Dardenne, Luc   103
Dargent, Ange   128
David, Lynch   65
Dawn of the Felines/Mesunekotachi (2017)   159, 160
Daybreak/Le Jour se lève (1939)   19
Dear Doctor/Dia Dokutâ (2009)   105–8, 203
death   164, 165
   concept of   176
Death by Hanging/Kôshikei (1968)   165
Death Note/Desu Nōto (2006)   144
Death Note: Light Up the New World/Desu Nōto Light up the NEW (sic) World (2016)   196
Death Note 2: The Last Name/Desu Nōto the Last Name (2006)   196
Deauville Asian Film Festival   4
découpage   48
Delamarre, Camille   10
Delépine, Benoît   131
De l'histoire ancienne (2001)   182
Demonlover (2002)   160, 161
Deneuve, Catherine   1, 2, 120, 174
Denis, Claire   24–31, 135, 182
Dentsu Creative X   45
Depardieu, Gérard   131
Departures/Okuribito (2008)   105, 123, 124, 144, 164, 201, 202
Dercourt, Denis   207, 208
Desser, David   10
The Diabolical Dr. Z/Miss Muerte (1966)   38–9
directorial style   51–2

The Discreet Charm of the Bourgeoisie/Le Charme Discret de la Bourgeoisie (1972)   38–9
The Diving Bell and the Butterfly/Le Scaphandre et le Papillon (2007)   126, 191, 207
Dodes'ka-den/Dodesukaden (1970)   168
Doisneau, Robert   121
drama   198–208
Drive My Car (2021)   3, 215
Dr Strangelove (1964)   203
Ducournau, Julia   162
Dulac, Germaine   147
Dumont, Bruno   145, 161, 162
Dupontel, Albert   207, 208
Duvivier, Julien   33
Dyer, Richard   173
Dying at a Hospital/Byôin de Shimu to Iu Koto   168

Eastman's Kinetoscope   8
Ebert, Roger   162
Ebouaney, Eriq   136
The Eel/Unagi (1997)   3
Eiga Hihyo (Film Criticism)   32
The Eight Hundred/Bābǎi (2020)   139
Eiichirō Hasumi   123
Eisenstein, Sergei   93, 170
Eizo Yamagiwa   32
Electric Dragon 80.000 V/Erekuto Rikku Doragon 80000V (2001)   65–6
Emmerich, Roland   183
Enter the Void (2009)   148, 150, 151
Eraserhead (1977)   65, 69
Eriko Kitagawa   122, 194
Eros + Massacre/Erosu Purasu Gyakusatsu (1969)   63–4, 154, 165
eroticism   146–51
Eternity/Éternité (2016)   169
Etienne, Pauline   124
Etsushi Toyokawa   140
EuropaCorp   10
European Coordination of Film Festivals (ECFF)   12
The Extraordinary Adventures of Adele Blanc-Sec/Les Aventures Extraordinaires d'Adèle Blanc-Sec (2010)   190, 191

family dynamic   181
Fantasmagorie (1908)   55
fantasy   147, 195–8
Fassbinder, Rainer Werner   147
Fat Girl/A ma soeur! (2001)   148
Father of My Children/Le Père de mes enfants (2009)   182
Fear and Trembling/Stupeur et Tremblements (2003)   124
female auteur   24–31
Ferroukhi, Ismaël   182
Festival de Cannes   4. *See also* Cannes Film Festival (2005)
Festival des 3 Continents   4
The Fifth Element/Le Cinquième Élément (1997)   21, 35, 74, 195
film festivals   4, 215
film-induced tourism. *See* contents tourism
filmmakers   145, 164
  nouvelle vague   115, 121
filmmaking, esoteric nature of   189
financial survival   106
Fireworks/Hana-Bi (1997)   13, 49, 123, 154, 173
First Growth/Premiers crus (2015)   186, 188
Five Dedicated to Ozu (2003)   126
flâneur   83
The Flowers of War/Jīnlíng shísān chāi (2011)   139
Fontaine, Anne   41
Ford, John   19
Forever, Mak P.   148
Foujita (2015)   41
The 400 Blows/Les Quatre Cents Coups (1959)   20, 115, 116, 138, 174
France
  cinema   181–8
  cinematic connections, Japan   1
  cinematic ecosystems   6–8
  global box office success   35
  institutional state support   40, 45–6
  international film festivals   12–13
  international profile   34
  international visibility   22–3
  nouvelle vague   20–3
  post-colonialism   34
  unemployment   98–105

Frantz (2016)   67
Fraser, Benjamin   182
Frontiers/Frontière(s) (2007)   22
Fukada Kôji   123
Fullmetal Alchemist/Hagane no Renkinjutsushi [Alchemist of Steel] (2017)   196–8
Full Moon in Paris/Les nuits de la pleine lune (1984)   100
Fumihiko Sori   196
Fumiko   117
Fumi Nikaido   123
Fumino Kimura   205

Gainsbourg, Charlotte   138
Gakuryû Ishii   65–6
Gance, Abel   33
Gao Qunshu   139
Gardner, William   33
Gheorghiu, Luminița   141
Ghost (1990)   127
Gilbert, Lewis   144
Gill, Tom   123
Girardot, Hippolyte   144
Girl Boss   212
Girlhood/Bandes de filles (2014)   26
The Girl on the Bridge/La fille sur le pont (1999)   66–7
global accessibility of films   5
global capitalism   105
Gloria Mundi   113–14
Glory to the Filmmaker/Kantoku: Banzai! (2007)   155
Godard, Jean-Luc   2, 4, 73–4, 135
Godzilla (1998)   183
Godzilla/Gojira (1954)   144
Godzilla vs. King Kong (2011)   192
Gondry, Michel   53, 128, 144
Goscinny, René   190
Gosho, Heinosuke   33
Gouriot, François   120
Gray, Jason   35
The Great Journey/Le Grand voyage (2004)   182
Guan Hu   139
Guédiguian, Robert   113–14
Guilty of Romance/Koi no Tsumi (2011)   151, 158, 212

Hajime Hashimoto 41
Hana and Alice/Hana to Arisu (2004)
  194
*Hana and Alice Lead the
  Investigation/Hana to Arisu Satsujin
  Jiken* (2015) 215
Hana-Bi/Fireworks (1997) 13, 49, 123,
  154, 173
Haneke, Michael 141, 164, 166, 182
Hansen-Løve, Mia 99–101, 182
Harmonium/Fuchi ni tatsu (2016)
  123, 126
Haroun, Mahamat Saleh 136
Harper, Graeme 130, 131
Harris, Carroll 215
Harry Potter 197
Haruki Murakami 169, 172, 173
Hate/La Haine (1995) 73
Hawks, Howard 21
Hayao Miyazaki 35, 144
Hazanavicius, Michel 68
Helter Skelter/Herutā Sukerutā (2012)
  162
Hendrix, Grady 49
Henry and June (1990) 213
Heroine Disqualified/Hiroin Shikkaku [aka
  No Longer Heroine] (2015) 61
Hidden/Caché (2005) 182
Hideaki Anno 195
Hillcoat, John 112
Himizu/Mole (2011) 110, 159
Hirokazu Kore-eda 1, 2, 127,
  174–81, 213
*Hiroshima, My Love/Hiroshima, Mon
  Amour* (1959) 20
Hitchcock, Alfred 2, 21, 154
Hitoshi Matsumoto 13, 66, 153
Honoré, Christophe 120
Hou Hsiao-Hsien 161
Howard, Ron 127
H Story (2001) 144
Hugo, Victor 185
Huillet, Danièle 147
Hulk (2003) 191
Hulot, Monsieur 125
human condition 164
Humanity/L'humanité (1999) 161
Hutchinson, Rachael 203

Ichi the Killer/Koroshiya 1 (2001)
  145, 153
identity, nation 5
ideological information 93–4
*I Have to Buy New Shoes/Atarashii Kutsu
  wo Kawanakucha* (2012) 121, 194
Ikiru/To Live (1952) 23–4
Iles, Timothy 107
imbalanced geographical system 105
Indochine 135
industrial genre 148
In Harmony/En équilibre [aka *In Balance*]
  (2015) 207, 208
'innocence of vision' (360) 80
In Praise of Love/Éloge de l'amour
  (2001) 73–4
Inside/À l'intérieur (2007) 22
institutional encouragement 39–45
institutional support 45–6
international art cinema 147
International Federation of Film
  Producers Associations (FIAPF)
  12
*Interstella 5555: The 5tory of the 5ecret 5tar
  5ystem* (2003) 56
In the Realm of the Senses/Ai no Korîda
  (1976) 145, 146, 154, 160, 165
*In This Corner of the World/Kono Sekai no
  Katsumi ni* (2016) 211
Intimate Enemies/L'Ennemi intime
  (2007) 135
The Intouchables/Intouchables (2011) 22
The Intruder/L'Intrus (2005) 182
Irreversible/Irréversible (2002) 145
Ishirô Honda 144, 191
isolation 105–13
Issey Takahashi 143

Jacob, Gilles 11
Jacobs, Alexander 127
Japan
  artistic integrity in 146
  censorship codes in 154
  cinema 214
  cinematic connections, France 1
  cinematic ecosystems 6–8
  confrontational cinema 147
  global box office success 35

international profile   34
masculinity   172
nūberu bāgu   23–4
obscenity laws   146
perceptions   164
political events   34
post-war period   36–8
presence at international film
    festivals   11–14
rebuilding   9
reputation   145
role of politics, cinema   93–4
2017, box office   6–7
unemployment   93–8
visual styles   47–8
Japan Film Commission (JFC)   45
*Japan Sinks: 2020, The Beginning of the
    End*   211
jazz-style   4
Jeunet, Jean-Pierre   121, 123
Joni's Promise/Janji Joni (2005)   204
Journey to the Shore/Kishibe no Tabi
    (2015)   127
Jun Ichikawa   12, 168
Jurassic Park (1993)   49, 190
Jury Award   211
Juzo Itami   165

kabuki   49–50
Kaji Meiko   212
Kang Je-gyu   139
Kassovitz, Mathieu   73
Katabuchi, Sunao   211
Katsutaro Inabata   8, 33
Kaufman, Philip   213
Kawase's hyperrealist style   51–2
Kazuhiro Yokoyama   148
Kazuya Shiraishi   159
Keaton, Buster   79
Kei'ichi Satō   193
Kenji Mizoguchi   2, 94, 215
Kentarō Ōtani   193
Kervern, Gustave   131
Kiarostami, Abbas   119, 126
Kill Bill Parts 1 and 2 (2003)   144
Kimi no Na wa/Your Name (2017)   7
*King Kong versus Godzilla/Kingu Kongu
    Tai Gojira* (1962)   191

Kinji Fukasaku   151, 152
Kiroku Eiga   32
Kiyoshi Atsumi   75, 83, 84
Kiyoshi Kurosawa   2, 94, 95, 98, 124, 127,
    140, 141, 172
Klapisch, Cédric   133, 134, 188
Kōhei Oguri   41, 65
Kōji Hagiuda   140
Kōta Yoshida   163
Krawczyk, Gérard   10, 124
Kriegel-Nicholas, Isadora   2, 9
Kubrick, Stanley   203
Kuhn, Annette   164
Kuniko Miyake   117
kyogen   80

Labyrinth of Dreams/Yume no Ginga
    (1997)   65
Lacheau, Philippe   7
Lady Maiko/Maiko wa Redi (2014)   119
Lady Snowblood/Shurayuki-hime   212
La Femme Nikita (1990)   183
La Haine   73
laissez-faire approach   101
The Lake House (2006)   127
Land of Hope/Kibō no Kuni (2012)   110
Lara Croft: Tomb Raider (2001)   190
Lartigau, Eric   182
L'avventura   2
Le bleu est une couleur chaude (Maroh)
    190
Lee, Ang   191
Lee Hyun-seung   127
Legrand, Gilles   187
Legrand, Xavier   182
Lehman, Peter M.   49
Le Maire, Jérôme   186
L'Empire des signes (1970)   34
Léon (1994)   35
Le Paquebot Tenacity (1934)   33
lesbian narrative   200
*Le Scaphandre et le Papillon/The Diving
    Bell and The Butterfly* (2007)   166
Les 400 coups/The Four Hundred Blows
    (1959)   2
Les Misérables (2019)   73
Let the Sunshine In/Un beau soleil intérieur
    (2017)   26–8

Levy, Shawn   190
liberal attitudes   213
Liberski, Stefan   124–6
life, contemplations on   174–81, 213
Like Father, Like Son/Soshite Chichi ni Naru (2013)   178–81, 183
Like Someone in Love (2012)   119, 126
Little Astroboy (2019)   41
Little Remi and Famous Dog Capi/Chibikko Remi to Meiken Kapi (1970)   206
The Little Soldier/Le petit soldat (1963)   135
Little Soldier Zhang Ga/Xiao Bing Zhang Ga (1963)   139
The Long Excuse/Nagai iiwake (2015)   203
Love Exposure/Ai no Mukadashi (2008)   164
Lubitsch, Ernst   88
Lucy (2014)   10, 21
Luhr, William G.   49
Luhrmann, Baz   121
Lu Over the Wall (2017)   211
Lynch, David   69, 162
Lys, Aalayna   136

Macbeth (Shakespeare)   203
Maggie Cheung   160
Makoto Shinkai   7
manga musical   6, 7, 40, 56, 121, 123, 127, 158, 162, 180, 189–201, 205, 213
Man's Pain/Ningen Ku (1923)   47
The Many Faces of Ito: The Movie/Itô kun A to E (2018)   205, 206
Marker, Chris   39
Marmaï, Pio   133
Maroh, Jul   190
Masaaki Yuasa   211
Masayuki Suo   119
Mastroianni, Chiara   120
McGregor, Ewan   149
mediation of reality   74
Meiji Restoration   8
Mei Kurokawa   140
Méliès, Georges   61
Mélo (1986)   61–2

Memoirs of a Geisha (2005)   144
Meyerhold, Vsevolod   170
Michael, Charlie   23, 35
Midnight in Paris (2012)   74
Miho Nakayama   122
Mika Ninagawa   162
Miller, Henry   213
Miret, Orso   182
Miwa Nishikawa   105, 203
mockery   82
Mone Kamishiraishi   119
monochrome   63–74
mono no aware (the pathos of things)   5
Mon Roi/My King (2015)   25, 87, 108–10
Mood Indigo/L'écume des Jours (2013)   53–5, 59
Moulin Rouge! (2001)   121
Mr Hulot's Holiday/Les vacances de Monsieur Hulot (1953)   75–88
Muddy River/Doro no Kawa (1981)   41, 65
Müller, Valérie   192
multi-screen megaplex   11
The Mummy (1999)   190
Mumon: The Land of Stealth/Shinobi no Kuni (2017)   204
The Murder Case of Hana and Alice/Hana to Arisu Satsujin Jiken (2015)   194
My Brother Loves Me Too Much/Ani ni Ai Saresugite Komattemasu (2017)   61
My Fair Lady (1964)   120
My Neighbor Totoro/Tonari no Totoro (1988)   144
My Summer in Provence/Avis de Mistral (2013)   167, 183, 184
My Uncle/ Mon Oncle (1958)   77, 78, 125
My Way/Maiwei (2011)   139

Nagisa Ōshima   145–7, 158, 165
Nakache, Olivier   138
Nakashima Tetsuya   7
Naomasa Musaka   140
Naomi Kawase   3, 11, 24–31, 127, 215
National Centre for Cinema   6
Netflix   214
Neuvic, Thierry   141

New Wave   152
Ni d'Ève ni d'Adam (Nothomb)   124
Night and Fog in Japan/Nihon no Yoru to Kiri (1960)   147
Night at the Museum (2006)   190
Nightmare on Elm Street   124
Night of the Felines   160
Nihonjinron   38
Nikita (1990)   74
Nikkatsu Studios   8
Nin, Anaïs   213
Nippon Hoso Kyokai (NHK)/Japan Broadcasting Corporation   45
Nishi, Yoshitaka   154, 155
Nōkanfu Nikki/Diary of an Undertaker (1993)   201
No and Me/No et moi (2010)   26
Nobody's Boy: Remi/le Naki Ko (1977)   207
Nobuhiro Suwa   122, 144
Noda, Shinkichi   32
Nodame Cantabile: The Final Score-Movie I/Nodame Kantābire: Saishu-gakushou-Zenpen (2009)   40–1
Noé, Gaspar   145, 148–50
Nornes, Abé Mark   11
Norwegian Wood/Noruwei no Mori (2010)   169
Nothomb, Amélie   124
nouvelle vague   10, 31, 115, 121, 152, 210
  before   20–3
Nowell-Smith, Geoffrey   181
nūberu bāgu   15, 23–4, 31, 210
Nygren, Scott   23–4

O'Brien, Adam   60
obscenity   158
Odagiri, Joe   129
O'Donoghue, Darragh   83–4
Oe, Takamasa   3
Oldeuboi/Old Boy (2003)   10
The Only Son/Hitori Musuko (1936)   116, 122
Ordre national de la Légion d'Honneur   2, 25
O'Regan, Tom   14
Osamu Mukai   122
Oscar awards   3, 148–50

Otoko wa Tsurai yo/It's Tough Being a Man (1969)   75
Otoko wa Tsurai yo: Torajiro aiaigasa/Tora-san Meets the Songstress Again (1975)   84
Our Little Sister/Umimachi Diary (Seaside Diary) (2015)   105–8, 127, 174
Outrage/Autoreiji (2010)   155
Outrage Beyond/Autoreiji: Biyondo (2012)   155–8
Outrage Coda/Autoreiji sai Shūshō (2017)   155, 158
Ozon, François   67–8

Pacific War (2007)   37
Pale Flower/Kawaita hana (1964)   24
Palme d'Or, Cannes   2–3
Palmer, Tim   145
Parade (1974)   77
paraplegic rider   208
Parasite (2020)   13
Paris I Love You/Paris je t'aime (2006)   122
Pauline at the Beach/Pauline à la plage (1983)   21–2, 100
Peranson, Mark   11
The Perfect Couple/Un couple parfait (2005)   144
Personal Shopper (2016)   184, 185
Pettersen, David   21
Pigs and Battleships/Buta to gunkan (1961)   23–4
Pirates of the Caribbean (2003)   190
Pistol Opera/Pisutoru Opera (2001)   68
Playtime (1967)   77–9, 87
Poelvoorde, Benoît   131
Polina/Polina danser sa vie (2016)   192
Porco Rosso (1992)   35
The Pornographers/"Erogotoshitachi" yori jinruigaku nyūmon [lit. "Pornographers": An anthropological introduction] (1966)   24, 153
Positif journal   9
Postcard/Ichimai no hagaki (2010)   50, 140
post-Second World War movies   50
Preljocaj, Angelin   192

pre-Second World War cinema   19
primacy of movement   170
The Princess Blade (2001)   212
Princess Mononoke (1997)   35
Princess Raccoon/Operetta: Tanuki Goten
      (2005)   53, 68
protagonists   83
Proust, Marcel   213
Psycho (1960)   2, 154
Pulse (2001)   124
Pure as Snow/Blanche Neige (2019)   41–2

Radiance/Hikari (2017)   29–31, 127, 167
Raging Bull (1980)   65
Raiders of the Lost Ark (1981)   190–1
Raid: Special Unit/Raid Dingue (2016)   7
Ran (1985)   38
The Rape of the Vampire/Le Viol du
      vampire (1967)   147
Rashomon (1950)   37, 49
Rayner, Jonathan   130, 131
reception   213–16
Red Alert (1958)   203
Red Sorghum/Hóng gāoliáng (1987)   139
Rémi: Nobody's Boy/Rémi sans famille
      (2018)   206, 207
Reservoir Dogs (1992)   173
Resnais, Alain   61–2, 144
Reunion/Itai: Asu e no Tōkakan (2012)
      110
R100 (2013)   153
Richie, Donald   146, 159, 213, 214
Riding the Breeze/Nanpū (2014)   140
Ringu   124
Rin Takanashi   119
Riva, Emmanuelle   20, 166
The Road (2009)   112
Rodriguez, Robert   191
Rohmer, Eric   123, 131
Rollin, Jean   147
Romance (1999)   148
Rosenbaum, Jonathan   77, 96
Ross, Kristin   79
Run Lola Run (1998)   52
rural community   113
Rust and Bone/De rouille et d'os (2012)
      101–3, 168
Ryoichi Kimizuka   110

Ryō Kase   156
Ryōko Hirosue   124
Ryoo Seung-wan   139
Ryō Wada   205
Ryuichi Hiroki   205
Ryusuke Hamaguchi   3, 215
Ryuzo and the Seven Henchmen/Ryûzô to
      7 nin no Kobun Tachi (2015)   155

Sachsé, Bernard   207
Sagnier, Ludivine   120
Saint-Amour (2016)   131
Samba (2014)   138
Sans Famille (Malot)   206
Sansho the Bailiff/Sanshô Dayû (1954)
      2, 6
Satoshi Miki   129, 130
Schilling, Mark   173
Schnabel, Julian   126, 166, 167
Schoendoerffer, Pierre   135
Sciamma, Céline   25
sci-fi films   69–70
Scorsese, Martin   13
Scott, Ridley   144
The Seashell and the Clergyman/La
      Coquille et le Clergyman (1928)
      147
A Season in France/Une Saison en France
      (2017)   136, 138
Seaton, Philip   116, 144
Seijun Suzuki   3, 4, 51, 53, 63, 122, 144
Sekiguchi, Hisashi   204
self-identity   5
self-Orientalising representations   23–4
Serikawa, Yugo   206
Serreau, Coline   25
Setsuko Hara   117
sexploitation   146–51
sexuality   158, 213
Shakespeare   203
Shanghai's Fundamental Films   10
Shimotsuma Monogatari (aka *Kamikaze*
      Girls, 2004)   7
Shin Godzilla/Shin Gojira (2016)   195
Shinji Higuchi   195
Shinobu Otake   140
shinpa films   49–50
Shinsuke Sato   93, 172, 173, 196, 212

Shintō Kaneda   140
Shin'ya Tsukamoto   65
Shirō Ōsaka   119
Shôhei Imamura   153, 158
Shoplifters/Manbiki Kazoku
   (2018)   2, 174
Shunji Iwai   193, 194, 215
Shun Nakahara   199, 200
Shūsuke Kaneko   144, 196
Signal: Luca on Mondays/Shigunaru-
   Getsuyôbi no Ruka (2012)   204
Silent Running (1972)   69–70
Sin City (2005)   191
Siri, Florent Emilio   135
Siworae/Il Mare/The Sea (2000)   127
Sketches of Kaitan City (2010)   128
Smith, Murray   151
Sommers, Stephen   190
Sonatine (1993)   173
Sono Sion   68–9, 71, 110, 120, 123, 145,
   151, 158, 159, 163, 164, 212
Spielberg, Steven   191
Spirited Away/Sen to Chihiro no
   kamikakushi (2001)   144
Spirit's Homecoming/ Gwihyang
   (2016)   139
Splash (1984)   127
Stagecoach (1939)   19
Stam, Robert   190, 191, 199, 203
Standish, Isolde   118, 122, 123, 153,
   158, 159
Still Walking/Aruitemo Aruitemo
   (2008)   175–8, 213
The Story of O/Histoire d'O (1975)   154
storytelling techniques   188
'straight-line' narrative   166
Straub, Jean-Marie   147
Stray Cat Rock   212
Stray Dog/Nora Inu (1949)   57–8, 172
Strip Mahjong: Battle Royale/Datsui-mâjan
   batoru rowaiaru (2011)   148
Strip Mahjong Idol: Warring States (Naked)
   Battle Royale/Datsui-mâjan Idol
   Sengoku jidai batoru rowaiaru
   (2015)   148
structured agreements   40–1
Subway (1985)   21
A Summer's Tale/Conte d'été (1996)   123

Sundome (2007)   148
Sundome 2 and Sundome 3 (2008)   148
Survival Family (2016)   110–13, 213
Sy, Omar   138

Tadao Sato   117
Tadashi Okuno   119
Tag/Riaru Onigokko (2015)   145, 151,
   152, 159
Taichi Inoue   125
Taiga Nakano   123
Takashi Miike   145, 153, 159
Takeshi Asai   195
Takeshi Kitano   123, 154–8, 173
Takeshis' (2005)   155
Takeuchi, Hideki   40–1
A Tale of Autumn/Conte d'automne (1998)
   131
Tale of Sorrow and Sadness/Hishū
   monogatari (1977)   51
Tales of Ugetsu/Ugetsu Monogatari (1953)
   2
Tampopo   165
Tamura, Shinya   205–6
Tanga, Bibi   136
Tarantino, Quentin   173
Tati, Jacques   15, 75–8
Tautou, Audrey   124, 180
Taxi 2 (2000)   10
Taxi Driver (1976)   13
A Taxing Woman (1987)   165
Tax Rebate for International Productions
   (TRIP)   40–1
Taylor-Jones, Kate   52
technicolour experience   63
Testud, Sylvie   124
Tetsuji Takechi   127, 146
Tetsuya Watari   122
That Obscure Object of Desire/Cet Obscur
   Objet du Désir (1977)   38
theatrical antecedents   61
Them/Ils (2006)   22
Thermae Romae I (2012)   144
Thermae Romae II (2014)   144
Throne of Blood/Kumonosu-jō (1957)
   203
Titane (2021)   163
Tokyo! (2008)   144

Tokyo Drifter/Tôkyô Nagaremono (1966)   122
Tokyo Fiancée (2014)   124–6, 170
Tokyo International Film Festival (TIFF)   13, 35, 42
Tōkyō Kokusai Eigasai (Tokyo International Film Festival)   4
Tōkyō Sonata/Tokyo Sonata (2008)   94–8, 107, 158, 172, 212
Tokyo Story (1953)   118, 158, 165, 174, 212
Tokyo Story (Ozu)   116, 118
Tokyo Trash Baby/Tôkyô Gomi Onna (2000)   205
The Tokyo Trial/Dōngjīng Shěnpàn (2006)   139
Tokyo Tribe/Tōkyō Toraibu (2014)   120
Tôkyô Yakyoku/Tokyo Lullaby   12
Toledano, Éric   138
Tomboy (2011)   26
Tomokazu Miura   129
Tony Takitani/Tonî Takitani (2004)   168–71
Tora-san (1969-95)   75–6, 79–88
Tornatore, Giuseppe   204
torture   153
Toshio Matsumoto   32
Toshiro Mifune   156
tradition of quality   208
Trafic/Traffic (1971)   77, 88
Trainspotting (1996)   149
Tran Anh *Hung*   169
The Transporter Refueled/Le Transporteur: Héritage (2015)   10
Triendl, Reina   151
Trintignant, Jean-Louis   166, 167
A Trip to the Moon/Le voyage dans la lune (1902)   61–2
Trouillot, Virgile   41
Truffaut, François   2, 72–3, 115, 117, 119, 208, 209
The Truth (2019)   1, 2
The Truth About Catherine   174
The Truth/La Vérité (2019)   174
Tsunagu Japan (2016)   144
Turim, Maureen   128
Tweedie, James   115, 121, 135
Twentynine Palms (2003)   145

The Twenty-Six Japanese Martyrs/Les Vingt-Six Martyrs Japonais (1930)   48
Two Days, One Night/Deux jours, une nuit (2014)   103–5
Tykwer, Tom   52
Typhoon Over Nagasaki/Typhon sur Nagasaki/Wasureenu Bojo (2012)   38

Udagawa, Daigo   148
Uderzo, Albert   190
Ugetsu Monogatari (1953)   5, 19
Under the Roofs of Paris/Sous les toits de Paris (1931)   33
unemployment
   France   98–105
   Japan   93–8
UniJapan   39
   Certificate   42–5
utsushi-e (Komatsu 1996)   8

Vagabond/Sans toit ni loi (1985)   131–4, 137
Valerian and the City of a Thousand Planets/Valérian et la Cité des mille planètes (2017)   7, 21, 190
Vanderschelden, Isabelle   121
Varda, Agnès   25, 131
Variety (2015)   189
Venice Film Festival (1951)   36, 37
Venice International Film Festival (1950)   13
Venice Silver Lion   19
Verbinski, Gore   190
Vertigo (1959)   2
Vietnam War   34
The Village Fair/Jour de fête (1949)   77
violence   151–62
Vivès, Bastien   192

Wada-Marciano, Mitsuyo   88
Warm Water Under a Red Bridge/Akai Hashi no Shita no Nurui Mizu (2001)   127
Warnier, Régis   135
Wasabi (2001)   22, 124
Water Lilies/Naissance des pieuvres (2007)   26

We Are Little Zombies/[lit.] *Watashitachi wa Ritoru Zonbī* (2019)   60–1
Wei Cui   139
Wei Te-sheng   140
Welcome to the Sticks/Bienvenue chez les Ch'tis (2008)   22
West, Simon   190
The Wheel/La Roue (1923)   33
The Whispering Star/Hiso Hiso Boshi (2015)   68–70
Why Don't You Play in Hell (2013)   123
wide-ranging   3
widescreen anamorphic lens   30–1
Wife of a Spy/Supai no tsuma (2020)   140, 143
Wingard, Adam   192
The Wolverine (2013)   144
Woman of Tokyo/Tokyo no on'na (2008)   88–9
Woman's Hole/Onno no anna (2014)   163

Yamamura, Takayoshi   116, 144
Yasujirô Ozu   116–19, 122, 165, 168

Yasuzô Masumura   165
Ying hung boon sik/A Better Tomorrow (1986)   13
Yôjirô Takita   105, 123, 164
Yoji Yamada   75
Yoko Suzuki   68–70, 72
Yŏngshì zhī mén/Warrior's Gate (aka *Enter the Warrior's Gate*) (2016)   10
Yoshiharu Tezuka   37
Yoshihiro Nakamura   204, 205
Yoshishige Yoshida   63–4, 154, 165
You Only Live Twice (1967)   144
You Will Be My Son/Tu seras mon fils (2011)   187, 188
Your Name/Kimi no Na wa (2017)   7
Yū Aoi   143
Yuki and Nina/Yuki to Nina (2009)   144

Zhang Yimou   139
Zucker, Jerry   127

www.ingramcontent.com/pod-product-compliance
Lightning Source LLC
Chambersburg PA
CBHW062133300426
44115CB00012BA/1901